THE
FRICTION-FREE
ECONOMY

THE FRICTION-FREE ECONOMY

Marketing Strategies for a Wired World

T. G. LEWIS

HarperBusiness
A Division of HarperCollins*Publishers*

HarperCollins books may be purchased for educational, business, or sales promotional use. For information please write: Special Markets Department, HarperCollins Publishers, Inc., 10 East 53rd Street, New York, NY 10022.

FIRST EDITION

Designed by Joseph Rutt

Library of Congress Cataloging-in-Publication Data

Lewis, T. G. (Theodore Gyle), 1941–
    The friction-free economy : marketing strategies for a wired world / by T. G. Lewis. — 1st ed.
        p.   cm.
    Includes bibliographical references and index.
    ISBN 0-88730-847-3
    1. High technology industries—Marketing.   I. Title.
HC79.H53L49   1997
620'.0068'8—dc21   97-13811

97 98 99 00 01 ❖/RRD 10 9 8 7 6 5 4 3 2 1

To Molly

Contents

Acknowledgments

I owe a debt to the corporate contributors, especially Dick Eyestone, Bay Networks; Paul Mehring and Deiter Haban, Daimler-Benz Research & Technology; Art Scott, Samsung Multimedia; Bruce Shriver, Genesis2; Manlio Allegra, TecMagik; Patrick Bonnaure, Bill Yount and Steve Perlman, WebTV Networks; David Boor, IBM-Multimedia Lab; Richard Brandt, *Upside* magazine; John Busch, Diba; Edward Christie and Paul Di Senso, SRI Consulting; Gary Franz, ViewCall America; Bill Gurley, Deutsche Morgan Grenfield; John Hiles, Thinking Tools; Neil Nored, IBM-Education; Doug Rosenberg, ICONIX Software Engineering; Wei Yen and Alex Yu, Navio Communications; Satoshi Sakashita, Hitachi Software Engineering America; Bill Gallagher, COM21; and Roger Schell, Novell. In addition, I would like to thank Peter Bormann, Eric Hall, and Todd Lewis, for reading early drafts of the book and making useful comments. Finally, Laureen Connelly Rowland doubled the quality of the manuscript through her ruthless editing and constant encouragement.

Preface

The Age of Revolution (1775–1814) was barely a spark of flint in 1776 when Adam Smith published the *Wealth of Nations*, a bestseller that ignited a conflagration no less important than the American Revolution that erupted that same year. Now the intellectual grandfather of today's bean-counting economic planners, Smith was a keen observer of his time—a kind of Alan Greenspan without an adoring press.

The Age of Revolution was the cauldron of capitalism. The *Wealth of Nations* was its user's manual.

The stuff of revolution was all over the place. Borrowing on a good idea from the inventor Newcomen, James Watt cobbled together the first practical steam engine, and in 1775 formed a partnership with Boulton to manufacture and sell the popular item. Watt may have been credited with scientific invention, but his real contribution was inventing the engine of capitalism. Science and technology joined hand in hand with economics to forge a new system—a new *economic* system that would define society for the next two hundred years.

Capitalism was the theory, and steam provided the practical application. The second half of the 1700s were fast times—too fast for some royalty and not fast enough for the masses, who, like Smith and Watt, were impatient to get on with it (*it* being the Industrial Revolution). But as Peter F. Drucker says in *Post-Capitalist Society*, even revolutions take time, about fifty years, to be precise. And the funny thing is, nobody knows what is going on until the revolution is over.

The second half of the twentieth century is a lot like the late 1700s. Revolution is everywhere and comprehension is scarce. The economics of Adam Smith is gone. The economics of Maynard Keynes is going. And the economics of the *friction-free economy* is coming. The friction-free economy is resetting economic theory for everyone—from high-tech companies like Intel and IBM to low-tech businesses like restaurants and used-car dealers.

Within the next twenty years we will come to fully understand the new laws of the friction-free economy. Fortunately, we've been warned. Take Netscape Communications, for example, which parlayed sixteen months of software development work into an IPO* valuation of $3 billion. Look at companies like Microsoft and Adobe Systems. Unknown a decade ago, they are now the darlings of the stock market. And the nouveau riche telecommunications companies like 3Com, Cisco Systems, and Bay Networks have turned from small-cap industries into powerhouses of the new century. These are the vanguard of the friction-free economy.

What we do know is that *something* is afoot. A new order is building that obeys a different set of rules, and is forcing all businesses to dance to a different tune. Here is a preview:

Civilization is hooked on speed: Living in Internet time means things happen fast. New industries and new ideas circle the globe in record time. Computer performance doubles every eighteen months, products get cheaper and better, and people's jobs go away. The personal car, the personal computer, the VCR, and cellular telephones are tomorrow's hula hoops and pet rocks. In fact, the rise and fall of products, within a very short time, becomes a requirement in the friction-free economy.

The principles of the friction-free economy depart from the past: Mainstreaming, Davidow's Law, the market-of-one, the formation of joint ventures and partnerships among enemies, and a return to tribal agrarianism, mark the new age.

- The tools of business have changed. Now everyone who wants to thrive in the friction-free economy must learn a set

---

*Initial Public Stock Offering: the point in time when venture capitalists cash out by letting novice investors pay 100 times what they paid for the right to risk their retirement savings.

of new tools: learning curves, marketing models, targeting, product space disintegration, mergers and acquisitions, and business-as-war.

- The consequences of the new economy are nonintuitive: Inverse economics replaces diminishing returns, volume pricing replaces premium pricing, narrowcasting replaces broadcasting and value chains are integrated. Instead, the friction-free economy marks a return to a kind of retro agrarian tribalism that superimposes a 1700s social structure onto a twenty-first-century technology.

- In this new era, marketing is a game of strategy: a New Lanchester Strategy that all businesses will need to adopt in order to survive. The New Lanchester Strategy says that the game ends as soon as someone gets 74% market share. Leaders emerge at 41%, and players are counted in when they achieve 26%. With less than 26%, you don't count!

What is a company to do? The fleet of foot use analytical skill to not only ward off competition, but to build empires. Businesses must learn the techniques of the friction-free economy to excel. They must master a new lexicon, culture, and way of life. It is no longer possible to conduct business as usual.

I have written this book for the conventional business person, the change-dazed manager, the displaced worker, the frantic product planner, the voracious stock picker, and the futurist in us all. It codifies the friction-free economy. It lays down the early principles. But it is up to you to put them into practice.

This book is perhaps the first attempt to show the way. Even though the ideas are unconventional, I believe you will benefit from the practical advice given in the following pages. Good luck on your journey, and I will see you in the twenty-first century!

Ted G. Lewis, Ph.D.

tedglewis@friction-free-economy.com

www.friction-free-economy.com

1

Living in Internet Time

OTHER PEOPLE'S MONEY

I woke up at 5:30 A.M. on August 8, 1995, tuned CNBC's Channel 37 to the Morning Business Report, and dumped thick cream into a bowl of Cap'n Crunch. The day would prove worthy of the cream. By 6:30 A.M. I was on the telephone to Charles Schwab, begging for a few crumbs of Netscape Communications Corporation (NSCP). But my best telephone effort fell far short of its mark, as nearly 40 million shares, promised at $28 per share, disappeared like a purse-snatcher on the Atlantic City boardwalk. Before the end of the day, NSCP was selling for $71 per share, leaving me and countless other wannabe shareholders in the dust. Within a few weeks, the price soared to over $170 per share, scandalizing the little old ladies in my investment club. My $40 bid was just a California Dream.

With sales barely more than a Microsoft engineer's pocket change (estimated $12M), the sixteen-month-old Netscape Communications was instantly valued at $2.8B—as in B for Billion! *Inter@ctive Week* said, ". . . the stock market created its own version of artificial reality." I figured that preseason investors like me were either being scalped by the Nasdaq, or the Netscape

Netheads* had convinced Wall Street that some little company in Silicon Valley was on its way to becoming the next Microsoft. What I had witnessed was in fact the friction-free economy in action.

WHAT IS THE FRICTION-FREE ECONOMY?

The idea that a fly speck of a company could topple Microsoft from its perch atop the computer software industry food chain is intriguing, to say the least. Why would anyone bet their retirement account on a small company next to Highway 101 when Microsoft and Intel Corporation had the world by the short wire of the mouse? Why was Netscape valued so highly? The answer: *the friction-free economy*.

Netscape was not the first indication of the existence of the friction-free economy, but it was the hit movie version of it. Netscape's pyrotechnic entry onto the *Wall Street Journal*'s front page was perhaps the most dramatic illustration of how the non-Keynesian, non-Newtonian, nonclassical economics of the friction-free economy shifts modern market-driven corporations into high gear.

Why is the friction-free economy non-Keynesian? It does not obey the supply-equals-demand rule of classical economics. Why is it non-Newtonian? What goes up does not come down. Newtonian mechanics cannot explain the phenomenon; only *mathematical chaos* can. This new brand of economics overthrows the postindustrial-age idea of efficiency, diminishing marginal returns, and cost-effectiveness. In short, it dumbfounds even the economists.

The trouble is, the friction-free economy seems to work. It churned out Microsoft, Intel, and hundreds of high-tech successes throughout the 1980s. It churned out the Japanese video game empires of Sega, Nintendo, and Sony. Practiced as an intuitive art in the 1990s, it is responsible for the rapid rise of the

---

*Denizens of the Internet are called Netheads. Netscape Netheads follow Netscape Communications' movements like panthers in the night.

Wired World* and the unfolding of electronic manufacturing and distribution on the Internet. Now it is rapidly becoming the invisible hand that will guide millions of more businesses in the next century.

THE FRICTION-FREE ECONOMY IS UNIVERSAL

The friction-free economy is not restricted to the software industry. It applies to hardware and service companies also. It even applies to governments. France used a limited form of friction-free economics when it built Minitel—the first national "Internet" system that provides WWW-like† information to all French households. Minitel won over 15 million consumers by giving away its telecommunication devices. Relying on the French government's pocketbook, Minitel terminals gained widespread acceptance faster than a socialistic version of Netscape. Giving away first-generation products in order to capture the lion's share of a market segment is known as *mainstreaming*. Minitel is as mainstream in France as the telephone is in the U.S.

Mainstreaming is but one principle of the friction-free economy. There are many others. To be highly successful, all companies must eventually apply the principles of the friction-free economy, principles that are well understood by such hardware companies as Intel, Bay Networks, Sega, Sony, Nintendo, and Matsushita. These same principles are practiced with a vengeance by such software companies as Microsoft, Netscape, Adobe, Macromedia, SpyGlass, CyberCash, and Marimba. And perhaps surprisingly, the service sector is quickly learning how to use these techniques to become leaders in the banking, financial services, consulting, and legal sectors.

---

*The Wired World is where bits replace atoms, information replaces people, places, and things, and virtual communities come together in tribal ritual. It is the hardware, software, and services of the Internet, and everyone who uses it.

†WWW stands for World Wide Web, which is everything humans know, converted into bits, linked together, and transported into the Wired World.

A FIELD OF DREAMS

The primary precept of the friction-free economy is simple: The more market share you have, the more you get. In other words, the rich get richer. Consider the revenues of two competitors in the on-line service provider segment of the network business (Figure 1-1). CompuServe started out ahead of all others, but America Online surged ahead in 1995 because it mainstreamed. AOL blitzed the market by giving away its PC desktop software by the millions. If you had anything to do with the computer industry, owned a computer, subscribed to a computer magazine, or had a cousin with an AOL subscription, AOL would find you and mail a diskette containing its free software to your doorstep.

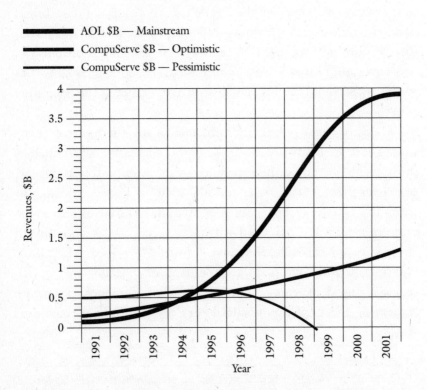

Figure 1–1. Mainstreaming versus languishing in the on-line services industry. AOL (America Online, Inc.) and CompuServe led the pack, but AOL mainstreamed while CompuServe did not.

Criticized for its high marketing expenditures, AOL succeeded in gaining market share at everyone else's expense. The revenues rolled in and the company is now a household word.*

The S-shaped curve of AOL revenues is characteristic of a mainstreaming company or product. It appears over and over again in all markets wherever a product or idea mainstreams.

To replicate AOL's success, businesses need to understand the first principle of the friction-free economy: The friction-free economy is (mostly) frictionless. That is, the cost of manufacturing, distribution, and support is much lower than in the old economy. This reduction in cost changes everything. Consider AOL once again. It beat out CompuServe by giving away its end-user software, called a browser†, to nearly everyone. During 1995 AOL included a free diskette containing its browser in every computer magazine printed. At a cost of $93 per user, getting customers was not exactly free for AOL, but the buildup in market share was astounding. AOL subscriptions accelerated while CompuServe floundered.

For simplicity's sake, the friction-free economy can be thought of as a kind of frictionless capitalism. This is where the non-Newtonian part comes in. Frictionless capitalism assumes zero production and distribution costs, no competitors, and the availability of unlimited resources. As Stephen Fleming of Alliance Technology Ventures says, the friction-free economy has "infinite shelf space, and zero marginal cost."[1] This idea has its limitations, but it is the fundamental gunpowder that blasted Netscape into orbit in 1995.

Maybe frictionless capitalism seems too idealistic, but in many ways it is ideal for the software age, where bits reign over atoms, information superhighways replace asphalt, and software standards mean more to Wall Street than P/E ratios. In some ways the new

---

*The household word is unprintable here. By 1997 AOL had so many customers that its on-line system became congested, leading some customers to complain to their attorneys. AOL was perhaps too successful as a mainstreaming company.

†A browser is a computer program that connects your computer to a service, via a telephone or network, so you can copy stuff from the service provider to your hard disk. Think of it as the dashboard of your Wired World vehicle.

economy is like a field of dreams—build it and sell it cheaply enough, and the customers will come.

THE CULT OF HIGH-TECH

At a fundamental level, infinite shelf space and zero marginal cost demolish the classical idea that supply equals demand. Throw this rule away. The friction-free economy violates such silly rules, but it has some silly rules of its own.

For example, the friction-free economy says to: drive prices to commodity levels, set standards at nanosecond intervals, target special interest groups, identify shooting ranges (and shoot), and appeal to tribalism. These guiding principles, and others, have achieved a cult status among marketing vice presidents. Some have names, in fact, such as Moore's Law, Davidow's Law, and the New Lanchester Strategy.

Moore's Law says that computer processing power doubles every eighteen months. This law sets the speed of the friction-free economy—a rate of change that has become known as Internet Time—and dictates a very important force operating in the friction-free economy: learning. Moore's Law is a kind of performance-learning curve that Intel and its competitors must follow. Moore's Law therefore is more than a techno-geek's mantra. It is a dramatic illustration of the importance of learning within the friction-free economy.

Davidow's Law is also a consequence of living in Internet Time, because it says, "The first product of a class to reach the market automatically gets 50% market share." Along with learning curves such as Moore's Law, it means that a company must render its own products obsolete before its competition does. Like Gordon Moore, William Davidow worked for Intel, where he observed the need for speed in obsolescing your own products.

The third major influence on the foundations of the friction-free economy came from a pioneer of the early 1900s. Londoner Frederick William Lanchester (1868–1946) designed England's first car, wrote *Aircraft in Warfare: The Dawn of the Fourth Arm*, and invented the mathematical theory of strategy in 1916. His ideas influenced Bernard Koopman, the father of operations research. W. Edward Deming introduced Koopman's and Lanchester's ideas to the Japanese in the 1960s, and academician Nobuo Taoka refined them into a marketing dogma for Japanese consumption. It has been codified as the New Lanchester Strategy, which describes the rules of warfare in the friction-free economy. When applied to business, the New Lanchester Strategy becomes a set of guidelines that tell a marketing manager how to defeat the competition.

Intel propels itself down the slippery slopes of Moore's Law by religiously applying Davidow's Law. Microsoft doubles the functionality of Microsoft Office while lowering its price faster than competitor IBM/Lotus Development. Netscape Communications evolves WWW standards while the standards committee ponders the next version of HTML.* Other companies like Adobe and Cisco stay out front through fleet-of-foot mergers and acquisitions.

In practical terms, applying these techniques catapults a product, service, or standard into the mainstream. And if you believe in frictionless capitalism—which you soon will—once a product achieves mainstream status, it is nearly impossible to dislodge. The product locks in its customers and brings enormous profits to the mainstreaming company. Hence, the goal of mainstreaming is *lock-in*.

NON-KEYNESIAN ECONOMICS

Mainstreaming is the single most sought-after goal of the friction-free economy. Netscape Communications may have demonstrated it in a dramatic fashion, but all businesses must strive to mainstream their products. The new era of the friction-free economy is based

---

*HTML is HyperText Markup Language. This is computer geek speak for the format that data must be in so that they can be stored, retrieved, sent, received, and viewed by WWW (World Wide Web) consumers.

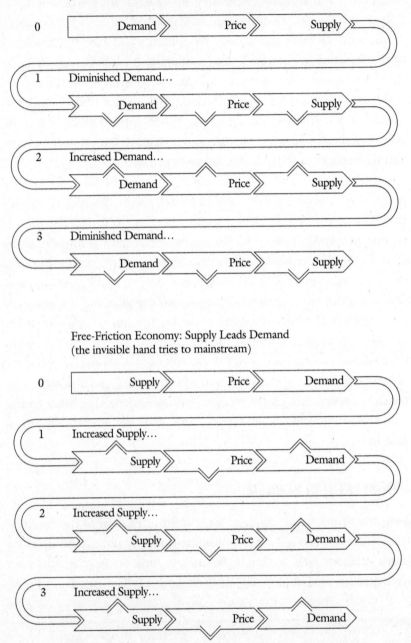

Figure 1–2. Classical vs. friction-free economies.

on the old idea of giving away the razors in order to sell the razor blades—or the reverse. Once millions of users are locked in to the company's product, they cannot escape. Mainstreamed products are dominant products in more than one meaning of the word. They simultaneously eliminate competition while they lock in the consumer.

Take Microsoft's mainstream product, called Office. It generates over $1 billion annually from routine upgrades. Users rarely consider abandoning the product because of the high cost of training, Microsoft's brand name, and the tribal community that holds Office users together.

But mainstreaming can be risky, because if it does not work, someone has to pay the bills. That is why it pays to understand the fundamentals of the friction-free economy. These principles are so radically different from the two-hundred-year-old principles stated by Adam Smith, Maynard Keynes, and other classical economists, they are often hard to believe. Sometimes they seem to violate the laws of physics; hence, they are also non-Newtonian. Yet, they can be seen in action in today's successful companies. They are the non-Keynesian "invisible hands" operating in the friction-free economy.

Subscribers to non-Keynesian ideas about market forces make idealistic assumptions that might seem absurd to a Stanford MBA. For example, what business school taught Netscape to start a business by giving away its cash cow? Netscape Navigator freeware propelled the company to 80% market share within six months of going public. Eudora, Qualcomm's e-mail client, is arguably the most popular freeware package in existence, yet Qualcomm sells thousands of copies of Eudora. McAfee Associates did not even think about making money from its installed base until it had 15 million users of its antivirus software! Most video game manufacturers such as Nintendo, Sega, and Sony lose money on the game machines, but make millions on the games. Sun Microsystems practically gave away its most important technological contribution of the decade, Java, and its stock doubled. Microsoft licensed its proprietary programming language called Visual BASIC to its competitors, and the next day its stock perked up. These examples point to one of the most confounding questions in the friction-free economy: *How can a company make any money if it gives away its products?*

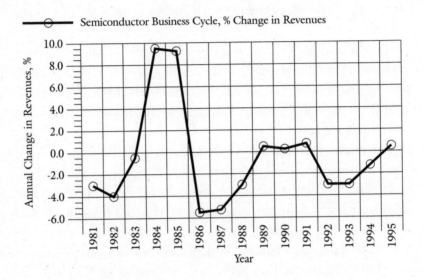

Figure 1–3. Business cycles in the semiconductor industry illustrate classical "supply follows demand" theory as it applies to chip manufacturing.

UPSIDE-DOWN ECONOMICS

Simplified diagrams of classical versus friction-free economics shown in Figure 1-2 attempt to answer the question, "How is friction-free economics different from classical economics?" In essence, classical economics has production dogging demand—the manufacturer *waits* for demand to rise or fall before adjusting production. This friction or delay introduces cycles and uncertainty into traditional markets, as illustrated by the semiconductor industry's ups and downs shown in Figure 1-3. In the classical economy, prices go down when demand goes down, forcing supply to also decline. In the friction-free economy, prices go down as supply goes up, forcing demand to increase.

In contrast, the friction-free economy turns the supply-equals-demand rule upside-down. Demand effortlessly follows production, because there is very little friction, and virtually no gravity. This leads to a radically different economy. A company either mainstreams or dies. There is little in between.

In the classical economy, prices go down when demand goes down, forcing supply to also decline. In the friction-free economy, prices go down as supply goes up, forcing demand to increase.

INCREASING RETURNS

Classical economics teaches the law of *diminishing marginal return*, or simply diminishing return. This means that as consumers get more and more food to eat, for example, they are less hungry. Full stomachs lead to less demand for food, hence, the diminishing return.

In the friction-free economy, consumers get hungrier as they eat more. For example, Microsoft customers want more and more software products from Microsoft. Why? Because users of software get locked into a particular word processor or publishing program. They do not want to learn a new system, so they keep buying the next version. Microsoft's profits grow as it releases new versions about every six months—feeding off of upgrades as well as new users. As users tell their friends about Microsoft's products, they too go out and purchase Microsoft products. Soon a product, service, or idea achieves a cult status. It becomes a fad, fashion, or "really cool product" in the eyes of the consumer. Before anyone knows it, it is a household name. When this happens, the product has reached the mainstream.

POSITIVE FEEDBACK

Lowering prices, locking in an installed base of users, and appealing to tribal instinct, all together stimulate demand. This kind of *positive feedback* mechanism piles more demand on top of previous demand. Instead of creating diminishing returns, a mainstreaming product, service, or idea gathers steam and generates more returns. Once this happens, there is no looking back. Production is constantly forced upward until market saturation is reached. Thus, the positive feedback inherent in the friction-free economy works in just the opposite way of the negative feedback, or diminishing returns of classical economics.

Positive feedback—fueled by low price—is why Netscape Communications was such a big hit. The brash young company applied the mainstreaming technique of frictionless capitalism in the extreme by *giving away* its WWW browser. Netscape purposely bought market share. "Free" is a very compelling price. By plunging the price of its WWW browser into the basement, Netscape hit the acceptance rooftop overnight, making the company the market leader. Now all businesses are stampeding to the WWW to give away their products!

RAZORS AND BLADES

The idea of giving away product to gain an edge has not escaped hardware-oriented companies either. Consider the "razors versus blades" approach employed by the hardware video game manufacturers. Sega, Sony, Nintendo, and Matsushita sell their game consoles at a loss of $150 or more, simply to lock in consumers and gain market share for their game cartridges. In the computer business this is known as creating an *installed base*. They make up for their losses by selling millions of games to their installed base.

Throughout most of the 1980s Microsoft used a similar technique when it licensed its operating system software to hardware vendors. Until the U.S. Department of Justice (DOJ) forced Microsoft to stop the practice, the company required that PC hardware vendors pay a license fee on every personal computer sold, regardless of whether or not it shipped with Microsoft's operating system. Even though Microsoft practically gave away its operating system, it required payment on every machine produced by the hardware vendor. In other words, IBM was required to pay a Microsoft PC-DOS license fee even when IBM shipped its PCs with IBM's own operating system in place of Microsoft's! This practice was ended as part of the settlement between the DOJ and Microsoft, but it illustrates how product managers combine friction-free economy principles with predatory thinking to generate a stream of revenue without even shipping a product.

LEARNING

The friction-free economy is about adding value to information. Adding value yields more information, and more information yields more added value. This cyclical process is a special kind of information-gathering called *learning*. Learning plays a central role in the non-Keynesian friction-free economy, because it replaces material advantage with know-how advantage.

Learning is a central part of the positive feedback mechanism at work in the friction-free economy. Generally, someone creates something new—an invention, computer program, or methodology. Then someone else improves the original. They have learned how to add value through a clever modification, enhancement, or application of the original. This fuels more innovation, adaptation, enhancement, add-ons, and improvements. More learning takes place, resulting in more value being added to subsequent generations of the product. This cycle of invention, learning, and adding value continues until the technology is exhausted or some other technology displaces the original.

The positive feedback effect of learning is nowhere more evident than in the computer hardware business. For example, when the original microprocessor was invented, hundreds of computer manufacturers added value to the basic invention by combining it with other chips to make a complete computer. These computers were used by people who invented new applications, which fed the microprocessor inventor/manufacturer with new information; i.e., the manufacturer learned. As a consequence, a newer, faster, smaller, cheaper microprocessor was manufactured to accommodate the new applications. The original microprocessor was not able to process video data, for example, but after several generations of invention, learning, and adding value, subsequent microprocessors handled not only video, but sound, fax, and telephones. This cycle continues today. In fact, the process has accelerated to the point where computer technology improves by a factor of 500 every decade!

INTERNET TIME

A consequence of learning is that entire societies get hooked on speed. Everything speeds up because learning is used to accelerate more learning. Thus, people, companies, governments, and other institutions must live in Internet Time—a time scale so brief that the interval between an event and a response to that event is imperceptible. Internet Time has been compared with the fast-forward life of a dog—seven human years equal one Internet Time year!

The learning process, along with the positive feedback mechanism that accommodates it, is described by a *learning curve*. Learning curves drive the friction-free economy. But what makes learning in the friction-free economy unique is that it is used on itself—learning is used to improve the learning process itself. Thus, the pace of change accelerates. Rapid learning rates of change are to the friction-free economy as banks were to the industrial age—they both compound their most valuable asset. Therefore, controlling learning rates of change is a key ingredient in the friction-free economy.

The compounding of learning rates has become a challenge to society because of the stress it places on humans. But in the friction-free economy, it is used like a hammer. Companies must plan and act within very short time periods—Internet Time—or else become as irrelevant as yesterday's headlines. Table 1-1 shows how we have come to Internet Time.

Fabrice Gropaiz, age twenty-five, helped raise money for AIDS research by donning a pair of in-line skates and skating around the world in 1996. Starting in San Francisco and skating eastward, first to the 1996 Olympic Games in Atlanta, Georgia, later to Europe, and then back to Los Angeles, he averaged about ten miles per hour, or sixty miles per day. At that velocity, Fabrice could circle the globe at its equator in 417 days, or in less than eighteen months. Without in-line skates, it takes three to five years for a human to walk around the world.

In earlier times, products, services, and ideas also propagated at the velocity of foot power. With the assistance of domestic animals, products, services, and ideas moved faster—an order of magnitude faster. Therefore, ideas circled the globe in less time, meaning that they could mainstream faster.

According to Table 1-1, the industrial age was ten times shorter than the agrarian age; and the postindustrial age was ten times shorter than the industrial age. In other words, the length of each age is tied to the rate of transportation and communication—the technology—of the age.

Given the friction-free economy equivalent of interaction, i.e., the Internet and global communications technology, it is possible to estimate the time scale of the friction-free economy. Curiously, it is extremely short, which suggests several interesting limitations to further speedup. Can we expect an age that is even shorter than three to five years? Unlikely.

Age	Length of Time (years)	Rate of Interaction (mph)	Time to Circle Earth (years)
Agrarian	3–5000 (Age)	3–5 (Human)	3–5 (Years)
Industrial	3–500 (Revolution)	3–50 (Horse-Auto)	.3–.5 (Months)
Post-industrial	3–50 (Trend)	3–500 (Airliner)	.03–.05 (Days)
Friction-free	3–5 (Fad)	3–5000 (Network)	.003–.005 (Hours)

Table 1–1. Ages and their lengths correlated with technology.

TERMINAL VELOCITY

For all practical purposes, the friction-free economy time scale (hours) is near the limit of human ability to absorb information and make decisions. Instead of being metered by technology, change in the friction-free economy is metered by human cycles of sleep, thought, and communication. Therefore, the friction-free economy is bounded by human frailty. Even if someday someone learns how to communicate faster than the speed of light, it is unlikely that significant groups of humans will be able to absorb the message and act on it in less time than the time scale of the friction-free economy. Without such fast reflexes, friction-free economy products cannot achieve mainstream saturation any faster than the three- to five-year time scale of the friction-free economy.

It is the age of *terminal velocity*. At terminal velocity, change is constant and so is the rate of change. The friction-free economy is the end of the line. It is the last of the major ages. But it will have a lasting effect, because it will permanently alter the global economy, leaving behind the principles of the friction-free economy.

John Trudel, a consultant from Portland, Oregon, who specializes in learning organizations, recognized this limiting factor in what he calls the information age. "I doubt there has been a time when there was so much frenzy and so little thought. Business performance and personal lives suffer from an Alice-in-Wonderland existence, where people run ever faster to stay in the same spot. Rather than doing things faster and cheaper, [managers] will invest to be different and better . . . we need new methods for business. The new ways will be as different from linear, reductionist, Machine-Age business as quantum physics is from Newtonian physics."[2]

THE DIGITAL *KEIRETSU*

Learning takes place most rapidly in groups in the friction-free economy. As a market space is divided into pieces by specialization and segmentation, and prices drop along a commodity price-learning curve, profits drop as well. This forces companies to join together in consortia, joint-ventures, and near-monopolies. Such a group is what I call a *digital keiretsu*, because it resembles the similar business groups of companies in Japan.

The digital *keiretsu* is a consequence of learning. Because the whole is greater than the sum of the parts, businesses in the twenty-first century will increasingly join together in order to tap the value of entire market spaces. For example, Intel and Microsoft work together to build high-end servers out of Intel hardware and Microsoft software. Both companies enjoy greater profits than either one on its own.

A digital *keiretsu* pumps value out of an entire market food chain. This process is called *value chain integration*, and is one of the emerging techniques used by hunter-gatherers of the friction-free economy. Learning is part of value chain integration—a concept that has a chapter all its own later in this book.

INVERSE ECONOMICS

Postindustrial society ran on a kind of topsy-turvy economic tread-mill called *inverse economics*. In simple terms, inverse economics means that products like cellular phones, TVs, or video recorders get better and faster as they get cheaper. Today's consumer expects this to happen. If next year's computer isn't faster and cheaper, sales lag until the computer industry offers a better, faster, and cheaper model.

Inverse economics, being non-Keynesian, has many nonintuitive consequences. One is its impact on mainstreaming. Understanding their relationship is key to understanding how to compete well in the friction-free economy. Adoption of a mainstream product is tied to price-learning. As a product commoditizes, it reaches 100% penetration into a market space—or else dies.

Take as an example the rapid conversion of the telephone system that is going on because of the rise of digital telephony, called CTI (Computer-Telephony Integration). The idea is simple:

Combine computer and telephone so that both data and voice can run over the same connections. With the appropriate hardware and software, and an Internet connection, anyone can place long-distance voice, data, and fax calls without paying long-distance charges! Such telephone calls hop, skip, and jump across the Internet to their destination without ever going through the billing computer that charges for the exchange. No wonder the Internet is growing so fast—it saves time and money.

The problem with CTI is that it requires special hardware and software. And not everyone is connected to the Internet. Progressive Networks, Inc., a software company that understands the friction-free economy, has been selling software that bypass industrial age telephone systems. With Progressive Networks' Real Audio Software and the proper connections, anyone can eliminate long-distance charges. However, the rate at which Progressive Networks can mainstream its products is determined by a declining price curve that forces both supply and demand to soar just as Figure 1-2 predicts. According to the friction-free economy, prices must decline in order to force unit volume up. This is indeed what is occurring in the telephone industry.

DAVIDOW'S LAW

Because inverse economics forces everyone to be a low-cost leader, and because quality must remain high regardless of the cost of production, every business is faced with the conundrum of being both a value and premium leader. There is only one way out: Davidow's Law.

Davidow's Law states that a business must be the first in its industry to render its own products obsolete. This is why Intel and other friction-free economy businesses work hard to replace their own products. Named after a vice president of Intel, Davidow's Law requires that a company be the first competitor to bring a new-generation product to market in order to dominate that market. It is better to leave out some feature or capability than to bring a new product to market in second or third place. Microprocessors from

Intel are not always the best or the fastest, but they are most often the first of their generation to hit the streets.

Intel nearly always demonstrates Davidow's Law when introducing new product lines. The one noteworthy exception was the company's failure to bring their RISC processor products to market before other manufacturers. The IBM/Motorola/Apple consortium beat Intel at its own game with the introduction of the PowerPC line. This sent powerful shock waves through Intel in the mid-1990s. In fact, in 1995 Intel purposely cut short the technological life of its wildly successful 486 processor to ward off the challenge of the IBM Power PC RISC product family. On April 26, 1995, headlines proclaimed, "To Aid Pentium, Intel Will Slow Flow of 486's." The article detailed how Intel applies Davidow's Law: "The decision reflects a long-standing Intel strategy of creating faster and smaller microprocessors before its competitors can catch up . . . then tries to drag computer makers and consumers along by cutting off supply of the older chips while lowering prices on its new, faster chips. Using this strategy, Intel has left behind many competitors that may not have developed microprocessors up to the new standard established by Intel."[3] Microsoft illustrates the same law—also called *versioning*—as it is applied to the software business. Instead of designing and writing the most powerful, feature-laden word processor, communication program, or electronic spreadsheet as a powerful first product, Microsoft and other software development companies use an evolutionary approach. Starting with a simple, straightforward version of a word processor, say, they work through a series of versions to get to the all-time best product. The software industry says it takes Microsoft at least three versions to get it right. Actually, Microsoft never gets it entirely right, because if it did, consumers would not need to buy the next version. Without versioning, Microsoft's sales would plummet.

Microsoft knows that it is better to be first of a kind than best of a kind. In fact, this has created a small industry of journalists and pundits who swarm around Microsoft, hoping to be the first to report on the next version of its products. Most computer magazines and publications in the industry owe their existence to these announcements. Perhaps the most flagrant example of this was the hype surrounding Windows 95. The press lavished nearly a year's worth of public relations on it. In reality, Windows 95 was an incomplete version of the full product. Microsoft will roll out Windows 97, and subsequent versions, before the full product arrives. This allows the software giant to obsolesce its own products.

The publicity that surrounds Microsoft is a dramatic example of how a company keeps its customers enthralled while contemplating the next version of its products. Enthralled customers don't buy a competitor's product, even if it is better.

How can your business keep up? Intel and Microsoft develop their next generation products concurrently with their next two or three generations. Although it is difficult to anticipate what features should go into future versions, it is better to make intelligent guesses and reduce the functionality of these products than to be late to market.

CANNIBALS IN THE WIRED WORLD

Davidow's Law and inverse economics play to the same side of the house. Take the CTI business again. In 1996 small companies like Progressive Networks, Third Planet Publishing, and VocalTech threatened huge and powerful AT&T with an innovative little software gadget that let anyone on the Internet place a long-distance telephone call for free.

These "net-phones" created a business that was estimated at $3.5 million in 1995, and expected to ramp up to $500 million by 1999. This may be mere pocket change to AT&T, but it scared the headsets off of the big telephone companies nonetheless. Tom Evslin, vice president of AT&T's WorldNet, said, "We intend to take a lead role in [this market], if anybody's going to cannibalize our revenue, it's going to be us." Spoken like a disciple of Davidow's Law.

AT&T WorldNet may be outwardly savvy to the friction-free

economy, but in 1996 there were plenty of industrial age reactionaries still in power. The American Carriers Telecommunication Association, a trade group that represents 130 regional long-distance telephone companies, petitioned the U.S. Federal Communications Commission to ban net-phones. This classical legal move, borrowed from the postindustrial age, did not work in 1996. Even if it had, fleet-footed businesses like VocalTech would have changed the rules and circumvented the regulations in some other way.

COMMODITY PRICES

Because of inverse economics and its relationship with mainstreaming, commoditization will become more influential as the friction-free economy kicks in. Consider the rumored Wired World entrepreneur who offered to send a riddle a day for 365 days to anyone on the Internet who asked to be tickled. Over 250,000 people mailed in $1 for the year-long subscription. Now our hero gets up in the Hawaiian early hours, conjures up a riddle, e-mails it, and goes to the beach! Not a bad way to make $250,000 per year!

Commoditization is alive and well in the real world, too. In 1996 the Kellogg Company rolled back the price of Froot Loops, Corn Flakes, and its other breakfast cereals an average of 19% in response to Post Cereal, which took 3% market share away from Kellogg in 1996 by lowering prices on its cereals. Three percentage points is $270 million worth of snap, crackle, and pop in the $8 billion American cereal business. Kellogg, with 36% of the market, dominates the breakfast tables of America. Its nearest competitor is General Mills with 26%, which gives Kellogg a big lead. In fact, sales of breakfast cereals were flat for years until Post started the 1996 price war that bagged market share for the third-place company. Post moved up from 13% to 16% two months after lowering its prices. This was war.

There is only one response to commoditization. General Mills soon lowered its prices, too.

PREMIUM BEANS

The riddle-a-day example illustrates the power of frictionless capitalism. However, commoditization is even more insidious than an industrial age economist can imagine. As it turns out, commodity products can surpass premium products in both price and quality, simply by applying principles of inverse economics, learning curves, and volume production within the friction-free economy. This is the lesson taught by coffee beans.

When Mr. Schultz returned from Italy, he was gonzo over European coffee. But back home in Seattle, coffee was like American beer—flat and boring. Worse still, Americans didn't know the difference between café latte and engine oil at an I-5 truck stop. Schultz had to educate people one cup of coffee at a time. Today his chain of Starbucks is serving 3 million caffeine heads per week from 800 stores. This number will double by the year 2000.

Starbucks is built on a foundation of quality. According to CEO Schultz, "What we noticed in our early years and maybe even more today is that the majority of products on the market today generally focus on a baseline of mediocrity."[4]

The friction-free economy mandates that products must compete on price as well as quality. This is a consequence of inverse economics and learning theory. However, because of high-tech manufacturing efficiencies and electronic distribution, inverse economics operates much faster and more voraciously in the friction-free economy than in the cereal economy or the coffee bean economy.

Information-gathering, or learning, plays an important role in making your business operate faster and more voraciously. Nonetheless, applying Davidow's Law, inverse economics, and learning theory may not be enough. You may still need to resort to branding.

PRODUCT BRANDING

In the friction-free economy, products are commodities, consumers are overloaded with data, and fads come and go too rapidly for consumers to make intelligent buying decisions. Planned obsolescence through the application of Davidow's Law may not be enough to engender customer loyalty. Therefore, businesses must use *branding*, i.e., associating a product name with a company to hold on to customers in a fickle world.

Intel's "Intel Inside" advertisements and Microsoft's image ads are examples of branding campaigns. The idea is to cut through the commodity-based market with a knife so sharp that the customer does not have to think before buying. The brand name becomes a fashion. It is fashionable to own a personal computer with "Intel inside" written on the box. It is cool to belong to the Apple Macintosh tribe.

Branding can sometimes attract easy money in the Wired World. Mike O'Connor of Saint Paul, Minnesota, owned a valuable piece of WWW property. His address on the Internet is www.television.com. Now, if you were CBS, NBC, FOX, or Turner, wouldn't it be nice to be synonymous with television? A WWW address like this should be worth millions, simply because it automatically brands whoever owns it. Two weeks after publicizing the auction of his address to the highest bidder, O'Connor turned down a $50,000 offer from CNET in hopes of a six- or seven-figure proposition from a larger media company. Look up www.television.com on the WWW and see who owns it now.

Product branding often comes into conflict with an antiquated legal system, too. Consider Philip Giacalone of Salinas, California, who wanted the WWW address Ty.com for his own. Giacalone staked his claim on Ty.com—named after his three-year-old son— for a virtual community called TechYard. The problem was, a company named Ty Warner of Chicago also wanted the address. Ty Warner makes stuffed animals for children.

Ty Warner held a trademark on "Ty," and Giacalone held the Wired World rights to the domain name "Ty." The postindustrial age legal system clashed with the friction-free economy squatter's rights when Giacalone filed in court, asking for $100,000 in damages, and the rights to Ty.com. "I'm not interested in selling it. It's my son's name. Maybe someday I will give it to him when I am through with it," said Giacalone.[5]

Smart businesses use various means of marketing to brand their products. If successful, the company's name rather than actual product is what really sells.

MARKET-OF-ONE

Jim Solomon was already a Silicon Valley guru when he dropped out of the high-tech business world and went into the restaurant business. He made millions in the computer-aided-design segment of the software industry after cofounding Cadence Design Systems in 1983. Then one day he walked out, saying, "I decided it was time to get a break and recharge the batteries."

Solomon had worked for the big names in technology—Motorola and National Semiconductor. He was known as an innovator, and later an entrepreneur. In addition to starting Cadence, he started a robotics company in 1994, and other companies in 1995. But in 1996 he had enough of straight-line corporate thinking. Instead, the friction-free economy's magnet attracted Solomon to the *market-of-one*.

In a friction-free economy, where inverse economics drives everything to a commodity, marketers must turn to targeted audiences. The smallest targeted audience is in fact a market-of-one. Is it possible to design, manufacture, market, and sell a product designed for a single person? In the friction-free economy, markets-of-one are not only possible, but required. Commoditization forces businesses to target individuals. Individualization and personalization are what distinguish products in the friction-free economy.

One of Jim Solomon's companies, Xulu Entertainment, is a chain of nightclubs that sell personalized entertainment and food. Customers are interviewed to find out what they like, how they like it, and with whom. They receive a personalized meal, a tailored adventure, and meet people of similar interests.

Xulu Entertainment nightclubs don't sell commodity products. They sell upscale, premium-priced entertainment that uses market-of-one techniques to thwart commoditization. In place of riding the commoditization learning curve, some businesses may choose to ride the market-of-one learning curve. The market-of-one principle is this: *Technology makes money when it is used to deliver high-quality products that are tailored to a market-of-one.* When coupled with inverse economics, the market-of-one principle can potentially produce higher revenues and provide a better defense against competitors than pure commodity-based products. However, market-of-one companies must not forget to obsolesce their own products.

NARROWCASTING

Marketing in the friction-free economy means finding a market-of-one and then targeting customers in that narrow segment of the market. This is called *narrowcasting*,* a word invented by Professor J. C. R. Licklider of MIT. In contrast to industrial age broadcasting, narrowcasting appeals to a narrow rather than broad audience.

Custom Clothing Technology, the software company that created technology for custom-fit blue jeans for women, invented the Personal Pair kiosk. With Personal Pair, a customer enters her measurements and style preferences into an ATM-like kiosk located in the store. Answering certain questions—do you like straight or tapered legs, do you like hip huggers, and so on—the customer defines what she wants through an interactive dialog with the machine. The kiosk suggests styles to try on, offers photos of the jeans, and accepts feedback.

Levi Strauss & Company thought Custom Clothing Technology had such a good idea that it bought the company, and now markets the kiosk through its thirty stores in the U.S.

Finding jeans that fit a single person is the first step toward a market-of-one philosophy. The next step is to manufacture them on the spot. Someday consumers might even trust a kiosk computer enough to let it keep personal records on their buying preferences.

---

*Narrowcasting is to broadcasting what a rifle is to a shotgun.

Even further in the future, the kiosk might be piped directly into consumers' homes by way of the WWW.

Fit Finder illustrates how friction-free economy technology is used to bring greater levels of personalization and tailoring to consumers—the whole idea of the market-of-one principle. Smart marketers use technology to create more options, more service, and more responsiveness to individual needs.

TANK COMMANDERS

The ultimate in market-of-one business is Peter Lewis's Progressive Insurance Company. Adjusters more or less live in Ford Explorers instead of holding down a desk. The Explorers are wired into a 24-hour computer that spits out settlements in minutes. Like tank commanders in Desert Storm, Progressive adjusters roll up to the accident scene while the rubber is still steaming, connect to their databases, and whip out a check on the spot.

Better still, call Progressive at 1-800-AUTOPRO and you get information on both Progressive's products and its competitors' products. In Florida you can compare Progressive's rates with those quoted by State Farm and Allstate. According to *Fortune* magazine (August 7, 1995), "Even if its price is slightly higher, the customer may choose to pay it out of gratitude for having been provided such friendly service."[6]

The friction-free economy is already operating in noncomputer, nonsoftware businesses. These are businesses of the future because of their marketing strategy, not because they use computers, the Internet, or high-tech consultants.

BAD BEER

Spring Street Brewing Company, makers of Wit Beer, was the first business to sell shares of its company in cyberspace. Spring Street's founder Andrew Klein bypassed stockbrokers and deal makers altogether when his IPO went out over the WWW in 1995. Klein's next move was to help other companies go public without the costly assistance of underwriters or brokers. Using his Web page (www.witbeer.com) as a weapon, former securities lawyer Klein created Wit Capital Corporation—a competitor to the New York Stock Exchange, Nasdaq, and American Exchange.

Then came the problem. According to Klein, "The goal is to fantastically reduce the cost of transactions."[7] Oops, Klein has completely missed the meaning of the friction-free economy. People don't want cheaper products; they want cheaper and more personalized products.

In the friction-free economy, personalization, individualization, and the market-of-one are winning ideas. Efficiency, lowering costs, and saving money are dying ideas. Had Starbucks cut corners and made cheap coffee, they would not be serving 3 million cups per week. If Levi Strauss succeeds with its kiosks, it will be because the customer gets tailored goods, personalized attention, and a perfect fit at Wal-Mart prices.

Contrast Spring Street Beer's approach to the stock market with that of Accutrade. In 1996 the discount broker, based in Omaha, Nebraska, gave away 120,000 copies of its stock market investor software and then started signing up customers at the rate of 800 per month. What did Accutrade have that so many investors wanted?

The Accutrade software turned individual investors into professional stockbrokers. Individuals could design complex trades that were automatically triggered when one or more stocks reached a preset value. Acting on behalf of its owner, Accutrade's simple browser automated some of the humanlike search and inference functions that were previously done by a human broker. "I don't believe it," was the reaction of some customers who needed to be reassured by Accutrade humans that the product really performed humanlike functions without a human.[8]

Accutrade attracts on-line customers because its services are personalized and tailored to the individual investor. Unlike Spring Street Beer's approach to buying and selling stocks, Accutrade targets a market-of-one.

VIRTUAL COMMUNITIES

A business must identify the personal habits, preferences, or tastes of a "typical individual" and build a product that is tailored to that individual. Then it must ferret out the millions of potential consumers and sell to them as if they were the most unique on the planet. But to keep those customers for more than a few microseconds, a business must appeal to their "shared experiences, values, or interests." In other words, create a sense of community. A successful marketing strategy must appeal to the tribal agrarian in us all.

ClariNet Communications in San Jose, California, is a perfect example. They "own" a tidy little tribal community of 1.3 million subscribers to e.News. According to their home page (www.clari.net/), "ClariNet e.News is an electronic newspaper: professional news and information delivered to your computer in the Usenet news format. Your site receives live news (including technology-related wire stories), timely computer industry news, syndicated columns and features, financial information, stock quotes and more."

ClariNet is a market-of-one company, because it delivers what you want, on your computer, without the need for you to log in, search, and download the results. The e.News content is site-licensed to corporations, schools, and ISPs (Internet Service Providers) without advertising.

More important, ClariNet is a tribal company, because its subscribers make up what is called a *virtual community*. Virtual communities are bound by the human need to be with birds of a feather. This notion will play an even more important role as technology connects people from anywhere in the world to products and services from anywhere in the world.

Ian Brown, host of the CBC (Canadian Broadcasting Company) radio show "Sunday Morning," writes about death and mourning on the WWW:

During one of my radio broadcasts recently, I mentioned that a friend of mine had died. His name was Yuri Rubinski, and he was 43 years old. A couple of days later, strange things began to happen. My e-mail began to pile up with messages from people I didn't know but who had known Yuri. They were short notes full of details. I knew Yuri too, they said. We met in high school. We listened to Sergeant Pepper together for the first time. He had a wild beard. That sort of thing. Now, in cyberspace, Yuri has never ceased to exist. Before long, Yuri had more of a presence in my computer than he'd had in my life. It was as if, over the Internet, people were still passing around his spirit. What I was witnessing, though I hesitate to use the word, was a resurrection—and a very believable one at that. The mourners at this digital wake could open up to one another fearlessly, because we did so in the invisible realm of cyberspace.[9]

Ian Brown experienced one of the most significant aspects of the Wired World—virtual communities are collections of people who form tribes that act out agrarian-age rituals. This kind of tribalism is more responsible for the rise of the WWW than the technology used to construct the Wired World.

Young Kelly Modica was living in Alabama with her soldier husband when she became pregnant with her first child. She was eight hundred miles away from home and did not know anyone, so she joined the August List—143 women from all over the world who expected their baby in August.

Kelly Modica's virtual community spanned the globe—from Norway to South Africa. "If I was living somewhere else where I had friends who were pregnant, it would be okay," she said, "but the August List has been the greatest resource for me, because I've been able to bond with all of these women."[10]

Virtual communities are a perfect match for the market-of-one principle. They are also loyal communities. For example, when Apple Computer got into trouble in 1996, 91% of Apple's customers said they were confident the company would recover. "We are devoted to the Mac," said Betty Baldwin of Space Science

Division at NASA Ames Research in Mountain View, California. "Our users would die if they told us we had to change from the Mac."[11] When asked why people in companies continued to buy Macintosh computers when it looked like Apple Computer was failing, Macintosh tribalism kicked in: "If Apple disappeared tomorrow there would be a lot of depressed graphics artists and publishers," said David Wu of Chicago Corporation.[12] Apple Computer led the PC industry in repurchase loyalty throughout its bad year. According to a survey conducted by Computer Intelligence InfoCorp, 87% of customers who bought a Macintosh in 1995 purchased another Macintosh.[13] Tribalism may have been the main reason Apple survived.

BRANDING AND TRIBALISM

Tribalism is alive and well in noncomputer industries, too. The Extended Family Database maintained by Saturn Automobile company allows Saturn customers to search for other Saturn owners by location and by model of car. One anonymous owner sent e-mail saying, "I hate cars, but I love Saturns. If I become rich and famous, I won't waste money on fancy, expensive cars, but instead buy a couple of Saturns every year."[14]

Virtual communities build brand name loyalty. The more that technology is used to create a sense of community, the more revenue and loyalty are returned. James Champy understands the importance of community and tribalism in the newspaper business. According to Champy, if newspapers want to survive in the friction-free economy and remain players in the Wired World, they have to "build electronic communities in employment [ads], home buying, and used cars to at least protect their classified advertising business—which can represent one-third of total revenues." Champy goes on to apply friction-free economy concepts to the survivability of other businesses: "Many other businesses will face the same stark choice—either to make their existing products obsolete through the development of on-line communities or to watch as other entities do it for them."[15]

In fact, the virtual community encompasses all of society. As the friction-free economy matures, everyone will become a part of some virtual community. When this idea becomes mainstream, many of the postindustrial rituals will give way to old-fashioned agrarian rituals. But I get ahead of myself.

LIVING IN INTERNET TIME

In the friction-free economy, new products, services, or ideas must achieve mainstream acceptance within a matter of years, not decades. Businesses must move at the speed of Internet Time—eighteen months. Home computers become obsolete in a matter of a few years; entertainment products are mere fads lasting less than a year; and few consumers remember the popularity of citizens band radios, big-dish satellite TVs, and Walkman tape players and radios.

A product must achieve widespread market acceptance in Internet Time, or it will never achieve widespread market acceptance. Netscape Navigator achieved 80% of the WWW browser market within months of its initial release. Microsoft's initial release of Windows 95 sold 10 million copies in its first year.

In fact, friction-free economy products are purposely rendered obsolete according to Davidow's Law. There are only two kinds of businesses: the quick and the dead.

The harsh reality of living in Internet Time challenges all businesses to learn the principles of the friction-free economy. Fortunately, you have this book to guide you.

Mainstreaming Henry Ford's PC

THE MEANING OF LIFE

After the Netscape IPO debacle, I mixed myself an orange juice cocktail laced with some medicinal alcohol,* and contemplated the meaning of life. I must not have been alone, because other stock market investors were left scratching their mostly bald heads throughout 1995 and 1996 as the high-tech sector propelled the Nasdaq and New York Exchange to ridiculous new heights. I felt compelled to understand this new age. My financial life depended on it.

In 1953, when mass production of computers began, the Dow Industrial Average was approximately three hundred. It took twenty-five years for NASA to put Neil Armstrong on the moon and the Dow to reach seven hundred—a little more than double its 1953 level. But as the friction-free economy began to kick in during the early 1990s, the Dow doubled between the time of the U.S. invasion of Iraq in 1991 and the Netscape Communications invasion of the Internet in 1996. Both were impressive events.

---

*Smirnoff.

Something was afoot, and I knew it, as I lined up behind blue-haired retirees at the Monterey Public Library waiting to use the card catalog computer. I needed to find an explanation for the surge in the market—especially the high-tech sector. How might I take advantage of the coming friction-free economy? Was it a bust, or was it "doomonomics," as *The Economist* said:

"[The friction-free economy stretches] a central principle of traditional economics, the law of diminishing returns. This says that, as production expands, every individual producer will eventually find that his costs per unit start to rise. The result is profound: firms stop growing, and competition can flourish. Production of software does not appear to obey this rule—or, at any rate, not in a straightforward way. Once a program has been written, it costs next to nothing to manufacture and market. That is why software companies can choose to sell their products very cheaply or indeed give them away. As [computer game] Doom proved, once market share has been gained, it becomes easier to sell follow-on products at higher prices."[1]

Doomonomics, named after the mainstreamed computer game Doom, is another word for friction-free economics. It is yet another illustration of increasing returns harvested from mainstreaming.

My pilgrimage to the library was beginning to pay off. The impact of the friction-free economy on the value of the stock market was becoming clear. But what were the underlying forces? I wanted a sound theory of the friction-free economy so I could beat out my investment competitors when the next opportunity presented itself. My search led me deeper into the library.

EVERYTHING'S GOING SOFTWARE

After several journeys to the library and hours spent in front of my computer viewing articles recovered from the WWW, I found a trail previously blazed by W. Brian Arthur, a former Stanford economist now at the Santa Fe Institute, and other expert economists, including Paul Krugman and Paul Romer. Arthur had already formulated a theory for explaining the friction-free economy. He had figured out where everything in the economy was going.

"Everything's going software," says Arthur, with a gleam in his eye.[2]

Chapter 1 of this book may have left you with the impression that mainstreaming can go on forever. Guess again. The friction-free economy may be non-Keynesian, but it is still subject to market forces.

Says James Aley: "The fact that increasing returns exists does not mean that diminishing returns doesn't. Far from it. Arthur argues that the two phenomena will always co-exist and are complementary."[3]

In fact, the friction-free economy merely delays the time when the effect of diminishing returns begins to kick in.

The Economist had more to say on this subject:

An economy ruled by increasing returns is a scary thing to contemplate. Free markets work well because they tend to reach equilibrium, with many companies competing and no one firm dominating for too long. In the world of increasing returns, this equilibrium would seem to break down: the big tend to get bigger without limit. Monopoly power becomes pervasive, and the need for vigorous regulation by government correspondingly great.

On the supply side, the software economics of production and distribution reduces the cost of entering the software market; technological ingenuity and a spirit of innovation will matter more than marketing clout, manpower and other expensive resources. The smaller the initial cost, the smaller the financial advantages of increasing returns. Increasing returns eventually run out of steam. Diminishing returns still kick in, just later than they might in other industries.

The economic implications of the digital revolution extend far beyond the software industry. Any information-based industry will be subject to the same forces as it automates and moves on-line. Banking, for example, has traditionally been a diminishing-returns business. But as banking moves on-line, the work of processing customers' business is done by cheap computers, not expensive staff. The bank that has the greatest reach and can spread its fixed costs over the largest number of customers will be able to offer the best rates and deals, thereby attracting even more customers. Enter increasing returns. The same can be said for all sorts of service industries, from processing insurance-claims forms to managing inventories. Whenever computers and networks can greatly diminish variable costs, volume suddenly becomes all-important: the more the better.[4]

My understanding was getting somewhere; but digging deeper, I found that the idea of mainstreaming itself was nothing new. In fact, mainstreaming and other principles of friction-free economics have been practiced for a long time. Even before computers and software were being mainstreamed, entrepreneurs were using mainstreaming to create market-leading businesses. Even before the postindustrial age, industrial age entrepreneurs used the same techniques as Microsoft's Bill Gates to build powerful empires, radically alter society, and leave a little for posterity.

THE FIRST PC

The first PC* was built and mainstreamed by Henry Ford. Ford set the standard for a new idea in the industrial age: a mass consumer product. But he did more than sell cars; he built an entirely new industry. By 1914 Ford Motor Company had 48% of the market for PCs. Starting in a garage, like many famous and not-so-famous Silicon Valley entrepreneurs, Ford rapidly grew to dominate the PC market within two decades, from 1905 until 1925.

---

*Of course, the first PC (personal car) was Ford's Phenomenal Machine—the Model T. If you missed the movie, read the book *The Death of Competition*, J. F. Moore, HarperBusiness, 1996, pp. 89–91.

Henry did not invent the automobile, but he did something more important. He invented *mainstreaming*. The PC (personal car) was one of the first mass-produced, mass-marketed, and mass-consumed products of modern times. It was so massive, it wiped out the carriage business in less time than it took to retrain most displaced carriage workers.

Mainstreaming is quantitatively described by an adoption curve that plots market adoptions as a percentage of total users, against time (Figure 2-1). Thus, 50% adoption means that one-half of the potential consumers of a product own the product. As time passes, the percentage changes. If the percentage tends towards 100%, we say the product mainstreams.

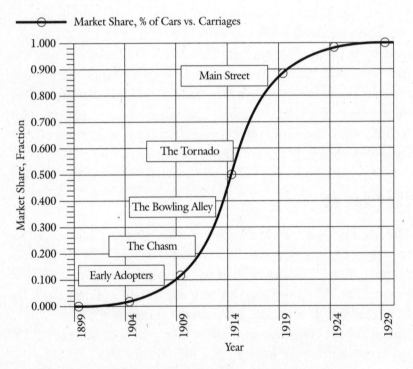

Figure 2–1. **Mainstreaming of internal combustion–powered automobiles versus horse-drawn carriage. (Courtesy U.S. Department of Commerce, Historical Statistics of the United States, Colonial Times to 1970, Washington D.C. Bureau of Statistics, 1975, p. 176.)**

SOMETHING NEW, SOMETHING OLD

The rise of the automobile industry is so similar to the rise of the computer industry that it is difficult to claim that anything is new under the sun. In fact, the story of the rise of the automobile industry parallels the modern story of Microsoft and Apple Computer.

Think of turn-of-the-century Ford Motor Company as today's Microsoft, and pre-1930s GM as Apple Computer. Compare the competitive landscape back then with today's computer market space.*

"Ford and Durant† rapidly became the two major forces in the nascent auto business. Over the next 20 years, near legendary battles between Ford and General Motors would erupt . . . by 1920 the General Motors ecosystem had nearly collapsed . . . Durant was ousted by his investors."[5]

Seventy years later, Microsoft and Apple Computer would become fierce competitors in the personal computer operating systems (OS) market. Within little more than a decade, the Apple Macintosh OS had lost its market to Microsoft's Windows OS. Like Durant's General Motors, Apple in 1996 "could not achieve sufficient economies of scale and was consequently stuck with high-cost structures and increasingly uncompetitive products."[6] And like Ford, Microsoft based its operating system on product simplicity and commodity pricing. Consequently Microsoft's OS sped past the Macintosh OS in terms of market share.

The game did not end seventy-five years ago, however. Alfred P. Sloan led GM back into the top tier by segmenting the market for autos, using classical targeting techniques. Continuing the battle for market share, the best-selling automobiles fragmented the market into six pieces. Yet, only fifteen models from six companies accounted for almost 5 million units per year by the 1990s.

---

*Market space is to whom and where companies sell their products.

†William C. Durant was another PC pioneer, who began building a small company called General Motors in 1904—four years before Ford Motor Company was founded.

Will Apple Computer rise again like a modern General Motors? Only if it masters the mechanics of mainstreaming. Will the computer industry fragment like the auto industry did? It already has. Will software titans like Microsoft, Adobe, Oracle, and IBM/Lotus survive the friction-free economy? Yes, as long as the economics of increasing returns does not implode.

How can a product manager use the principles of the friction-free economy to grow another Apple Computer, Microsoft, Oracle, Lotus, or Netscape? To answer, we must explore the story of Ford's phenomenal product.

THE INVENTION OF MAINSTREAMING

Until the Great Depression got in the way, almost everyone dumped their horse-drawn carriage and bought a car between 1905 and 1925—a very short time. In 1914 Ford's company produced more than 267,000 cars, capturing a 48% market share. Ford mainstreamed the personal car, and at the same time built an industry. How? First, Ford used learning theory. His factories produced twenty cars per employee verses the industry average of four cars per employee. Lower production costs meant lower consumer prices. Compared to his contemporary competitors, Ford was literally giving away his product. Sound familiar? It should. Like product giveaways by software companies eighty years later, Ford's low-priced cars simultaneously mainstreamed the horseless carriage, and captured a major share of a new industry (see Figure 2-1).

Figure 2-1 and Table 2-1 provide some raw data from Henry Ford's era. The number of autos produced from 1899 through 1914 grew from 3,000 to 548,000 units, while the number of carriages declined from 905,000 to 568,000 units. That is, car production matched the level of carriage production in a mere fifteen years! Within another fifteen years, automobiles displaced carriages altogether, leaving coach builders either out of business or hastily converting their factories to manufacture other products. Not only did the production of cars eliminate the production of carriages,

Year	# Cars (000)	# Carriages (000)	Fraction
1899	3	905	0.003
1904	22	937	0.023
1909	124	828	0.130
1914	548	538	0.505
1919	1652	216	0.884
1924	3186	30	0.991
1929	4455	4	0.999

Table 2–1. Empirical data for Figure 1. The fraction equals the number of cars divided by the sum of cars and carriages for each year. Data are in thousands of units sold.

but car production exceeded the original carriage production by many times.

MAINSTREAMING AND THE CHASM

Mainstreaming may not be new, but it is fast becoming more important as the influences of the software industry infiltrate modern business practice. Technologists have known about the S-curve shape of market-share mainstreaming for many decades. In fact, they have given names to sections of the curve shown in Figure 2-1. I have used names similar to those suggested by Geoffrey Moore in *Crossing the Chasm* and *Inside the Tornado*.

In Moore's terminology, a new product starts out by attracting the early adopters, who will try almost anything new and novel. These pioneers want to be the first kids on the block to own the product, use the service, or espouse the idea.

The Chasm, as Moore calls it, is the lull in the market that occurs just after the pioneers have bought the product, but just before it catches on with a wider audience. This lull must be crossed or else the product, service, or idea will die for lack of broader acceptance. The Chasm forces a business to reevaluate who the customer is, what the product's benefits are, and how to hit a marketing home run. While this phase is a "time of great despair," according to Moore, it is also an opportunity to fine-tune the marketing approach.

The Bowling Alley is where a business does targeting. An appropriate niche and a target consumer are identified and pursued. This is a good place to address the needs of a community of consumers.

The Tornado is where things get hectic. The product takes off, hits a home run, and rapidly gains market share. Everyone wants it. This is the path to the mainstream.

Main Street is what Moore calls the aftereffects of mainstreaming. Here the product, service, or idea is well-accepted by the market, so the only thing left is for a business to build upon it. This is where Henry Ford's phenomenal machine ended up, twenty short years after the Ford Motor Company opened its doors. It is where classical economics gains control. It is where diminishing returns become a reality.

The mainstream adoption curve provides a yardstick for marketing directors. The shape of this curve shows how well—or poorly—a product is doing. It also identifies where a product is in its life cycle. And it provides an early warning system when a product or company is going downhill.

THE FRICTION-FREE ECONOMY ABHORS A MONOPOLY

While seemingly a good spot to be, Main Street is a dangerous place. A near-monopoly becomes a target for competitors. It suffers from diminishing returns. It invites competition. It attracts new businesses that change the rules, reverse-engineer its product, or traverse the learning curve faster than it does. Main Street companies risk losing their competitive edge.

Successful mainstreaming does not automatically imply a monopoly. In fact, a smart business will stay away from excess market share. This intriguing idea is not only a curiosity, but necessary for long-term success in the friction-free economy.

Somewhere between the Chasm and Main Street lies Nirvana. To get a foothold on the slippery slopes of the mainstreaming curve, all businesses must slide along the learning curve.

LEARNING EQUALS MAINSTREAMING

Ken Ruggles, president of Systems West, Marina, California, has a doctorate in meteorology from MIT, but his education really shifted into high gear when his compact, easy-to-use, affordable, and rugged computerized satellite weather systems began to sell like bibs at a Boston lobster feast. Formerly president of Global Weather Dynamics and a graduate of the Naval Academy, he is an authority on weather satellite systems. But it was not until Systems West learned a lot about its own business and customers that the company started to cross the Chasm.

Systems West first began selling its product to commercial fishermen who worked in cramped and harsh conditions aboard small fishing boats. This is where learning began. "The fishermen really taught us a lot," said Dick Reins, vice president of engineering.[7] Soon the compactness and ruggedness of the product was attracting sales from the U.S. Army, British Army, Canadian Navy, and Swedish armed forces.

The company's first system cost $250,000, but then Systems West began traveling down a steep learning curve in the direction of mainstreaming. When the learning curve lowered the price of its more powerful weather system to $55,000, TV weather stations in Japan started ordering. The product was crossing the Chasm and was well on its way to the Bowling Alley.

Nowadays, when you see the colorful weather map on your favorite TV weather broadcast, it is most likely generated by one of Systems West's products. Weather data broadcast from weather satellites is transformed into computer graphics, which are integrated into the weather report. Simple sounding, but it was not that easy before Ken Ruggles came along. Knowing that ease of operation would open up bigger markets, Ruggles says, "We believe the only thing the operator should do is turn on the power switch."[8]

Systems West illustrates the connection between mainstreaming and learning:

- Learning is essential in the friction-free economy, because learning is how a business gains markets.

- Price-learning curves contribute to gaining market share by commoditization.

While price-learning curves are not the only ones that gain market share for a company or product, they are the most prevalent.

VOLUME ECONOMICS

Classical economics does not associate learning with mainstreaming. Diminishing or increasing returns relate cost to demand, but fail to explain why the friction-free economy rockets forward even when cost and demand are not factors. A company that gives away its products, like Netscape Communications, cannot be explained by cost and demand curves. Only learning curves can explain why giveaways lead to success. So learning curve theory is the foundation of mainstreaming, and hence of central importance to the friction-free economy.

Learning curves, discovered in the 1930s by airplane manufacturers, explained why airplane manufacturing costs dropped by 30% when the *accumulated volume* of production doubled.* Suppose a manufacturer produces 1,000 units per year. The accumulated volume of production doubles in the second year, from 1,000 in year

---

*Accumulated volume is the sum total of widgets produced. It starts at one, then goes to 1+2, then 1+2+3, and so on until you have a pile of widgets.

one to 2,000 in year two. This forces the cost of production downward by 30%. In other words, the second year's cost declines to 70% of the first year's production cost, because the accumulated volume doubled. By the end of the third year, the accumulated volume equals 3,000 units. By the end of the fourth year, the accumulated volume reaches 4,000 units, double that of year two. Thus, production cost declines to 70% of year two.

If production cost is initially $100,000 per airplane, and 30% is the learning rate, then volume-doubling forces the cost to $70,000 after the second year, and $49,000 (0.7 times $70,000) after the fourth year. This is a savings of $51,000 over the initial production cost. Notice how the saving compounds like a snowball gathering snow as it rolls downhill. At 30% per year, a $100,000 snowball gathers over 50% savings in a very short time. This is also known as *volume economics.*

Learning compounds. The first time a doubling occurs, cost is reduced by the learning rate. Upon a second doubling, cost is reduced even more, because the savings are piled on top of earlier savings. This is why the friction-free economy is also the economy of living in Internet Time.

The aircraft industry's 30% *learning rate* was a bit higher for some companies and a bit lower for others. Learning rate averages for specific industries are affected by many factors. For example, the first airplane off the production line is not as well made as the next one. As accumulated volume mounts, workers, managers, salespeople, and customers apply their acquired experience to making better and better airplanes. Some improvements may increase quality, others lower cost, and still others involve learning what the customer really wants. There are many ways to improve production, marketing, maintenance, and service. All of the improvements combined define the learning rate.

THE PRICE-LEARNING CURVE

Since the early days of airplane manufacturing, the learning curve theory has been rediscovered, reinvented, and generally repeated thousands of times in other industries. Some companies follow a 25% learning rate, others a 50% rate. Some industries give it different names, such as Moore's Law* in the semiconductor industry, or *kaizen* in Japan. Yet, the learning curve idea is the same.

Both Ford and Durant were trying to lower their production costs so they could reduce the price of their new cars. A low-cost car appealed to more people, thus expanding their market. The faster they lowered costs, the faster they could lower prices. Low prices lead to high sales, and high sales lead to market share. Market share is the name of the mainstreaming game.

Learning how to lower costs, and then how to lower consumer prices, becomes a competitive race. If Ford's prices drop faster than GM's, then Ford gains market share and GM loses it. This is the idea of the price-learning curve. It is an old technique for gaining market share. What is new is the idea of accelerating the price-learning curve to beat out the competition.

The relationship between price and mainstreaming is a fundamental building block of the new software economic theory. It replaces diminishing returns, supply-and-demand equations, and other classical economic models that fail to describe the effects of a friction-free economy.

In a friction-free economy, price and market share are inversely proportional to one another. They are different facets of the same thing. A mainstream adoption curve can be obtained from a price-learning curve, and vice-versa. Given one curve, we can find the other.

Henry Ford used a sharp decline in price as a weapon. As a consequence, he forced the automobile industry to learn how to build a commodity-priced car. As the price declined, the volume of units increased, automobile manufacturers improved their production processes, which in turn decreased cost, leading to lower prices.

---

*Gordon Moore was a cofounder of Intel Corporation. Actually, this is his first law. Later, Moore realized that the cost of building fabrication plants was also doubling along with performance, so he made up his second law, which states that it will eventually be too expensive to build faster and faster microprocessors because the fabrication plants will cost an arm and a leg.

This feedback mechanism was self-fulfilling—the more prices were lowered, the more they could be lowered.

Companies that follow a price-learning curve eventually end up as commodity players. As prices decline, costs can be lowered, because production volume goes up. In the friction-free economy, learning is continually accelerated, lowering prices to the point where a commodity price is eventually reached. (See Figure 2-2.)

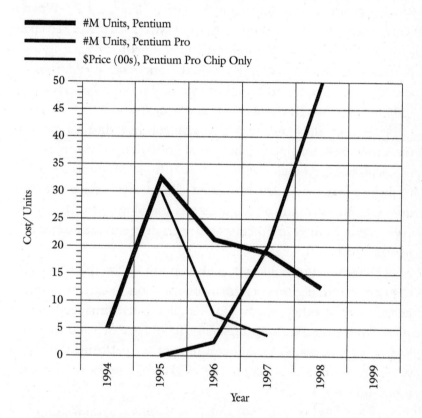

Figure 2–2. Declining prices and increasing unit shipments of the Intel Pentium and Pentium Pro processors over time. By changing prices, Intel controls the rate of mainstreaming of its chips.

TECHNOLOGY LEARNING CURVES

The friction-free economy is driven by learning curves that describe industrywide learning. They are a kind of benchmark for each industry segment. A business must beat the industry benchmark, go under, or settle for a minority share of the market. Aggressive companies like Intel and Microsoft set the pace of their industries by manipulating learning rates of various technologies. Consider the heart of the personal computer: the microprocessor.

Following Davidow's Law, Intel introduces a new processor before its competitors, and then adjusts the rate of obsolescence of its own products by controlling their price (Figure 2-2). When a competitor starts to creep up on it, Intel lowers the prices of its processors, and lowers the boom on the competitor. When its own products get in the way, Intel raises the prices on its old product, and lowers the prices on its next generation products. Intel walks a thin line between Davidow's Law and mainstreaming.

Figure 2-2 illustrates how Intel controls its industry by setting the benchmark for prices. The volume of older processors rises as prices plunge, and then reaches a peak as Intel kills its own product to make room for its new processor. The new processor sales volume (see the Pentium Pro line) starts out slowly, and then rises even higher as Intel smothers its older product and mainstreams its new product.

Of course, Intel could not make a profit if it were not possible to manufacture higher-performance processors in each succeeding generation. In other words, Intel applies a performance-learning curve to its manufacturing capability, to create a demand for faster and faster processors. Coupling a hunger for performance with a declining price-learning curve has worked like magic in the computer industry.

THE PERFORMANCE-LEARNING CURVE

Moore's Law is an example of another kind of learning curve—the performance-learning curve. The semiconductor industry has followed Moore's Law for decades. Instead of doubling accumulated volume, the semiconductor industry aims to double the speed of its products. So Moore's Law defines a performance-learning curve that says, "The performance of a microprocessor doubles every eighteen months." Actually, it is not clear whether the learning needed to achieve performance doubling is due to increasing volume production or the reverse. The semiconductor industry has been increasing both.

The doubling of performance law first articulated by Gordon Moore is used by the PC industry to fuel ever-increasing sales, as earlier and slower models are rendered obsolete by faster models. The most astounding feature of Moore's Law is that it has worked for over a decade! In recent years, performance has been doubling at nearly sixteen-month intervals, due to competitive pressures on market-leading Intel.

THE SECOND PC

PC vendors rush to produce faster computers so they can coax buyers into discarding their perfectly okay old PCs in favor of buying newer, faster, and sexier machines. Outdating PCs through spiraling speed jumps has worked for decades in the PC industry. Owning the fastest PC on earth has become a marketing mantra. But will this work forever?

Moore's Law may be running out of volts. Sometime early in the next decade, performance is expected to level off. The semiconductor industry will have to find another way to render its products obsolete.

One remedy for the approaching end of the line in PC performance is to add multiple processors to single PCs. This approach will no doubt appeal to many vendors, but it has problems. For one thing, additional performance may not motivate consumers. They may be tiring of the *technology treadmill.** The home PC segment will reach mainstream saturation about the same time that overall mainstreaming, due to the flattening of the performance-learning

---

*Like miniature electronic mice laboring on a treadmill, consumers are condemned to running forever toward faster, cheaper, and more fashionable widgets.

curve, pushes the entire industry to its limits. Both of these trends bode ill for the PC industry.

The year 1996 was a historical landmark because it was the first year in which PCs outsold TVs in the U.S. market. In 1996, 24 million PCs were sold—slightly more than the total number of TVs. But only 40% fell into the hands of consumers—the same people who already own 90% of the world's TVs. While the business PC market continued its lead, the home PC market still had some growing room. This idea has occurred to PC vendors, who have begun targeting home buyers even more intensely than before.

Consumers are very sensitive to prices, however, so the semiconductor industry must learn to manufacture commodity-priced products instead of performance-priced products. In other words, the PC industry must switch from a performance-learning curve to a price-learning curve if it wants to address the consumer market. This transformation is underway as we approach the next decade.

In 1996 a segment of the computer industry started to address price-sensitive consumers. Touted as the Internet PC, Network PC (NC), or simply an on-ramp to the Infobahn, the NC began its ascent along a mainstreaming curve. The NC is a price-learning-curve product, and the industry that produces such products must ride the declining price-learning curve.

The computer industry has much to learn about commodity markets. Even if it does, a classical breakdown in the industry may occur around the year 2004. This is the time when the doubling law becomes very difficult to maintain. Think of the breakdown this way: In one year, around 2004, performance must increase by more than all previous increases in the entire history of microprocessors. Doubling performance every eighteen months is a tough act.

LOCK-IN

One of the most controversial consequences of applying learning curves to marketing is the resulting lock on customers. The lock can be so tight that customers cannot afford to let go of your product. This is known as *lock-in*,* a common practice in the friction-free economy. Lock-in is the process of capturing a dominant market share by captivating customers.

"We need consistency, and the weight of inertia keeps us on Intel platforms," said Howard Warren, senior systems analyst for an Arkansas insurance company.[9]

"We prefer to buy from one PC maker, because it's just one company to deal with," says Paul Steel, director of information systems for the U.S. Senate in Washington.[10] Lock-in might just be a code word for inertia and laziness.

Ford and Microsoft each created an industry from a single product—the Model-T and MS-DOS, respectively. But Microsoft lives in the friction-free economy, which means that it has an advantage that Ford lacked. Microsoft has lock-in. In fact, the friction-free economy rules that Microsoft lives by equating mainstreaming with lock-in. In effect, the purpose of mainstreaming is to gain lock-in.

Microsoft, and other smart software companies, get lock-in by dictating a file or interoperability standard, operating system, or application program. Its customers get "addicted" to Microsoft products because it is too expensive to retrain users, ignore the Windows standard, or go against such a powerful company.

The lock that Microsoft has on the PC industry is comparable to Ford Motor Company owning the rights to the internal combustion engine, thus forcing its competitors to buy all of their engines from Ford. It is comparable to owning all of the water rights in the Sahara Desert and taxing every sip. It ranks with cornering the petroleum market when everything runs on oil.

The annual PC Forum attracts some of the biggest names in the computer industry. It is a watering hole for computer industry big wheels who annually gather to make deals and schmooze. When fric-

---

*Ahem, I avoid the term *monopoly*, but just barely. Lock-in is what happens to a customer when he or she has no choice but to buy your product.

tion-free economy expert W. Brian Arthur reached the podium to give his speech in 1995, he had to utter only one word to freeze a hundred conversations in midsentence: "Microsoft." Microsoft has reached software nirvana, where the word *lock-in* and Microsoft have become synonymous. More than three-quarters of PC "productivity applications"—the largest packaged-software category, including word processors, spreadsheets, and databases—comes from Microsoft. Even Coca-Cola only has half of the soft-drink market.

Microsoft's lock-in comes from its ownership of the dominant operating system for PCs. This may seem innocent enough, but Microsoft exploits its ownership of Microsoft Windows by inserting a secret code that helps its own applications run better or work together better—locking out competitors.

Much of the software world is convinced that Microsoft simply does not play fair. For most of the 1990s, competitors badgered antitrust authorities with complaints about Microsoft's alleged monopolistic abuses. Yet, a series of investigations by the U.S. Department of Justice ended without action. The postindustrial age legal system simply cannot cope with the friction-free economy.

Lock-in is a very powerful positive feedback that can propel a business to a monopoly position and shut out smaller, less successful competitors. This partially explains the rapid rise of the S-shaped mainstreaming curve, because:

> *Change in market share is proportional to existing market share.*

Not only does lock-in hold on to customers, but because of the cumulative effect of repeat buying patterns, growth of market share accelerates. Market share acceleration pushes a product, service, or idea across the Chasm, into the Tornado. (See Figure 2-3.)

Figure 2-3 illustrates the sharp climb in market share when a company has a lock on a market segment. Microsoft's change in market share between 1994 and 1995 started from a strong base of 62%—a near-monopoly. Within one year its share was 77%.

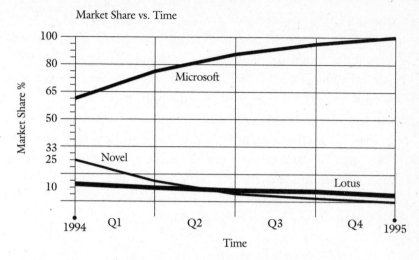

Figure 2–3. Microsoft's share of the word-processing market soared as MS-Word locked out competitors Lotus and Novell. WORD went from 62.2% share in 1994 to 77.1% in 1995.

By the end of 1995 Novell and Lotus got out of Microsoft's way entirely. Lotus sold out to IBM, and Novell sold its word processor to Corel, both in anticipation of their defeat. This example illustrates the powerful effect of lock-in operating in the friction-free economy. It also illustrates some of the forces that shape the mainstreaming curve. Therefore we can say:

> *The goal of mainstreaming is lock-in.*

SATURATION

Superstore retail outlets such as Borders, Crown Books, B. Dalton, and Waldenbooks are taking over like a bad joke at a Shriners' Convention. U.S. book sales increased from $18 billion in 1989 to $24 billion in 1994. Over the next five years, book sales are expected to increase by about $10 billion, reaching $34 billion. There is little evidence that paper books are being replaced by electronic media such as CD-ROMs or the WWW.

Chain bookstores are mainstreaming America. Maybe it is

because of the vast wasteland called TV, the high cost of going on-line, or simply because people like big bookstores. For whatever reason, independent bookstores are losing market share. In 1994, 21.4% of adults bought their books at independent bookstores. One year later, 1995, that share had dropped to 19.5%.

In fact, the trend toward large retail chains has been in play for years. In 1991 chains commanded 67% of the adult market. By 1994 it was 78%, and in 1995 it was almost 81%. It does not take a computer to compute the trend, but does this mean that large conglomerates will lock in consumers? How long will it be before independent bookstores go extinct? (See Figure 2-4.)

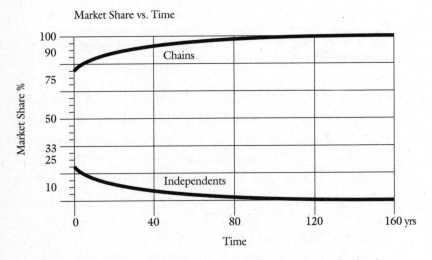

Figure 2–4. Mainstreaming of chain bookstores versus the demise of independents.

Figure 2-4 shows the trend as a mainstreaming curve. Surprisingly, it will be over 160 years before chains annihilate independents! Why? This example illustrates the second factor that determines the shape of the mainstreaming curve.

Change in market share is proportional to the amount of market share that remains available to a company.

This rule says that market share is proportional to the amount of slack in the market. When two or more companies own large chunks of market share, and they are competitive businesses that can hold on to their shares, little market share remains "available." But if some or all of a company's market share is fragile, that share becomes available. That is, it is up for grabs by anyone. I call this the *available market share.*

Figure 2-4 illustrates how the growth of market share is slowed by saturation—the complete penetration of a market segment by a product, service, or idea. When a market share reaches 90% or 95%, or approaches 100%, further growth of market share is flattened out by the above rule.

The decline in available market share becomes a major force in mainstreaming. In fact, declining available market share can overtake an installed base, whether it is locked in or not. This effect will become part of a deeper explanation of competition in the friction-free economy.

THE MAINSTREAMING PRINCIPLE

Confused? On the one hand, you may argue, growth in market share is accelerated by an installed base of locked-in customers, and on the other hand, growth is limited by the lack of growing room. These two factors seem to contradict one another. They are not contradictions, however, because one factor kicks in at the beginning and end of the mainstreaming curve, and the other factor kicks in throughout the middle. Acceleration is due to "lots of available market" at the beginning of the curve, and deceleration at the end of the curve, when there is "little remaining market." Rapid growth occurs in between because of the installed base of customers.

Change in market share is proportional to both existing market share and the remaining market share.

POSITIVE FEEDBACK AND MAINSTREAMING

The previous example of Microsoft versus Lotus and Novell illustrates the positive feedback of the friction-free economy. Feedback comes from two sources:

- The existing market share of a product, i.e., its installed base.

- The remaining market share, i.e., what share the product does not already have.

Negative feedback is like a brake that holds back when you travel too fast. Negative feedback is drag, friction. In classical economics, negative feedback is drag in the form of demand holding back supply, friction in the form of diminishing returns, and a brake in the form of normal costs of manufacturing, distribution, and marketing.

Positive feedback is the opposite. The mainstreaming formula is loaded with positive feedback that initially accelerates rather than retards change in market share. This formula says, first of all, that the more market share a product has, the more it will get. That is, change in market share is proportional to how much a business already has.

The second influence involving the "remaining share" is a gas pedal when market share is small, and a brake when it is large. It explains why the law of *increasing returns* works initially, and the law of *diminishing returns* works eventually. For example, if a product has an initial market share of 1%, then the remaining amount is 99%. This increases the change in market share; i.e., it is the law of increasing returns or positive feedback. If the product has 99% market share, then the available market share is only 1%; and the product's change in market share will decrease. This is the law of diminishing returns, or negative feedback.

MASTERING THE UNIVERSE

In the late 1990s a wave of multimedia, video, and picture-phone devices began their climb up the mainstreaming curve. These devices combined camera, microphone, speakers, and a computer into what science fiction writers used to think was far into the future—a telephone that transmitted motion pictures and data. Combining video and telephony takes computing beyond the videophone, because it can connect multiple people at multiple locations, mix voice, video, and data, and still do the tasks expected of a computer.

The problem with personal video systems was price. In the early 1980s these things cost nearly $100,000. Then volume economics, Moore's Law, and sharp engineering began whittling away at the cost. Soon consumer prices began to plunge along a learning curve, and in the late 1990s, price points reached commodity levels. Video teleconferencing came of age.

The emergence of video teleconferencing illustrates how a fast learning curve can plunge prices very quickly, and raise market acceptance just as quickly. If you want to control your segment of the market, set the pace of the learning curve, and in so doing, meter the rise of acceptance via mainstreaming. Pacesetters are masters of their universe.

The mainstreaming concept may appear to be simpleminded, but it is in fact a complex effect that can be used to explain everything from taking market share away from a competitor to making money on the stock market. But the most profound facet of the theory, yet to be explored, is the nonlinearity of the friction-free economy. This nonlinearity causes some nonintuitive side effects— bumps in the night—that we simply cannot ignore. Keep this in mind as you rush to the next chapter.

3

Battling the Warriors of the Wired World

MUSASHI, THE GREAT WARRIOR

Shinmen Musashi No Fujiwara No Genshim, or as Westerners commonly know him, Miyamoto Musashi, was born in 1584 and lived during the "Wild West" period of Japanese history. Musashi has been a legend for four hundred years in Japan. He is now becoming a legend in the minds of business strategists everywhere. Musashi was a great warrior whose writings influenced generations of warriors. His success is attributed largely to his skill as a strategist.

His *Book of Five Rings* describes strategies of combat—the so-called *heiho* ("Hei" means "soldier," and "ho" means "method"). For example, the "flowing water cut," "continuous cut," and "fire and stones cut" describe various ways to whack your opponent exactly when he or she is least likely to suspect it—an even more useful skill in today's Wired World than in Musashi's Japan. For you see, success in the friction-free economy is a question of strategy.

BUSINESS AS WAR

Musashi provides one of the earliest studies of strategy. But his teachings are as modern as the Wired World. The current *kendo* (knife fight) among the software giants is a kind of bloodless sport where the object is to render the other company inconsequential or obsolete.

But Musashi was merely a warrior. It would take greater intellectual skill and another three hundred years before the art of war would be raised to the level of scientific discipline, until the new science of operations research would evolve, quantifying warfare tactics, strategy, and power. And another fifty years would have to pass until World War II put Musashi's ideas, and the analytical techniques of operations research, into practice. As the end of the cold war diverted attention from physical combat to business combat, strategy and analytical skill merged. The result: *business-as-war*.

The warriors of the Wired World use the same analytical techniques as a modern battlefield commander, but instead of the swiftness of supersonic bombers, precision of laser-guided smart weapons, and destructiveness of death rays, today's business commanders rely on the swiftness of mainstreaming, the precision of targeted marketing, and the destructiveness of business tactics. Most of these techniques lend themselves to mathematical formulation. So a smart warrior must use computers and mathematical models as weapons of business-as-war. Like everything else in our technological society, marketing has become an analytical science. We owe much of our current knowledge of this science to a great inventor.

THE GREAT INVENTOR

In 1916 Frederick William Lanchester (1868–1946) wrote *Aircraft in Warfare: The Dawn of the Fourth Arm.** This book established the

---

*Lanchester may be dead, but he lives in cyberspace at www.lanchester.com.

discipline that led to the mathematical analysis of warfare, and later to the field of operations research (OR). Lanchester is considered by many to be the father of OR, and it is his theory of warfare that would make him a hero of the friction-free economy.

Ironically, this great scientist is not well known in the Wired World, yet, his theories are even more appropriate today than they were a century ago. Lanchester might be called the architect of the friction-free economy, or at least the designer of its marketing strategy.

THE NEW LANCHESTER STRATEGY

Lanchester's work was introduced into Japan in 1952 through the writings of W. Edward Deming. Subsequently, Dr. Nobuo Taoka and other descendants of Musashi evolved the theories of Lanchester. Columbia professor Bernard O. Koopman used the Lanchester Strategy for the U.S. Navy, and others honed the "New Lanchester Strategy."[1] In particular, Taoka applied Lanchester's theories to sales and marketing. Considering market share as a kind of troop strength, and sales and marketing budgets as a kind of weapon, Taoka's extensions of Lanchester's theories have been providing Japanese businesses with the analytical tools and techniques necessary for success in the friction-free economy. The New Lanchester Strategy is a weapon for warriors of the Wired World. It is a tool for taking aim, firing, and then capturing market share.

KEEPING SCORE

The New Lanchester Strategy often gives some unexpected results and unusual insights when applied to modern-day software economics. Take the definition of a monopoly, for example. According to the New Lanchester Strategy, a monopoly exists when a business has a mere 74% share of a market. Monopoly is, of course, the holy grail of every ambitious company. But why stop at 74%?

Achieving a market share of 90%, 95%, or 100% seems the most desirable goal for any business. While few companies reach such heights, total annihilation of the opposition is every competitor's ambition. In fact, the original Lanchester Strategy advocated boosting market share to its highest possible level. But overwhelming domination should not be the goal of a smart business in the friction-free economy. According to the New Lanchester Strategy, when a company's market share *exceeds* 73.9%:

- It becomes difficult to stimulate more demand.

- The company invites competition from other industries or specialty companies.

- The correlation between market share and profitability disappears.

IBM's fall from dominance of the computer industry in the 1980s may be an example of this law. Today IBM is struggling to be noticed in the Wired World. Without the lock-in that IBM established in the decades prior to the 1980s, the company would have long ago fallen victim to the cut and slash of the warriors at Microsoft.

Interestingly, Microsoft's domination of the personal computer software market may now be sowing the seeds of its own destruction. In 1996 Microsoft had over 85% of the operating systems market, and an even higher percentage of the so-called office suite market. Instead of jumping for joy, Microsoft must protect its flank from competitors, stimulate more demand when more demand is most difficult to create, and keep on generating high returns, or else risk the wrath of the stock market.

Contemplating the downfall of Microsoft may seem like folly, but look at where the money comes from: about half from licensing its Windows operating systems, and about another half from MS Office (actually, in the first quarter of 1997 $1B of the $2.2B came from Office). It is truly amazing how little product Microsoft has. One slip in Windows 95 and/or NT, and the company could be forced to slash its workforce, or else come up with 50% of its revenues from somewhere else. Another slip in Office sales, and the company would be looking for assistance from the federal government. If it could happen to Chrysler Corporation, it could happen to Microsoft.

Mike Brown, CFO of Microsoft, admits, "We have the issue of saturation there" when describing the Office dependency.[2] He told Wall street gurus that Office sales got a boost from the introduction of Windows 95, which stimulated replacement sales of the near-monopoly product. In 1996 Microsoft was starting to act like a 1980s failing IBM—using lock-in to pump revenues from existing customers. After the effect of the introduction of Windows 95 tapered off in 1997, Office leadership began to wither as Lotus and Corel started chewing away at Microsoft's monopoly. The New Lanchester Strategy could be seen in action.

WINNERS AT 41%

When a company's goal is to dominate its competitors, it usually attempts to gain at least 50% of the market. The New Lanchester Strategy refutes this, saying that only 41.7% is needed. Therefore, the target of a *market leader* is to capture more than 41% of the market. Why? The gap in profitability between the market leader and its rivals widens when the leader's market share exceeds 41.7% but is less than 73.9%.

In 1995 McAfee Associates achieved 41% market share of the PC network management suite market by merging with Saber Software. McAfee clearly used its merger to achieve market leadership. Symantec is another company that uses this technique. M&A (mergers and acquisitions) is a game of strategy. It is a tool of savvy businesses in the friction-free economy.

PLAYERS NEED 26%

A company that has more than 26.1% of a market, but less than 41%, is considered a *player*. Such a company must keep its chin above the 26% minimum, even though it is not a leader, to maintain its position as a competitor.

A company's viability as a profitable entity weakens if its market share dips below 26.1%. Instability means that the company's position can be reversed by a competitor. Companies in this category are called *unstable players*.

Once a company exceeds 26% it begins to break away from the crowd. It is in a position to mainstream its products. Profitability changes, as does its market share.

Soon after the IBM PC was introduced, it took off the way all mainstreaming products should, and reached a leadership plateau of 41%. This was good. This was just like a replay of the Model T. Then IBM lost control of its operating system. Just as quickly as it had gained leadership, IBM's share of the PC market slipped to less than 10%. Microsoft essentially took IBM's market away, and gave it to clone manufacturers—for a fee.

THE THREE SHOUTS

Wired World warriors, like the great Musashi before them, might resort to shouting to gain a competitive advantage. Musashi's original recipe specified *The Three Shouts*, divided into "before," "during," and "after." Before the battle, the prescription is to shout as loudly as possible. During the fight, shout in a low-pitched voice. After the battle, crow! Computer industry leaders such as Larry Ellison (Oracle), Scott McNealy (Sun), Jerry Sanders (Advanced Micro Devices), and T. J. Rodgers (Cypress Semiconductor) provide ample evidence that the three shouts are alive and well practiced in the computer industry.*

The three-shouts technique is perhaps useful in sales meetings or new product launches, but for more positive results on the play-

---

*Ellison shouted early in the network computer phase of the Wired World battle by announcing his vision of a low-cost PC for browsing the Internet; McNealy is outspoken on the struggle between Microsoft and the rest of the industry; Sanders is well known for being fired by Intel founder Robert Noyce because he wore a pink shirt to an IBM sales call; and Rodgers has been accused of shouting at anyone who will listen on matters of political correctness. This is only a small sample of the activism and eccentricities of some of the friction-free economy's prime movers.

ing field, use the New Lanchester Strategy. The three shouts of the New Lanchester Strategy are:

- Using tactical maneuvering to reach the minimum target of 26.1% market share.

- Crossing the Chasm to reach 41.7% or more.

- Mainstreaming to monopoly position at 73.9% or more.

How does a business rise from ground zero, reach 26.1%, then 41.7%, and finally 73.9% in the friction-free economy? What principles let the friction-free economy entrepreneur start out as a slug and end up as Bill Gates?

CUT AND SLASH

According to Musashi, "To cut and to slash are two different things." Cutting is decisive with spirit, slashing is nothing more than touching the enemy. Cutting is precision planning, slashing is risk-taking. One is based on a sound strategy, while the other is based on gambling. Winning in the friction-free economy is all about strategy. And the first step in applied strategy is to have a plan.

Cutting, in the friction-free economy, is done with analytical tools running on personal computers—often located in garages. In the software industry, a start-up business needs only a computer, spreadsheet, Web connection, and creativity. But today's warrior of the Wired World must master the *Kendo* of numerical methods. Invincibility among the samurai of software depends completely on a thorough understanding of math.

Business-as-war demands that marketing gurus use the tools of war. These tools are computerized models of combat. In the following, replace "an army" with "your business," and "war" with "marketing."

The war potential of an army is proportional to its tactical strength plus strategic strength times production strength.

Direct competition is where tactical strength comes in, while indirect or infrastructure strength is where strategic strength lies. Think of tactics as the art of getting shelf space for your new box of cereal. Think of strategic moves as the art of getting brand name recognition. Production strength is related to budget—the player with the largest advertising budget has greater production strength. The player with the greatest revenues carries the biggest production stick.

PC WARS—WHO IS WINNING?

The PC market is a good example of an industry where nearly all of the competitors are on the lowest rung on the ladder to monopoly. Figure 3-1 shows the rather low market shares of the leading manufacturers during the first half of the 1990s. Surprisingly, market share curves reveal no trends, no mainstreaming S-curves, and no straight lines. It reveals almost nothing about who might win and who might lose in the PC market space. Instead, Figure 3-1 provides an opportunity to apply the New Lanchester Strategy.

All competitors in the PC space are unstable, because none has over 26% market share. To break away from the pack, a PC vendor would have to become the first competitor to reach a market penetration of 26.1%. Therefore, all PC manufacturers are trying to sprint to the magical 26.1% level. But how?

PLAYING THE NEW LANCHESTER GAME

The first step in deciding how to apply the New Lanchester Strategy is to find out where your company stands in comparison to the competition. This requires that you collect data on yourself and your competitors. Table 3-1, for example, shows total revenues and market shares for the top competitors in the PC Wars in 1995. Suppose we use these competitors to play a few rounds of the New Lanchester Strategy Game. In this game, market share is used as a measure of a combatant's tactical strength, and revenues are used as

Market Share vs. Time of Leading PC Vendors: All Competitors Are Unstable

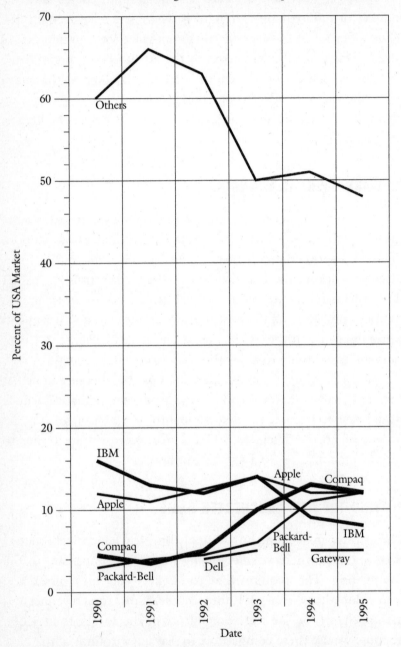

Figure 3–1. USA market share of the leading PC manufacturers from 1990 through 1995. Notice that nobody had reached the minimum target of 26.1%

Company	Revenues in 1995, $B	1995 Market Share, %
Apple	11.1	11.5
Compaq	14.9	11.7
Dell	3.5	5.0
Gateway	3.7	5.1
IBM	71.5	8.2
Packard Bell	7.5	11.6

Table 3–1. PC competitors, their market shares, and their production strengths.

	Defender					
	Apple	Compaq	Dell	Gateway	IBM	Pack-Bell
Attacker						
Apple		player	leader	leader	mono	player
Compaq	player		leader	leader	mono	player
Dell	player	player		player	leader	player
Gateway	player	player	player		leader	player
IBM	player	player	player	player		player
Pack-Bell	player	player	leader	leader	mono	

Table 3–2. Relative positions of PC Wars competitors in the New Lanchester Strategy Game. (Mono = Monopoly)

a measure of production strength. Notice that none of the companies held 26.1%, nor did any of them come close. But as competitors, they are far from equals, as Table 3-2 shows.

Table 3-2 tells the vice president of marketing where his company stands relative to the others. Remember, according to the rules, the food chain is made up of unstable companies at the bottom, and monopolies at the top. The hierarchy is: unstable, player, winner, and then monopoly.

Table 3-2 should be read row by row. For example, the first row says Apple was a *player* relative to Compaq and Packard Bell (Pack-Bell), and a *leader* relative to Dell and Gateway. Apple was a *monopoly* relative to IBM, because Apple's market share was relatively high compared to its low revenues (strength), indicating that in 1995 Apple performed very well in contrast to a much richer IBM. IBM should have had a larger market share than Apple, in proportion to its revenues, because revenues translate into production strength in the New Lanchester Strategy. In a sense, Apple, Compaq, and Pack-Bell were more efficient than IBM in terms of gaining market share.

Of course, this is unfair to IBM, because the total revenues of IBM were used instead of the much smaller revenues of the IBM PC Company, the division that makes the IBM PCs. But it works in the example.

THE MAGINOT LINE

André Maginot was France's minister of war after World War I (1930), when occupying French troops began leaving the Rhineland. He decided the only way to avoid another conflict with Germany was to build an impenetrable fortification along France's eastern border with Germany—a fortress that became known as the Maginot Line. Unfortunately, Germany simply bypassed the Line when it attacked at the onset of World War II. So much for impenetrable defenses.

In the friction-free economy, major competitors are always constructing impenetrable fortresses against competitors. Microsoft's huge market share of the personal computer software business is the most obvious example. Intel commands 80% of the microprocessor market, so the combination of Microsoft software and Intel hardware draws a kind of Maginot Line across the PC industry landscape. It has become known as the *Wintel monopoly*.

Since World War II, the Maginot Line has become a symbol of how an impossible obstacle can be overcome by strategy. Nowadays, warriors and marketing managers both see the Maginot Line, and its failure to stop the advances of a technologically superior force, as an incentive to fight against an overwhelming opponent by changing the rules. The current struggle among combatants in the PC Wars is centered on this idea. Anti-Wintel competitors are trying to change the rules of the computer industry in order to take market share away from the Wintel monopoly.

Is the Wintel monopoly permanent? Is it possible to change the rules, and thereby go around Microsoft and Intel? If it is, it can be done only through a combination of changing the rules and applying the analytical techniques of the New Lanchester Strategy. In the friction-free economy, rules are broken every day, but this may not lead to victory. Still, the question lingers: Is it possible for a company to move from being an unstable competitor to a player or leader, even when it faces a monopoly? The answer is yes, and the technique was articulated by the Great Warrior many centuries ago.

TO SOAK IN

According to Musashi, when further advance is made impossible by an impenetrable barrier or counterforce, you *soak in*, meaning that you become one with the enemy. You bide your time while waiting for the opposition to make a mistake. In the *Book of Five Rings*, Musashi advises, "Research this well."

Actually, it turns out that Microsoft itself has researched this well. Microsoft used the strategy of soaking in very effectively in 1996, when its dominance was threatened by anti-Wintel forces that attempted to change the rules of the PC industry. In fact, Microsoft used the phrase "absorb and extend" to describe its strategy. Microsoft's embrace and extend strategy has been so successful in dealing with competition that it has become one of the maxims among high-tech competitors. This strategy is very instructive.

Sun Microsystems' fortunes suddenly turned for the better

when it stumbled onto a use for a research language it developed called Java. Java was a skunk works project being developed in the back room by James Gosling, a Sun Microsystems Lab lizard. Gosling and coworkers had a video-on-demand appliance product in mind when they started Java, but their work was quickly overrun by events that changed everything. Instead of building a video-on-demand system, Sun decided to throw Java at the Wired World.

The first breakthrough came in 1995, when Netscape Communications licensed Java for its Navigator Web browser. What a stroke of luck for Sun and Java, because Netscape was in the process of mainstreaming its browser. Sun's Java hitched a free ride to the top.

Of course, Netscape licensed Java and other technologies so it could link up with Sun Microsystems, SGI, and other anti-Wintel forces to overthrow the Wintel monopoly. Using the Maginot Line as inspiration, Netscape's managers wanted to bypass Wintel by "going around." They would accomplish this impossible task by changing the rules. And Java was a perfect technology for changing the rules, because Java could run on anything. Java did not depend on Microsoft's operating systems nor its applications to work. It worked just fine without Microsoft's help. It was platform neutral.

Jim Clark, cofounder of Netscape, was quoted as saying, "I suppose the dissemination of the client [browser] electronically with no charge to some extent was influenced by the knowledge that Microsoft had a huge installed base. And the one way to do that was to give away our client."[3]

But the anti-Wintel forces did not anticipate soaking in. Microsoft soon abandoned its Maginot Line and licensed Java, too! Although Java was a direct competitor to Microsoft's OLE technology, commanders at Microsoft soon realized that they could not move their Maginot Line, either. So they adopted a strategy of soaking in. By licensing Java and then adapting OLE to work with Java, Microsoft bought valuable time and market share. In a double dose of marketing genius, Microsoft spin doctors changed the name of OLE to ActiveX and joined in the main-streaming parade started by Netscape. Without changing a single line of code, and licensing Java to work with OLE, Microsoft's ActiveX became an instant player. The anti-Wintel challenge was temporarily neutralized.

Microsoft absorbed Java just like a warrior of the Wired World. But it did more. Before the end of 1996, Microsoft began its campaign to extend Java. In its first volley, Microsoft's version of Java had features that Java's creator, Sun, could not believe. Microsoft's Java worked better on Microsoft's operating system than on anyone else's. By absorbing and then extending Java, Microsoft remained the Musashi of software.

TO ADVANCE

It is good to soak in as long as you end up on top. In the New Lanchester Strategy, landing on top means achieving 41.7% of the market before anyone else does. This is the so-called equilibrium, or stable, state. I call it the *market leader* state.

How does a business achieve 41.7% of its market in the friction-free economy? Once an opponent soaks in, it must focus its energy on advancing. A foothold of 26.1% proves that a business is a stable player, but it needs to advance to 41.7% to become a leader.

A leader is a company with greater strategic than tactical strength.

A leader can overwhelm others because it has a lock on the market, a brand name, a big budget, or owns the standards of its industry. It does not need tactical war potential; that is, it doesn't need to lower its prices, practice guerrilla marketing, pull cheap tricks at trade shows, or manage the press. Leaders pull ahead of other players and begin to mainstream their products. They throw their weight around. Leaders shift from informative product ads to brand awareness–building image ads.

ENDING THE GAME

To end the game a leader must become a monopoly of its industry. It must marshal strategic superiority to overwhelm all opposition. But in the friction-free economy, ending the game is not quite as simple as brain-bashing warfare. Another example will demonstrate how a market leader moves into a monopoly position and begins the final stages of ending the game.

In 1996 the client side of the client-server segment of the PC software market was divvied up among Microsoft, Borland, Powersoft, and Centura. This market space is the software development tool bazaar where programmers buy their wrenches, screwdrivers, and measuring tapes for plumbing an enterprise system that runs a major business. It is at the heart of the so-called business computing market, where nearly 900,000 boxes of software tools are sold every year. A Wired World warrior can pocket some significant yen by growing into a monopoly here.

Microsoft and Borland were the major competitors in this market because they held the lion's share of customers. At 62%, Microsoft (leader) was far ahead of Borland at 16% (player). Everyone else was unstable. No company was a monopoly; therefore, the game was not over.

If Borland drops and Microsoft gains a few more market share points, the game will come to an end. Microsoft can achieve a monopoly in this segment of the software market. In fact, by the time you read this, the deed may have already been done. In early 1997 Borland was on the ropes, showing big losses, slashing its workforce, and struggling to get a new product out the door. Del Yokum, an Apple Computer veteran making his reputation as a corporate turnaround artist via Tektronix, was pulled in to save the company, but in my opinion his best shot is to sell Borland to a deep-pocketed Microsoft competitor.

The question for Borland was, "How can David slay Goliath?" The question posed by Microsoft in 1996, however, was just the opposite: "How can Microsoft gain enough additional market share points to end the game?" Answering these questions illustrates another rule of the New Lanchester Strategy.

THE TRAFALGAR TECHNIQUE

Lanchester was intrigued by the art of warfare. In particular, he had a fascination for Lord Nelson's victory at Trafalgar. As it turns out, Lanchester was on to something.

British Admiral Lord Nelson defeated a much larger French and Spanish naval force at the Cape of Trafalgar in 1805. What was Nelson's trick? He concentrated all of his smaller fleet on a single weak point in the Franco-Spanish line. After breaking through the weak point, he picked off the stragglers, who were no match for the bully British. Mopping up like a professional antiques dealer at an amateur estate sale, Nelson systematically diminished the opposition.

When a competitor wants to take business away from another competitor in the friction-free economy, it uses the Trafalgar Strategy to target a weak point, gain market share, and systematically parlay small gains into one big gain. This is the severest cut of all, according to the *Book of Five Rings*.

The key to the Trafalgar Strategy—or targeted marketing, as modern bully Brits might call it—is to find a weak point and concentrate your efforts on this weakness. Finding and targeting a weakness in an opponent is called finding the *shooting range* in the friction-free economy. Here are the rules that tell strategists how to find the shooting range:

- In a two-company battle, if Company A has a market share less than three times that of Company B, then A is in the shooting range of B.

- In a battle among more than two companies, any pair of companies within 1.7 times market share of each other are in each other's shooting range.

Before a company can target a weakness, it must find the weakest competitor. In a two-way contest such as the Borland versus Microsoft software tools struggle described above, Borland would need at least 19% market share—Microsoft's 62% divided by three—to even contemplate a Trafalgar Strategy. In 1996 Borland was three percentage points shy of the mark. Therefore Borland could not hope to overcome its Goliath.

Another way of phrasing the first rule in terms of the Borland versus Microsoft competition is:

- In a battle between Microsoft and Borland, if Microsoft has a market share less than three times 16%, which equals 48%, then Microsoft is in the shooting range of Borland.

Too bad for Borland—Microsoft is not in its shooting range. Borland cannot hope to reverse its position with respect to Microsoft, because Microsoft had 62% market share, which was far above the 48% goal. (See Figure 3-2.)

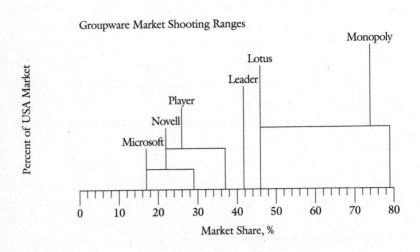

Figure 3–2. Shooting range diagram for the groupware market circa 1995. Lotus was clearly a market leader with Notes, and in fact, monopoly was within shooting range. Microsoft and Novell overlapped, indicating they were in each other's shooting range.

Look at another example from the PC software industry that illustrates the second rule. IBM liked Lotus Notes so much it bought the company and renamed it. Domino is simply Lotus Notes retreaded as an Internet groupware product. But back in 1995 the outcome of the groupware war was not so obvious. However, the shooting ranges were easily selected using the second rule of the Trafalgar Strategy. Figure 3-2 shows 1995 market shares in the competitive groupware market segment.

Overlapping blocks in Figure 3-2 illustrate the 1.7 rule: targeting opportunities exist whenever market shares are within a multiple of 1.7 of one another. Monopoly was within the shooting range of Lotus Notes. Indeed, by 1997, reincarnated Notes was pushing toward 9 million customers, and had left the other players in the dust. Microsoft and Novell had each other in their gun sights, but IBM/Lotus sped toward the finish line with visions of monopoly dancing in its head.

TAKING AIM

Selecting the right competitors to include in your shooting range is a major part of surviving in the friction-free economy. Once you have identified all competitors within your shooting range, you must further refine your marketing strategy before going into battle. This is the art of *taking aim*, and it is one of the most powerful techniques of the Trafalgar Strategy. Consider the rough and dangerous health care business as an example of taking aim.

Patient care is a multi-billion-dollar business in the U.S., and getting bigger. One reason is that the high cost of medicine is driving consumers to become their own caretakers. Why go to a physician when you can administer your own tests, and get advice on the Web?

Consumers may not be rushing to take out their own organs, but they are spending over $4 billion annually to do things like test their insulin level and urine acidity. This trend has not been overlooked by companies like Johnson & Johnson, Bayer, Boehringer Mannheim, and Abbott Labs. In fact, the $4 billion home patient care segment of health care is a hotly contested market. Like warriors of the Wired World, smart marketing managers of drug companies aim at weak points in their competitors' line of defenses to gain market share.

By systematically targeting the weakest competitors, gaining share, and then turning attention on successively stronger competitors, a ruthless attacker can rise to a monopoly position. This is another fundamental law in the friction-free economy:

> *Strong companies get stronger by aiming at the weakest companies first, followed by stronger and stronger companies.*

THE SQUARE LAW

How does a warrior of the Wired World decide who is weak and who is strong? How does taking aim actually work? Lanchester's early work mathematically showed that Army A could always defeat Army B if A had a force large enough to overwhelm B. Back in 1917, victory was obtained at high cost—both sides slugged it out until all soldiers of one side were destroyed. Army A won by surviving the onslaught of Army B.

Wars of attrition differ from marketing wars of strategy, but the idea of overwhelming the enemy still works. The question posed by Lanchester was this: "How much more powerful does Army A have to be to overwhelm Army B?" The answer:

> *Army A can overwhelm Army B if the strength of Army A is greater than or equal to the strength of Army B squared.*

The word *squared* always scares folks a little, but the concept is really quite simple. For example, if the strength of a company is three, then a competitor needs a strength of nine—three times three—to overwhelm it. This is called Lanchester's square law. What it means to businesses in the friction-free economy is:

> *Company B's marketing budget must be the square of Company A's budget in order to take market share away from Company A.*

The square law defines the basic non-Keynesian forces at work in the friction-free economy. It quantifies a marketing manager's model for how to win against impossible odds, and it establishes the foundation for an analytical discipline of marketing. The New Lanchester Strategy and its square law turn marketing into a science. It makes it possible for a garage start-up in Silicon Valley to do battle with nothing more than a personal computer and a telephone connection to the Wired World.

MERGERS AND ACQUISITIONS

If a company is able to compete effectively and grow its market share, then it can hope to become a player, then a leader, and finally a monopoly. When a company becomes a monopoly, the game is over. Finding a shooting range, taking aim, and then firing at the weakest competitor is one way. But there is more than one path to world domination. Mergers and acquisitions are a shortcut to a monopoly.

> *Mergers and acquisitions are appropriate when they move a company from unstable to player, player to leader, or leader to monopoly.*

Consider again the groupware market example of Figure 3-2. This is particularly instructive, because Lotus was acquired by IBM essentially so IBM could gain share in a market that was going to be dominated by either Lotus, Microsoft, or Novell. IBM had to act quickly or be completely shut out of the desktop software segment of corporate America.

Microsoft and Novell were at best unstable warriors in this narrow market segment. Had they been interested in playing the New Lanchester Strategy game, either one could have attacked the other by merging with Lotus. This would have changed their status from unstable to leader.

In reality, a merger between Lotus and either Novell or Microsoft would not have worked, because Lotus would not have significantly increased its market share. However, a merger between the groupware divisions of Microsoft and Novell would have created a more aggressive competitor to Lotus—but not competitive enough. A Microsoft/Novell pairing would violate the strategy of taking aim. The merged business would become a player, but not a leader.

As it turned out, IBM saw an opportunity to gain a foothold in the broader desktop software market space by acquiring Lotus. The resulting IBM/Lotus company failed to change the status of Lotus, but it made IBM a strong leader in this segment.

WINNERS AND WEENIES

Merging and acquiring can be used to gain an overwhelming market share when movement has become static. For example, when competitors are so locked in mortal combat that nobody's market share changes, M&A activity may be the only avenue for advancement.

The M&A game can also be used to predict who might be a winner and who might be a weenie in the friction-free economy.* Perhaps your stock portfolio needs a tune-up, or your brother-in-law needs a tip. In any case, the determination of which businesses are going somewhere, and which ones are not, may be useful.

Suppose 1995 data is used to predict what might happen in 1996 or later. The M&A game can be used as a kind of crystal ball. For example, the portable PC segment of the PC market was dominated by Toshiba, but NEC was hot on its heels in 1995. What happens if the M&A game is played among these competitors?

- Toshiba, NEC, or Compaq could have gained an advantage by merging their portable computer divisions. The resulting business would have become a player.

What actually happened? In 1996 NEC merged with Packard Bell to form the largest global PC vendor in the friction-free econ-

---

* *Weenie* is marketing talk for a loser.

omy. NEC used M&A to leapfrog over Toshiba in the portable segment, and advance on everyone else in the desktop segment. Combining the portable PC segment owned by NEC with the desktop segment owned by Packard Bell turned out to be a winning strategy. In fact, after NEC merged with Packard Bell to form the Packard Bell NEC company, Toshiba decided to enter the desktop segment!

Look at another example. In 1995 Microsoft Windows NT began to threaten the UNIX marketplace by eating into UNIX sales. Prior to the Windows NT challenge, UNIX vendors were lined up behind Sun Microsystems for market share. What were the possibilities for UNIX vendors to become stronger?

- Hewlett-Packard could have bought out Santa Cruz Operations (SCO)—the largest independent UNIX vendor in 1995. The resulting merger would have made HP a player just like rival Sun, but it would not have placed HP in a leadership position.

Did this actually happen? No, but almost. Novell sold UNIX to SCO later in the year, and HP became a partner, with SCO, in the further development of UNIX by SCO. Short of a buyout, perhaps, but not by much. SCO could still be merged into HP's operations in the coming years.

Still not convinced that M&A is a game of strategy? Consider this:

- In 1995–96 the Macintosh was the leading Web publishing platform, but nobody dominated the Web server market. Apple's acquisition of NeXT was driven as much by its need for a modern operating system as it was by WebObjects— NeXT's Web construction software.

- Adobe led in 2D, but lagged in 3D, graphics software in 1996. Autodesk was a player in 3D, but not a player in 2D. A merger of Adobe and Autodesk would have formed a monopoly of the image-editing segment of the software market, and ended the game. By 1997 no mergers or acquisitions had occurred, and neither company had changed position.

WARRIORS IN THE WIRED WORLD

Business is war. Business in the friction-free economy is thermonuclear war. From the sword-fighting days of Musashi to the analytical weapons of the New Lanchester Strategy, business has evolved into a game of strategy. And the strategy of the friction-free economy requires analytical tools and techniques previously employed by armies and now aimed at companies. In addition, the computer age introduces even more sophisticated tools involving measurements of market share, revenue growth, and targeted marketing. Still, these tools are only a starting point. They lead to even greater marketing tools being wielded by warriors in the Wired World—tools you will need to thrive in the friction-free economy.

4

Mining the Friction-Free Economy

This is how I now see us. Do you also see us in the same way? Or have I, as I now am, really ceased to be one of you?

—*John Maynard Keynes, 1883–1946*

A POOR GYPSY

According to Robert Heilbroner and Lester Thurow, the three greatest economists were Adam Smith, Karl Marx, and John Maynard Keynes. "Their vision still define the field of economics for everyone, right and left alike."[1] These historical figures defined what modern society calls economics. Their ideas have permeated everyday thinking to such a great extent that it is easy to believe they are universal truths. What are these truths, and why are they no longer valid in the friction-free economy?

Adam Smith started life in the fast lane. Born and raised in Kirkaldy, Scotland, in 1723, baby Smith was kidnapped by gypsies who gave him up after a few hours, declaring, "He would have made, I fear, a poor gypsy."[2] On another occasion, student and scholar Smith was so absorbed in thought that he stepped into a pit while walking deep in discussion. Later in life he would meet the great minds of his age, travel, and publish his masterpiece, *Wealth of Nations*.

Smith wrote the *Wealth of Nations* over a period of ten years, after a distinguished career as an absentminded professor at the University of Glasgow, Scotland, and tutor for Lord Townsend. Worried about self-interested, profit-hungry, "mean and rapacious" individuals who preyed on others, Smith worked out in detail how such selfishness and money-grubbing might actually benefit all of society. Smith believed in the market system, which he called the *Invisible Hand*—a self-regulating mechanism that would produce what society needed, at a price society could afford.[3]

We learn two things from Adam Smith. First, competition is not only good, it is the hidden mechanism that makes economics work as a self-regulating system. This idea assumes a direct relation between supply and demand, and sets the philosophical basis for classical economics. But self-regulating systems reach stable or equilibrium states, and we know that the underlying invisible hand of the friction-free economy is not stable, nor self-regulating. Thus, Smith's first idea does not apply in the friction-free economy.

Second, Smith believed the demand for labor would be matched by the supply of laborers. He was the first to realize that "supply equals demand" really defines monetary value. Money quantifies the point where a supply curve crosses a demand curve. But in the friction-free economy, money is not so easy to define. Other factors, such as market share, product lock-in, and value-add, define money. Therefore, Smith's second idea no longer applies in the friction-free economy.

If Smith was an optimist, Karl Marx was a pessimist. Marx saw the invisible hand as a powerful, money-grubbing hand of the capitalist in the pocket of the worker. Instead of evolving toward greater wealth for all, Marx postulated an economy where the rich get richer, until an equilibrium point is reached with all of a nation's wealth concentrated in a few powerful people's hands. Marx came closer to characterizing the friction-free economy than did Smith, perhaps, but he failed to understand its chaotic undertow.

Keynes was the mathematician who tried to explain both of his predecessors. Using sophisticated linear mathematics that few people understood at the time—or today—he showed that both were right—the invisible hand led to two stable equilibrium points. One point expanded the economy forever (Smith), thus increasing the wealth of a nation, and the other point led to chronically high unemployment and a concentration of wealth (Marx). Mathematically speaking, the economy could end up as Smith hoped or as Marx predicted. Keynes's solution to the Great Depression involved government spending in order to dislodge the economy from one of its equilibrium points (depression), and send it on its way towards the other equilibrium point (prosperity).

Keynesian economics has ruled for over a half century; but in fact, economics is still the dismal science it was originally thought to be, and modern markets rarely obey the truths set down by these great thinkers. The friction-free economy, by nature, disputes some of the so-called absolute truths of economics, and demands that smart businesses understand how it is different, in order to compete and succeed.

THE BOURSE, OF COURSE

The purest of the pure markets are stock exchanges. Historically, stock exchanges like the Paris Bourse—built at public expense—were open to all buyers and sellers. The colonial capitalists of New York gathered under a big buttonwood tree down by the wall and traded stock like baseball cards. But when the NYSE (New York Stock Exchange) officially opened in 1792, trades had to be brokered through twenty-four intermediaries. These "members" controlled the "free enterprise system" for almost two hundred years, until trading was partially opened up to the public once again. In 1975 discount brokers were allowed to resell equities. Twenty years later, 25% of the business was being conducted by the "outer circle" of discount brokers and non–Wall Street bankers. By the early twenty-first century, the NYSE, Nasdaq, and many other exchanges throughout the world will be as open as the Bourse, of course, because of the Internet.

In the friction-free economy, stock market buying and selling will return to the public. The market will be wide open. Transactions will take place in the Wired World at friction-free economy speeds. For example, 75% of all money ever invested in mutual funds up until 1996 poured in from 1992 through 1996—only four years! This flow of wealth could not have happened under the buttonwood trees, nor through the pocketbooks of exchange members. The Wired World is rapidly taking us back to the open and public stock exchange. And in the case of the stock markets, trading will become increasingly retro—as if it were under the buttonwood tree. Only, this time it will be via a network appliance.

These open and public stock markets are the closest thing to friction-free capitalism. There are few brakes to hold them back. This is why the stock market is such a good illustration of why the classical theory of free enterprise no longer works. Stock market behavior cannot be explained by anything but the friction-free economy.

Stock markets behave chaotically, and therefore demonstrate the chaotic nature of the friction-free economy better than any other market system. Their economy is being guided by an invisible hand of *mathematical chaos*. If a business can understand how this invisible hand operates, it can also understand how the friction-free economy works.

THE BOOMLET OF 1996

Never much of a gambling man, I really had no idea how to make money in the stock market before I understood the friction-free economy. I was the central character in that old joke, "If you want to make a million dollars in the stock market, start with 2 million." But the run-up of the Nasdaq and NYSE between the autumn of 1995 and the late spring of 1996 compelled me to join in the fun. The fun, as it turns out, was discovering that the stock market is yet another example of how the friction-free economy operates.

The boomlet of 1996 was an opportunity to put my money where my mouth was. Like the friction-free economy I had come to understand, the stock market is the ultimate in friction-free capitalism. It is a pure bazaar, where marginal costs approach zero, products can have infinite shelf life, and production costs are nil. What better laboratory than this to test my theories?

The behavior of the economy in the friction-free economy is nonlinear, which means that change does *not* progress smoothly from one value to the other. Instead, changes jump about, much like the Dow. This notion propelled me to ask, "Can the ups and downs of the stock market be anticipated by the nonlinear mainstreaming equations of the friction-free economy?" The answer is, "Most of the time."

Figure 4-1 shows the stock market boomlet—in terms of the Dow Industrial Averages—for the first half of 1996. The data were sampled at one-month intervals, so they give only a rough approximation—valid perhaps for demonstration purposes only. Had I sampled the closing price at the end of each day, the curve shown in Figure 4-1 would be much more erratic. As it turns out, even with the smoothing of infrequent sampling, the rise of the Dow illustrates a chaotic behavior. The Dow average exhibits a well-known mathematical phenomenon known as *mathematical chaos theory*.

Good-bye Keynesian economics, hello mathematical chaos. The behavior of a product, service, or idea mainstreaming in the friction-free economy can be understood only in terms of modern mathematics. The burgeoning field of mathematical chaos explains how the friction-free economy works. Businesses that understand chaos, or accidentally stumble onto its principles, will prosper and grow. Everybody else will wonder what happened to them.

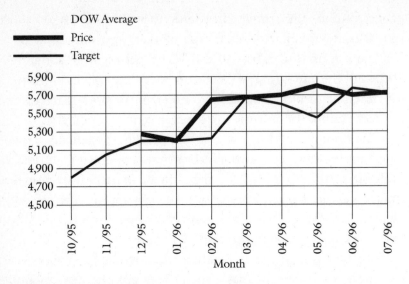

Figure 4–1. The DOW jumped over 1,000 points, or over 20%, in the 9 months between October 1995 and June 1996.

A LITTLE BIT OF CHAOS

Mathematical chaos is not a difficult concept to grasp as long as you ignore the mathematics. Here is how it works. The first time I drove a car, I wandered back and forth across the centerline like an alcoholic. I overcompensated for each bump and curve in the road. My problem? First I aimed too far to the left, then I swerved too far to the right to compensate. In other words, my feedback system was out of control. Without the assistance of my father, I would have oscillated uncontrollably back and forth until attracting the attention of a police officer.

After a while I learned to control my steering. Instead of a jerky left or powerful right turn of the steering wheel, I learned to moderate each adjustment. It took a few harrowing practice trips in my 1949 Ford Coupe before I developed a more subtle touch. But in fact, minor adjustments did the trick. Eventually my internal feedback control mechanism calmed down and I was transformed into a normal ten-year-old without a driver's license.

Suppose I had not learned from my driving experience. I might have continued to oscillate from side to side as I drove down the road. If these oscillations had been more or less the same distance back and forth, they would have been considered *unstable* behavior at most, and violations of traffic laws at least. Such oscillations demonstrate a kind of chaotic behavior that sometimes occurs in systems that are inherently *unstable*. Mathematicians call this *unstable* chaos.

It could have been worse. Suppose that each time I attempted to correct my poor aim, I had overshot more than the time before. The oscillations would have gotten bigger and bigger until I might have landed in the ditch. My driving would not only have been unstable, it would have been chaotic. Mathematicians call uncontrollable oscillations *chaos*.

Driving, buying, selling, and gaining market share inherently behave according to the rules of nonlinear systems. And some nonlinear systems are prone to becoming chaotic. A *chaotic system* is a nonlinear system that tends to become unstable or chaotic, much like my early driving. The friction-free economy is such a system. The nonlinearity of the friction-free economy is the major reason the classical theories of Adam Smith, John Maynard Keynes, and others no longer work.

Mathematical chaos is the field of study that tries to understand nonlinear systems. It is the nonlinearity that makes these systems unstable or chaotic. Chaos is common in physical systems. Everyone has heard about the butterfly that caused tidal waves in Maui by flapping its wings in Tokyo. Of course, this is a ridiculous example of chaos in global weather patterns, but it dramatizes how nonlinear, nonlinear systems are! Hence, nonlinearity means that cause-and-effect linkages can behave in unexpected ways. In the absurd case of a butterfly, the long-distance effect of its flapping wings is far more dramatic than expected using a simple linear model. In nonlinear systems, cause-and-effect is also far more dramatic than intuition leads us to believe. The friction-free economy is governed by nonlinear cause-and-effect, so our intuition cannot be trusted when it comes to making business decisions.

GAMBLING WITH CHAOS

The Nasdaq reached its local high of 1254 on June 6, and then corrected to a low of 1008 on July 16. The Dow hit 5,833 on May 23, and then fell to 5,182 in July. The 165-point Dow drop in one day on July 5 ended the boomlet of early 1996.* The Nasdaq Composite had its second-biggest point decline ever on July 15. The boomlet was definitely bust. Only the crash of October 1987 exceeded these two resounding thumps.

The front page of *Business Week*, June 3, 1996, asked the question, "Never before have so many people had so much riding on the market. Should we worry?" After the July 5 thump, the popular press was asking, "Where can we hide?" The oscillations continued throughout 1996. Stock market personalities made good fodder for TV shows, and analysts everywhere were eager to explain why the market went up, and why it went down. Unfortunately, most of them were wrong. Why? Only chaos theory had the power to explain these oscillations.

Both markets alternated among unstable, stable, and sometimes chaotic states throughout much of the second half of 1996. These ups and downs did not surprise me, because both markets were simply demonstrating mathematical chaos theory. During the middle of June 1996, when the Dow exceeded 5,700 points, I sold over $40,000 in various equities. In August, when the boomlet was clearly over, I bought back in—gaining about 12% over a period of several weeks. Throughout the turbulent days to follow, I bought and sold at "mostly the right time," according to my broker. By the end of the year, I had gained 22% over a six-month period, and when the Dow reached 7,000 in early 1997, my portfolio was up by one-third. How did I do this? What timing method did I use to buy and sell?

Figure 4-1 contains a curve labeled "Target." This curve comes from mathematical chaos theory. It can be interpreted as "where

---

*Of course, there were subsequent boomlets later in 1996, but let's take one boomlet at a time.

the market wants to go."* Like a reservoir of water that seeks its own level, the target is the "correct" level of the market. If the actual price is above the target price, then it is above what it "should be." Conversely, if the actual price is below the target, it is below where it "should be."

STRANGE ATTRACTORS AND FIXED POINTS

Chaos theory deals with nonlinear equations that behave, well, nonlinearly. But even when behaving erratically, a nonlinear system tends toward a fixed point called a *strange attractor*. This is a point around which oscillations fluctuate, or where a stable system converges. Suppose we think of the stock market as a nonlinear chaotic system that behaves like a coiled spring. A spring can be smoothly stretched, up to a point—stretching is linear—but when the spring is suddenly let go, it bounces back. Indeed, it oscillates, just like an overextended stock price. When pulled too far, the spring breaks, which is an even greater calamity. Like an overextended spring, the Dow average can be overextended, too. When the Dow "breaks," it sends the average plunging to alarming lows.

Is it possible to predict when a spring will break? In practice, the answer is "most of the time." Why not all of the time? If you try to determine how far a spring will stretch before it breaks by experimenting with a lot of springs, you will discover that the amount of required force varies from spring to spring. This is due to slight differences in materials and construction among the coils. The breaking point may be different for each spring, but on the average, a spring's breaking point can be estimated by any graduate student of physics or engineering. As long as we understand these slight variations, we can estimate the breaking point "most of the time."

The ups and downs of the friction-free market called NYSE or Nasdaq are like the stretching of a spring. If you go up too far or too fast, the coiled steel reaches its breaking point, and collapses. If

---

*The market will go where it wants to. My job was to predict where it wanted to go.

all force is removed while extended, the coil also collapses. Similarly, the stock market can reach its breaking point and crash. It can also collapse when all force (demand) is removed. Finally, it oscillates about its fixed point, when some—but not all—force is removed.

Chaotic systems are like coiled springs because they have points that can be reached but not exceeded. They behave as expected up to these points, but anything beyond the breaking point results in chaotic behavior. These are the fixed points of chaotic systems. In the stock market, they are the fixed points of a stock price. In the friction-free economy, they are the market share percentages of companies.

Remember, not all springs stretch the same distance, nor do they break at the same point. Similarly, not all stocks rise or drop at the same time. This is why it is possible to compute a fixed point most of the time, but not all of the time. This uncertainty is what makes buying and selling so much fun! But if you are right most of the time, you can make money most of the time. You can also lose money some of the time. But on the average, it is possible to beat the market if you can predict when the coiled spring of a stock is about to snap, leading to a price decline.

BOUNCE THEORY

The coiled spring analogy with the stock price of a Dow or Nasdaq stock illustrates why the classical theory of the economy no longer works. Stock prices, market shares, and the value of money itself are governed by nonlinear systems that behave like nonlinear coils of spring steel. This is what I call the bounce theory of the market, and it is a form of mathematical chaos that also describes many of the behaviors of businesses in the friction-free economy.

To illustrate bounce theory, consider again the stock market example. What determines the bounce in the price of a stock? Fear and greed. Fear and greed stretch and contract the coiled spring of a stock price. They do so in a nonlinear, mathematically chaotic manner.

Investors like to make money in a bull market, but they become edgy and nervous if the market goes up too fast. They start to toss and turn at night, wondering when the run will end. The higher the market, the more they worry. Torn between greed and caution, investors become erratic. They start buying and selling. They introduce unstable behavior. This erratic behavior gains momentum. It pushes the coiled spring to its breaking point. This creates havoc on Wall Street. Investors call it volatility; I call it chaos.

Investors are torn between fear and greed. Therefore, change in buying urges are proportional to the desire to avoid a loss (fear), and the desire to earn a profit (greed). The larger the fear, the more likely an investor will run. Similarly, the larger the potential for profit, the more likely he or she will pour more money into a stock. This "law" is very similar to the mainstreaming law:

> *Change in buy/sell behavior is proportional to both fear of a loss and profit potential.*

When this simple rule is turned into an equation, it belongs to a famous class of mathematical chaos formulas. It is nonlinear and nonclassical. In fact, this kind of equation completely upsets the theories of the great economists, such as John Maynard Keynes and Adam Smith.

GOOD-BYE, MR. KEYNES

John Maynard Keynes was a gambling man, too. In his early years as an economist, he played various British markets. Often using other people's money, Keynes won some and lost some. In some cases, the losses were so sizable that he had to resort to real work to repay his investing partners. Over the years, however, Keynes made a fortune in the foreign exchange markets. Every morning he would spend a few hours in bed, reading and calling his broker. A few hours per day were sufficient to make him a very rich man. Perhaps his forays were in the interest of science. Mine were motivated by greed.

Keynes was more than an economist. He was a mathematician. And he was a renowned author long before he became the father of modern economics. Keynes's book, *The General Theory of Employment, Interest and Money*, was published at just the right time to pull the world out of the Great Depression. While it was far too complex for the average economist to read, it preached a simple message: Economic activity was determined by the willingness of entrepreneurs to make investments. Like the pure-play stock market, economic activity of a whole nation is driven (or dies) by how much money is in the system. And, like the friction-free economy, the more money in the system, the more activity. One feeds the other, in a spiral of economic growth.

As good as Smith, Marx, and Keynes were, they lived in a world with fewer complications. Their world could be modeled as a linear, dynamic system. Such a world view no longer explains the nonlinear dynamic behavior of modern economics. The friction-free economy is fundamentally different from the classical economic system of the past because its underlying mathematics is described by nonlinear mathematical chaos. But there are even more differences, which the classical economics of Smith, Marx, and Keynes are unable to explain. For example, Keynes had no concept of learning and process improvement. His was a world of tangible goods, supply-and-demand for these goods, and a linear progression from one state of the market to another. There was no such thing as a breaking point or oscillations about a strange attractor. Keynes may have been prone to fear and greed just as any other human, but his theories never incorporated such factors. In simple terms, classical economics lacked bounce.

WAVE THEORY

The mathematical chaos of the friction-free economy leads to the bounce theory of how stock prices, market shares, and product adoptions fluctuate. But it also introduces a side-effect—waves. Bounces create waves, and waves transmit chaos to all other ships.

Wave theory says that oscillations created by a sudden change in one stock price propagate to other stock prices. Oscillations in the market share of one company can end up capsizing another company.

Consider the waves caused by a bounce in market share. A high market share bounce means a company is doing well, but if the bounce is too high, the business may be in danger of creating chaos. Interestingly, a dominant company can introduce chaos into the mainstreaming of another company without much impact on itself. The reason: A group of competing companies form a large, complex system of learning/bouncing competitors—a system that may become unstable or even chaotic due to "too much" bounce. When such a group of companies compete with one another, chaotic behavior in one company can propagate to all others. Only the strong companies are able to withstand these waves of changing market shares.

If a company has a large market share, it is less susceptible to unstable waves that pass through the systems of competitors. Weaker companies may get whiplashed, but companies with lots of market share have the inertia to stave off these waves. If a company has lock-in, then it is nearly immune to chaos—but not entirely.

So much for theory. Here is an illustration. Consider another market segment that is becoming dominated by Microsoft. The UNIX operating system was perhaps the first software product of the friction-free economy. Its creator and one-time owner was AT&T, a company that thought UNIX was nothing more than an idle experiment. It was given away to universities in the late 1970s and 1980s, much the way Netscape gave away its early Navigator browser software. Soon UNIX-trained students infiltrated business, and a few, like Bill Joy, formed new companies like Sun Microsystems. Naturally, they wanted to use UNIX, because they already belonged to the UNIX tribe.

Others licensed UNIX from AT&T, but AT&T never really made any profit from these licensees. Eventually UNIX was sold off to Novell, but Novell could not compete against its own licensees.

So Novell sold UNIX to The Santa Cruz Operation, a small company that attempted to keep UNIX alive at exactly the same time that Microsoft introduced its UNIX killer, Windows NT.

By the late 1990s UNIX occupied the workstation and server market along with Novell's NetWare, IBM's OS/2, Microsoft's Windows NT, and various other versions of UNIX (OSF/1, Solaris, HP-UX, AIX, etc.). The problem was, Microsoft's Windows NT began gobbling up market share as Microsoft changed from a PC company to an enterprise company.

The dominance of UNIX and Novell NetWare in the server segment began collapsing as Microsoft's NT began to mainstream. In less than one year, from 1994 to 1995, the market share of Microsoft Windows NT versus Novell NetWare and UNIX radically shifted, creating extreme fear among UNIX vendors. This shift gained momentum in 1996 and into 1997, forcing UNIX vendors to huddle together against the odds. In fact, the share of NT accelerated so fast that it sent waves through the server market. Microsoft was gaining market share too quickly, and the result was mathematical chaos.

As a consequence of the waves sent out from the rapid climb of Windows NT and the rapid decline of its competitors, everyone's boat began to rock and roll. Even Microsoft's share began to oscillate as Windows NT rode a bumpy road to greater market share in 1997. Beyond 1997 Microsoft's market share of the server segment will oscillate around its strange attractor, causing oscillations in the market shares of UNIX and NetWare well into the next decade. That is, chaos will continue unless something happens to supress the waves emanating from Windows NT.

THE FOG OF MAINSTREAMING

Rapid growth in market share can become chaotic, just like a stock price. When this happens, wave theory predicts oscillations in the shares of competitors as well as the company that is crossing the Chasm. But wave theory is just that—a theory. In practice, chaos is dampened by competition. Competition is a kind of friction, retarding the coiled spring so that it snaps back slowly when let go. Competition introduces friction into the friction-free economy. Competition introduces drag. Competition reduces the friction-free economy to something resembling classical economics, but with a very important difference: The underlying mechanisms are nonlinear. Because of competition, the fundamental law of main-streaming in the friction-free economy reads like this:

Change in market share is proportional to both existing market share and the remaining market share. But competition introduces drag; competitive mainstreaming is dampened by drag.

A second look at the Microsoft Windows NT competition illus-trates this rule. Keep in mind that this market has an underlying nonlinearity—a kind of invisible hand that is guiding its behavior. In other words, the invisible hand of Adam Smith has been replaced by the invisible hand of chaos.

Because competition introduces drag, it pulls the friction-free economy back from the brink of chaos. Not everything is perfect, free, or easy in the friction-free economy. Sooner or later, a com-petitor comes along to foil plans of world domination. Nowhere is this more obvious than in the network server segment contested by Microsoft, Novell, and the many UNIX vendors. Therefore, Microsoft can thank the friction of competition for reducing oscil-lations in its market share as Windows NT heads towards a monopoly of 75% or more. Microsoft's lock-in makes it immune to bounce, but its smaller rivals may get swamped by waves of fluctu-ating market share. Many of them will capsize.

Novell practically invented PC LANs (Local Area Networks) for departmental computing. They were the Microsoft of network operating systems, having an overwhelming share of that market segment before Microsoft noticed how much money could be made. Ray Noorda, founder and CEO of Novell, paid homage to

Bill Gates, founder and CEO of Microsoft, during the late 1980s and early 1990s. Noorda tried to talk Gates into looking the other way while Novell mainstreamed to victory. Instead, Noorda and Gates set out to destroy each other. Noorda lacked the analytical foundation of the New Lanchester Strategy, and his company failed the transition from a single mainstream product to a mainstreaming-in-the-large industry.

Maybe Noorda argued that the world should be divided into two pieces, like the Line of Demarcation drawn by Spain and Portugal. Maybe Gates had visions of merging with or buying Novell at some point in his empire building. Perhaps nobody will know for sure, but for some reason Noorda and Gates broke off negotiations, and by 1995 Windows NT 3.51 was ready for combat. Novell's NetWare was definitely in Windows NT's shooting range.

UNIX is a different story. It already had a grip on the high-end enterprise servers when Windows NT came along. Few UNIX vendors took NT seriously, because it began life as a toy. Lacking many of the industrial-strength features of UNIX, NT had to settle for a niche market serving small networks and work groups. But then the Internet came along and changed the technical balance. A special kind of server—*Web server*—found a home in big companies.

Microsoft wasted no time finding its shooting range, aiming, and shooting to kill. In a classic divide-and-conquer move, Windows NT was split into two products—one called Windows NT workstation for desktops, and the other called Windows NT server, for enterprise applications. Like Janus, the two-headed god, Windows NT would look both ways: at the future desktop, and at the enterprise server segment. The server version would drive a wedge between Novell NetWare at the low end and UNIX at the high end. And while Microsoft was at it, IBM's OS/2 would sink into the setting sun as Windows NT wooed IBM's faithful Fortune 1000 customers. The strategy was perfect, and the timing coincided with the rise of the Internet.

Chaotic mainstreaming introduced instability into the server market space. But competition stabilized the market. Microsoft's steady advance against its competitors was a pure power play that worked. NT took the market lead away from low-end UNIX in 1996, and will surpass Novell by 1998 at its current rate of adoption. By the year 2000, Windows NT could reach solid leadership status, and be on its way to mainstreaming at all levels.

Where did Novell and UNIX go wrong? Novell missed the rapid onset of the Wired World. NetWare had a zero market share of the Web server segment of the network operating systems market in 1995, and a slim 9% in 1996. Windows NT established a two-to-one lead over NetWare in this important subsegment, early on.

UNIX could not help itself. A relic from the 1970s, UNIX was simply too complex, too costly, and too big to hold on to its lead in any other than the very high-end server and engineering workstation segments. But these are the techie segments that constitute a very small part of the broad market for servers. UNIX could not apply Davidow's Law fast enough to keep up with Windows NT.

HOW THE COOKIE CRUMBLES

Traditional economics centers on monetary policies, valuations like market capital, and manufacturing costs. These are outmoded measures for an economy hooked on value-add. In the friction-free economy, money is nearly meaningless because it is possible to churn out abundant goods and services at ever lower cost. This is just how the cookie crumbles in a civilization that can produce goods and services of higher and higher quality at lower and lower cost. Consider Netscape, which gave away its software product (zero price), and produced as many consumers as desired (infinite supply). It was able to do this because of the friction-free economy of the Internet. Making more copies of Netscape Navigator was as simple as copying bits from Netscape's server disk to your own. The marginal cost of manufacturing and distribution was zero, therefore Netscape was able to produce an infinite number of them.

What, then, is the meaning of money in the friction-free economy? Money, of course, still means *something*, but interestingly, the friction-free economy runs on *value-add*—adding value to something else. Most high-tech businesses today are links in a value chain that runs from basic technology companies like Intel, to midlevel value adders like Microsoft, to end-user links like Wells Fargo Bank.

> *Money is made in the friction-free economy by adding value along a value chain—and then extracting money from one or more links in the chain.*

The replacement of money with value-add does strange things to the economy. Cash revenues and profit mean very little. Instead, every business that expects to compete in the friction-free economy must make a compelling *value proposition* in order to survive. Instead of providing a product at a price that large numbers of consumers will pay, successful businesses must add enough value to enhance the *entire* chain.

Perhaps the most publicized illustration of confusion between making money and surviving in the friction-free economy is provided by Apple Computer. Up until the very end of its long string of successful quarters, the company was awash in revenues and profits. In 1995 it was selling in excess of $10 billion worth of products—much larger than Microsoft. In fact, Apple Computer's revenues were greater than Intel's, Microsoft's, and the IBM PC Company's throughout much of the company's first twenty years.

Apple stumbled on the realities of the friction-free economy that says, if you don't add value to a value chain, you cannot survive even if you make a profit. Apple Computer failed to add value to the mainstream PC value chain, and in 1996 it reported a loss of nearly $1 billion! By 1997 the company was laying off engineers like workers at a pet rock factory. It was not Apple's only problem, but confusion over revenues versus market share did the company in. A misunderstanding of value-add was the culprit.

COUNT THE WAYS

If absolute money is now only the equivalent of a scorecard, how does a business become "wealthy" in the friction-free economy? There are many ways, a few of which follow:

- A sizable market share is valuable to investors when a company like Netscape goes public with 80% of the browser market in its back pocket, and only $12 million in sales. How else did Netscape's market value soar to almost $3 billion on such small sales? In this case, Netscape added value by defining an entirely new market segment—browsers— and capturing the lion's share of it. Investors paid handsomely for a piece of this locked-in installed base, hoping to cash in—along with Netscape—on the follow-on products.

- A huge lead in product development was a value-add when Sun Microsystems released its nouvelle Java language. Sun's stock value doubled even before Java proved itself. In fact, Sun created an entirely new value chain. As a consequence, there is now a "Java industry" of software vendors and merchants adding value to the original product. Thus, Sun's value-add is to produce a "Java dial-tone," meaning Sun's Java is a content-delivery mechanism just as the telephone is a distribution mechanism for business transactions.

- Favorable product reviews by the automotive press are added value to Ford, Chrysler, GM, Toyota, and Mercedes-Benz when they announce a new product. Not exactly money in the bank, but such reviews eventually translate into sales. Therefore, an entire industry of public relations firms, journalists, and analysts has sprung up to feed the automobile consumer. Perhaps a bit intangible, PR, image, and reputation are as valuable as gold was a hundred years ago.

- Speed is a value-add in a number of ways in the friction-free economy. One of the most intriguing facets of this is how fast a company can invert the cost of its products and services while increasing the quality. The speed with which a company can pull off inverse economics is one of the most valuable assets it can have. This is so important that it is known as the upside-down effect in the friction-free economy.

UPSIDE-DOWN ECONOMICS

Keynes and other classical economists find it difficult to explain why products and services get better as they get cheaper. The reason for their difficulty is simple—their models are all wrong. Classical models do not incorporate the learning curves that drive mainstreaming. In fact, inverse economics—a consequence of learning—introduces yet another nonlinearity. As in the previous examples, learning curves reveal some unusual nonclassical side effects in the friction-free economy.

Inverse economics dictates that products, services, and ideas get better and cheaper. Unlike those in earlier ages, products in the friction-free economy achieve the impossible: Their quality goes up while their price goes down. How is this possible? In the good old days, craftsmanship was hard to come by, and quality building materials were more expensive because they were more rare. In short, quality was a value-add. A better product created a greater demand, causing its price to go up.

Today quality goes up as costs go down, for a number of reasons. Sophisticated manufacturing tools and modern statistical sampling theory are obvious explanations. But in the friction-free economy, learning curves count for more than even statistical sampling. Things are not as linear in the friction-free economy. It is possible to produce a premium-quality product at a commodity price in the friction-free economy, causing the old idea of "quality equals value" to become obsolete.

Take Mercedes-Benz and Toyota, for example. Clearly, a Benz is a premium-priced product and a Toyota is a commodity-priced product. But a 1996 Toyota is probably a better car than a 1976

Mercedes-Benz. The technology of 1996 permitted Toyota to build higher-quality cars that year than in 1976—as good as premium-priced cars of twenty years earlier. Yet, the 1996 Toyota is still a commodity-priced product.

The reason Toyota is able to produce a high-quality car at a commodity price is inverse economics. The reason inverse economics drives prices to lower and lower levels is volume economics. Recall how the aircraft manufacturers lowered their cost of production each time their accumulated volume doubled? They increased their quality through sheer numbers. Similarly, the higher production volume of Toyota cars allows the Toyota company to learn faster than Mercedes-Benz. If properly managed, learning can be used to produce better and better cars at lower and lower cost. Simply by manufacturing large numbers of vehicles, Toyota is able to speed through price barriers faster than a lower-volume producer.

Learning curve models predict that a commodity-priced product will eventually overtake a premium-priced product simply because of higher production volumes. If Toyota makes enough cars, eventually Toyotas will be both better and cheaper than same-year Mercedes-Benzes! It is as if Toyota were able to produce a 1999 model car in 1996, while Mercedes-Benz is able to produce only the best 1996 car.

Over time and many generations of products, a volume producer can learn faster than a premium producer through sheer numbers. Because Intel produces 60 million microprocessors, compared to 4 million for Motorola, Intel has an advantage over Motorola. Boeing produces more commercial airplanes than anyone else, making it the lowest-cost manufacturer and a tough competitor. In any industry, everyone has equal access to know-how and resources. But the volume producer has access to faster learning curves.

Once a product is mainstreamed, its manufacturer can leverage its volume-economics advantage. The commodity producer can reinvest savings obtained from volume learning. That is, instead of lowering prices, the commodity price can be kept constant, and the savings can be put back into the product in the form of improved quality. The product undergoes constant improvement—*kaizen*—instead of constant lowering of its price.

A very fast learning industry, such as the computer and communications industry, can make a commodity product that pulls ahead of a premium-priced product simply by outproducing it. A business might produce ten times as many widgets as a premium-priced competitor, and still sell them for one-third to one-fourth as much. Therefore:

> *In a fast-learning industry, volume economics can be traded for quality, thus making it difficult for premium-priced products to compete. In a slow-learning industry, volume economics is not as much of an advantage; premium-priced products therefore can compete on the basis of quality rather than price.*

JUNKYARD DOGS

Nonlinear inverse economics has enormous implications. Think of the premium Macintosh market versus the leading Wintel commodity market. Simply by selling ten times as many boxes as Apple, Wintel roared past the Macintosh. At one time, Wintel machines were no better than a junkyard dog. But after rapidly climbing the learning and performance curves of the computer industry, Wintel machines are both cheaper and better than higher-priced machines. Consumers can buy a commodity Wintel box that is almost as good as a Macintosh, has more memory, larger screen, and bigger disk drives, but is priced lower. Apple's failure to understand inverse economics cost it its leadership in the industry.

Combine inverse economics with the near-zero-cost manufacturing and distribution capabilities of the Wired World, and you get extremely high volumes, extremely low pricing, and extremely fast learning. This explains, from a different point of view, high rates of success among Wired World companies such as Netscape Communications and products such as Java from Sun Microsystems. In the friction-free economy, inverse economics generates extremely cheap, yet high-quality, products, services, and ideas.

THE VALUE OF TIME

Another way to define value is by measuring time. In Adam Smith's day, speed and timeliness were not so important because the industrial age moved in decades, not hours. In the friction-free economy, the clock runs at Internet Time speeds. As a result, time is more precious than dollars.

Time waits for no one, and Internet Time waits even less. Decisions and actions are limited to certain windows of opportunity. These windows are very valuable. Take the concept of double time, for example.

DOING DOUBLE TIME

A product, service, or idea that misses its window of opportunity is worthless. Alternately, a product that hits its window is golden. This idea can be combined with inverse economics to add value to a product, service, or idea. In particular, combining timing with inverse economics leads to the concept of *double time*. Double time is the length of time it takes a product, service, or idea to double its market share. This is usually the same time it takes to double accumulated volume. Remember, learning takes place whenever accumulated volume doubles.

Like Hubble's Constant for estimating the rate of growth of an expanding universe, double time explains how fast an industry or product is expanding along some mainstreaming curve. But unlike Hubble's Constant, double time is not a constant. It varies along the nonlinear mainstreaming curve.

The time it takes to double market share depends only on learning rate. Since market share is limited to 100%, it is impossible to double more than once after reaching a 50% share. At the other extreme, doubling a small market share might take a very short time. Therefore, double time changes as market share increases up to 50%, and then it becomes meaningless.

For example, the double time of the common household telephone was over sixty years! Henry Ford's Model T doubled its market share in about two decades, and the VCR doubled in less than a decade. Products and services with doubling times within the two- to three-year Internet Time scale of the friction-free economy can be found in abundance in the computer industry. Multimedia PCs, game machines, computer networks, and Internet host products and services fall into this category. But these opportunities won't last, because by the year 2000 most of them will have reached their midpoints. For example, the number of Internet users will double in the next two to three years, but after 2000 it will be too late to double it again. Similar markets are viable until around 2002, when doubling becomes impossible. We are living in a unique time, when products, services, and ideas have such a short double time that they render themselves obsolete! And an obsolete product is worthless. This is why venture capitalists in Silicon Valley live and die by the following rule:

The value of a product is inversely proportional to its double time. A product, service, or idea that cannot double its share of the market within the time scale of its era has no value.

THE VANISHING PHYSICAL WORLD

Another dimension is added to the abstract concept of value-add in the friction-free economy—physical size is inversely proportional to value. In the friction-free economy, small is beautiful. Computers that consume less power, take up less space, weigh less, and make less noise are valued more than their larger equivalents.

In the spring of 1997 Apple Computer CEO Gil Amelio proudly announced the fastest portable computer in the universe to a throng in Japan. But the mostly Japanese reporters attending the Tokyo unveiling were disappointed. They had expected Amelio to announce the smallest portable! In the crowded buses and subways of Japan, a small portable computer is more valuable than a larger, faster one.

Weigh the value-add of a lightweight, portable computer. For approximately the same capabilities—memory capacity, processor speed, disk storage capacity, and accessories—a consumer was willing to spend at least $1,000 more on a laptop than a desktop computer in 1996. The premium increased in midrange machines, and then came back down a small amount as the upper end was reached. For example, consumers paid a $2,000 premium in the $3,500 range, and a $1,500 premium in the $5,000 range.

The Sony Walkman may have been the first product of the friction-free economy to demonstrate the high value placed on the vanishing physical world. The main selling point of the Walkman was its size. Not only does the friction caused by delivering material goods, services, and ideas diminish in the friction-free economy, but the material goods and services themselves vanish! Furthermore, as less and less of a good or service is sold, its price (value) goes up! Like the advertisement says, less is more in the friction-free economy.

THE VALUE OF MARKET SHARE

Market share, of course, is highly valuable in the friction-free economy—but what is less obvious is that market share is perhaps the most valuable product of the friction-free economy. Market share increases the utility of a product, service, or idea, rather than decreasing it, as in the classical economics of Smith, Marx, and Keynes. In their world, the more of something everyone has, the less valuable it is. If everyone has all the bread they can eat, bread prices go down. If the streets are paved with gold, cement becomes more valuable than gold. Scarcity is equated with value, and abundance equated with cheapness and accessibility.

In the friction-free economy, abundance makes a product more valuable.

This is yet another example of upside-down economics at work. But how can something increase its marginal return when there is more and more of it?

Automobile, TV, and appliance manufacturers deal with the value of commodity products by appealing to fashion. A new car is purchased when the old one still works, because styles change. You purchase a new TV because it is newer, even though the old one still works fine. Appliances generally last twenty years or more, but the average household purchases new ones after about twelve to fifteen years, simply because the reliable old one is no longer hip.

Mass-market manufacturing has lessened the value of things, but the friction-free economy works in the opposite way. In fact, the more abundant a product, service, or idea becomes, the greater its possibility of lock-in. The widespread abundance of Microsoft Word is what makes it valuable. The abundance of computers running Windows makes Windows more valuable than UNIX. The abundance of VHS-format tapes and video cameras makes VHS VCRs more valuable—not less.

Gilder's Law of the Telecosm (aka Metcalfe's Law) demonstrates the utility of abundance in the Wired World. A newly purchased computer has utility because it is used to track finances, process digital images, and write letters to friends. Computers are better and cheaper than owning a calculator, camera with darkroom, and typewriter. If a computer is connected to other computers by a network, its utility goes up by the number of other computers it connects to. In fact, Gilder's Law says the value of a computer increases by the square of the number of other computers that are connected to it by a network. Abundance wins over scarcity once again.

An abundance of computers connected together in the Wired World contributes to the value of each individual computer. The increase in value-add is nonlinear—it is exponential. This illustrates yet another nonlinear, non-Keynesian effect of the friction-free economy.

THE VALUE OF MOMENTUM

In 1994–95 penetration of CATV (Cable TV) into American homes reached 62%, and then stayed there. By 1995–96 major CATV businesses were losing money and reaching for new ways to make up the losses. This is one reason Time Warner, TCI, and others began merger and acquisition activities as well as entered the business of telecommunications. They needed an impetus to grow. They needed an injection of vitality. They needed the Telecommunications Bill of 1996, which deregulated telephone and CATV empires.

CATV's problem is that the industry never reached the critical market share needed to turn a bunch of companies into an industry. It left too much market share up for grabs. This invited competitors such as PRIMESTAR and DIRECTV to enter the market traditionally held by CATV operators, because there was room at the top. CATV ran out of gas—its market momentum slowed or stopped.

A business cannot become an industry leader in the friction-free economy unless it has *momentum. Market momentum* is the product of market share and rate of change of market share. In the case of CATV, adoption reached 62%, but the rate of change of adoption slumped to zero. Thus, CATV's market momentum also dropped to zero. This placed CATV in jeopardy.

In the friction-free economy, a business must keep up its momentum if it wants to dominate its market. It does this by having a positive rate of change of market share. Momentum has to build as a product mainstreams, reaches a maximum, and then declines. Therefore, it is essential that market share constantly inch its way upward. When peak momentum is reached, a product is poised to become so dominant that a business can create an entire industry. But if that business does not achieve dominance in all aspects, it invites someone else who will.

A business can optimally convert its product into an industry standard at the maximum momentum point. Failure to do so may jeopardize its chances to become a monopoly and end the game.

BATTLE FOR INDUSTRY

In the early 1980s I hung out with the pocket-protectors* of Hewlett-Packard in Corvallis, Oregon. One pocket-protector group was doing research in a field that seemed at the time to have very little to do with computers. Take Greg Wilson, for example. His job was to squirt fluid from a small nozzle onto a flat surface and figure out how to control it. Greg used powerful parallel computers to model flowing fluids, and evangelized a programming language called OCCAM. OCCAM died, but fluid flow went on to become a mainstream industry.

It turns out that ink is a fluid and a piece of paper makes a reasonably flat surface. If the ink squirts at the right speed, hits the paper just right, and dries as soon as it hits, squirting machines make very nice printers. HP's foray into fluid flow paid off when the need for high-quality, low-cost printers coincided with the rise of small office computing.

If you want to dominate the ink-jet printer industry, you need to understand fluid flow. You also need to understand momentum in the friction-free economy. HP used several learning curves to build an overwhelming momentum for its ink-jet printers and become the dominant force in the overall printer market. Their color ink-jet printer business grew at a rate of 167% between 1994 and 1995, while laser printers advanced at a rate of 22%. Today HP literally owns the ink-jet market.

The names of HP, Microsoft, Intel, and other industry leaders have become synonymous with their market-leading products. The

---

*You can usually tell an engineer from a marketing type.

generic ink-jet printer is not called a hydrodynamic printer, but instead its name derives from the HP InkJet. HP's brand name has achieved marketing immortality—it is synonymous with the ink-jet printer. HP assigns a very high value to its brand name, because brand name recognition is better than a rise in the company's stock price. And because of their brand name, dominant companies like HP become an industry unto themselves. This is exactly the point.

The key word here is *industry*. There is a big difference between growing an industry versus growing a company. Microsoft is an industry. Apple Computer is a company. Cisco Systems is an industry; Bay Networks is a company. The distinction is important because the rewards of growing an industry are much greater than the rewards of growing a product. Specifically, when a company transforms itself into an industry, its value transforms into a gold mine.

Microsoft and HP beat out their competitors through a simple strategy of building an industry in addition to a company. Today the "Microsoft industry" consists of the mother ship plus thousands of third-party developers, partners, and followers. The "HP printer industry" thrives on HP's dominance. Their brand name adds value to their products. This is one more way in which the friction-free economy differs from the classical theory, which does not even try to quantify the value of a brand.

MINING IN THE FRICTION-FREE ECONOMY

Money is no longer a good indicator of value. It has itself become a commodity to be used like labor, materials, and knowledge. In its place, the friction-free economy substitutes value-add.

> *Value is multiplied in a value-add value chain. Businesses can optimize their return on investment by integrating their products into established value chains.*

The gold is in the value chain. The more links of the value chain a business owns or controls, the more gold it gets. This is the golden rule. If a business wants to mine the friction-free economy, it must mine the value chains of one or more market spaces.

Video game merchants were perhaps among the earliest high-tech companies to establish this trend—one that will continue to expand in the friction-free economy. The actual game console may be sold at a $150 to $200 loss so that the vendor—Nintendo, Sega, Sony—can lock in customers to their value chain. Then these companies rake in the profits from the game cartridges—and even more money from one or more links in the chain—tie-ins with movies, fast food restaurants, and toy manufacturers.

When Netscape Communications gave away its browser, it planned to make money in the entire value chain. In particular, its game plan was to give away the client software (the PC side), and sell the server software (mainframe or enterprise side). The company had an unexpected surprise—it also made about 40% of its first year's revenues from browsers!

Netscape understood the importance of milking profit from value chains. Hence, in 1996 it spun out a company called Navio Communications to exploit additional links in the value chain created by their Internet standards. Navio's job was to dive deeper into the value chain by building a software platform for consumer products. Hardware developers would pay a tax on every box sold with Navio system software on it. Thus, Navio attempted to turn the value proposition around—taxing the basic technology vendors for the rights to Navio's software platform.

CLIMBING THE LADDER TO SUCCESS

The friction-free economy violates many rules of classical economics, principally because it behaves according to nonlinear rules and therefore is subject to chaos. The techniques that once worked in the classical world may not work in the new world. Value is no longer strictly defined by money. Diminishing marginal return no longer works on scarcity. Products sell for more if they are less; that is, smaller, lighter, and cheaper. Markets are more segmented and their value continues to decline, forcing companies to tax the entire market space. This explains why so many businesses are joining in partnerships with rivals.

MARKETING IN THE FRICTION-FREE ECONOMY

Given that the friction-free economy obeys different rules, it is no surprise that marketing in the friction-free economy also obeys different rules. In fact, marketing is turned upside-down, too. In general, the nonlinearity of the friction-free economy and the need for maximizing the return on value-add is driving product space and market space in two different directions:

> *As product spaces become modularized, componentized, and compartmentalized to address the individual, customized, targeted needs of niche markets, the corresponding market space, and the value chains in them, become more integrated. In a sense, products become disintegrated while markets become integrated. This is forced onto businesses by the commoditization of products, and ever more expensive value chains.*

This is perhaps the most profound impact that the friction-free economy has on business in this decade. It is of such major proportions that it will infiltrate subsequent discussions. But first, what does it mean?

Competing products form a product space, and the environment in which they compete forms a market space. In the old days, large companies integrated along vertical lines in order to lock out competitors and maximize their return on the value chain. This does not work anymore, because of the high demands of learning, inverse economics, and short doubling times. Instead, large and small companies must segment their market space, which leads to componentization of the products and the formation of horizontal integration—what J. F. Moore calls value integrating.[4]

The desktop PC product space is a well-known example. Product specialization has severely segmented the desktop PC market space dominated by Intel and Microsoft–Wintel. The "product" in this space is not a monolithic PC, but rather a collection of cobbled-together products. The monitor, modem, sound card, disk drive, printer, network, scanner, keyboard, mouse, operating system, word processor software, drawing program, e-mail program, and spreadsheet program can be purchased separately. In fact, the segmentation of the desktop PC market space is so severe that it is often difficult for a consumer to make the parts work together.

This is why it is rare for a TV manufacturer to combine a VCR recorder with a TV, or for a fax machine to be combined with a printer or answering machine. It is why automobiles do not have built-in telephones, and home appliances are sold as separate pieces of furniture. In fact, product space integration occurs in any industry where the competition is so fierce that nobody dominates. When everyone must scramble for market share, product spaces disintegrate and value chaining forms complex and interwoven alliances, associations, and partnerships.

The segmentation of the PC market space, and the corresponding unbundling of the products in this space, are the result of rapid technological advancement, of course, but they are also the result of optimization of the value chain. The problem with this optimization is that it renders almost every link in the chain unprofitable. Optimization drives out profits, because inverse economics requires that each product get better and cheaper on a vicious time scale.

How can a modem vendor make a profit on the sale of a $100 modem? How does Nintendo profit from the sale of a loss-leader? The solution is to integrate the value chain so that everyone in it can make a profit. This is why the value chain integrates. This is why companies form partnerships and work within a business ecosystem,[5] or what I call a digital *keiretsu*.

Marketing in the friction-free economy is much more complex

than this, but the fundamental difference between today and yesterday is the notion of value integrating. This idea depends on product space disintegration, because without specialized products, the vice president of marketing has no bargaining chips. He or she must go it alone, and in the friction-free economy, loners rarely survive the wolf hunt.

Marketing in the friction-free economy means value chain integrating. Microsoft and Intel must work together to milk optimal return from their complementary products. The 60,000 third-party vendors that work with Microsoft depend on value chaining to sustain their business. They provide highly specialized and targeted products that enhance the mainstream Wintel product—at each link in the chain. However, within each link, individual companies struggle with the underlying chaos that is the foundation of the friction-free economy.

5

Making Money in the Wired World

WELCOME TO CLUB MODE

The setting was an exclusive Hollywood party hosted by fashion designer Vito Brevis. I wandered through the crowd, running into an undercover cop looking for a drug lord. Reeling, I then turned to go through an archway leading into the bedroom where I bumped into a CNN reporter, two models, and an artist lounging in silk pajamas. One of the models asked if I was interested in seeing her photographs of Brad Pitt. They were back at her flat. Well, one thing led to another, and I ended up buying $50 worth of perfume while she was in the shower.

It was a party. It was a puzzle. It was a fantasy. It was Club Mode.

Club Mode is not only a place for netizens* to spend their money, it is a place for marketers to learn how to take netizens' money.

Club Mode isn't real, of course. Rather, it is a virtual world spun onto my screen. Invented by Animatics Multimedia of Ottawa, Canada, and financed by a joint venture among Corel, Global

---

*A citizen of the Wired World is called a netizen.

X-Change, and Animatics, Club Mode started life as a CD-ROM. Now it is on a small screen near you.

But Club Mode and thousands of Web pages like it are more than multimedia in your face. They are a harbinger of things to come. They are what will make the Wired World go around. They are the malls and market spaces of the friction-free economy.

BILLBOARDS IN THE WIRED WORLD

Animatics' president, Alfredo Coppola, uses real actors and real props to film Club Mode action. But unlike in a movie, his interactive socializing takes place in a simulated make-believe world. When you first enter Club Mode, a moody graphic proclaims: "You have entered Club Mode, the first truly interactive drama on the Web. It's a fifteen-part series where you can lose yourself in the messy fun, mystery, and sexy adventures of a loose collection of barflies and gadabouts. Club Mode is the companion piece to MODE, the hit CD-ROM by Corel and Animatics."

Where do you want to go today? Club Mode will take you there—for a price. In addition to Mode adventures, customers can interact with other customers in the Mode Meet section of this Wired World. Photographs and short biographies may be posted as an added inducement. In 1996 Club Mode's target was 50,000 customers. Traffic is the game, and building advertising revenue is the goal.

One way to create wealth in the Wired World is to post ads—billboards—along paths leading to information and entertainment. Banner ads generate revenues for Club Mode advertisers, but many other revenue streams can be tapped. For example, lifestyle products occasionally and subtly appear in the story line. Club Mode derives an income from the clothes that virtual humans wear, the virtual furniture, and the virtual beer that is consumed in the virtual reality. Product placement involves carefully integrating a company's products into the story line at just the right place to attract the targeted consumer.

Advertising revenue is big business in the Wired World. "The market for on-line advertising will be worth some $4.8 billion by 2000," boasts Bill Bass of Forrester Research.* Yet, banner ads and product placement are peanuts compared to the targeted marketing opportunities available to the Wired World. The big bucks are in software that tracks what each customer does while talking to virtual humans in Club Mode. Marketers can discover a lot about buying habits and consumer desires from conversation—even if it is with an electronic mannequin. In the friction-free economy, marketers will use technology to target a market-of-one.

Animatics' Coppola says, "Keeping people coming back is a key to success with interactive dramatic media. This is not a gamer's game, this is not about visual 3D action—this is about socializing—it's about people. There's no point in trying to shove an arcade game onto the Net. We don't believe that. We believe people want to know about people."[1] In other words, entertainment in the Wired World is provided by the customers—netizens—themselves. Such a deal!

BIGGER THAN ELVIS

Whatever your opinion about Club Mode, it is a prototype for future market spaces. It is an experimental virtual mall aimed at the year 2000, where shopping, interacting, and consuming will take place in real time. Jim Clark, cofounder of Netscape, speaking at the Fifth International World Wide Web Conference held in Paris in 1996, said, "There is at least a $5 trillion industry up for grabs," in reference to only the telecommunications portion of the Wired World. Telecommunications revenues represent only a fraction of the total revenues that the Wired World will generate in the next century. The Wired World will consume the market space of the physical world. It is simply growing too fast and getting too big to do otherwise.

---

*Total ad revenues within the U.S. were $200 billion in 1996, according to *Communications Week*, Sept. 16, 1996, p. 70.

Clark should know. He was a pioneer in creating the gang of companies that combined multimedia with the Web and came up with a way to make money from advertising, transacting, and socializing. Before Clark's company, Netscape Communications, was founded, netizens thought the Web was a gift from the U.S. government. In fact, they protested in 1994 that nobody had the right to make money on the Internet. Netscape led a group of companies that transformed the Internet into a commercial marketplace. As a consequence, nobody today questions whether the Internet is for capitalists or socialists.

The Wired World is more than hardware routers, wires, and computers. It is an entirely new product space. It is an entirely new market space. The Internet product space, combined with the World Wide Web market space, establishes one of the most powerful platforms ever contrived for doing business. The Wired World is to the friction-free economy what the interstate highway system, air cargo system, and telephone/fax system were to the old economy. In fact, it is bigger than Elvis.

THE WIRED WORLD DISINTEGRATES PRODUCTS

The Wired World is significant because it provides a near-infinite supply of products, services, and ideas, at a near-zero cost—a near-frictionless economy. The Wired World is exactly what the friction-free economy needs:

> *The Wired World implies major ramifications, not the least of which is the disintegration of the product space and the corresponding integration of market space value chains.*

The Wired World accelerates the drive toward products that must become increasingly modular, specialized, and componentized in order to compete in the friction-free economy. Companies are driven to expand monolithic products into a *range of products*, and as they do so, their monolithic product disintegrates. Disintegrating products are replaced by a family of components or highly specialized products. The Wired World will be built from Tinkertoys that have special functions, and correspondingly special market niches.

Product disintegration can take many forms. The modular stereo, the differentiated product line, and the customized golf club. So-called generic products disintegrate into a family of products. Since Henry Ford's "any color you want as long as it is black" cars disappeared, the auto industry has been disintegrating their products. Now it is impossible to buy a simple car. There are compact cars, midsized, medium-sized, large, sport utilities, vans, light trucks, trucks, off-road, sport, and utility vehicles. Automobiles fit a lifestyle niche, not a general transportation need.

The computer industry is in the midst of a major product disintegration phase, too. The so-called *appliance computer* is an example. As the information industry matures and segments, more and more monolithic products will disintegrate and be replaced by components. These components must work together, of course, so the trend towards disintegration must be accompanied by interoperability standards.

Disintegration achieves a number of important objectives in the friction-free economy. First, it permits the best-of-breed component to be swapped in and out of a system. The best audio speakers, best TV monitor, best application program, and best storage devices can be substituted into the system to take advantage of individual technology learning curves.

Second, modularity provides shorter cycle times, which in turn accelerates the time to market, so vital to competitiveness. This is particularly important in the computer network segment where Cisco, Bay Networks, 3Com, and Cabletron are battling it out for dominance. This explains why Bay Networks struggled to sell its grand network architecture rather than point products to customers. If Bay Networks could convince customers to buy into a modular, disintegrated product approach, under the umbrella of an all-encompassing architecture, then its customers could get off of the technology treadmill. At the same time, Bay Networks would succeed against Cisco Systems because the standard-setting initiative that propelled Cisco to the lead position would pass to Bay Networks.

INTEGRATING MARKET SPACES

At the same time that products are disintegrating, leading to market segmentation, the value chains that make up a market space are integrating. In fact, segmentation forces value chain integration; otherwise, how is a business to make money from a smaller and smaller segment? This peculiar state of affairs has led to joint ventures and partnerships among seeming competitors, as well as cooperation in one product line and bitter competition in others.

Market space integration is how highly segmented products make a profit for their owners in the face of segmentation. Integration means extracting revenues from more than one link in a value chain. It is yet another way for a company to squeeze profit from value-add. Market space integration will pick up speed as everyone gets wired.

MADE FOR THE FRICTION-FREE ECONOMY

Okay, so the Wired World is large, brash, and untamed. It can't be stopped, so it must be accommodated. But the question remains, "What will netizens buy?" Will the Wired World be profitable? Will the Wired World replace the physical world of commerce? The short answer is yes, the Wired World will eventually have as profound an effect on the world economy as the Industrial Revolution had on the Renaissance economy.

The Wired World is made for the friction-free economy. Electronic networks are highways for zero-cost distribution systems, roadside billboards for light-speed selling, and pervasive shopping malls with infinite shelf space. The laws of the friction-free economy properly model the Wired World's nonlinear, chaotic behavior. The Wired World rewards niche product targeting—even accelerating the disintegration of product spaces. It builds the virtual communities needed to integrate market spaces just as the automobile created urbanization. And it drives everything to a commodity price level.

WHAT DO NETIZENS WANT?

The Wired World is now such a driving force in the software age that it often sends its netizens to extremes. Richard Weideman spent eighty-eight days locked in a glass cubicle in Cape Town, South Africa, to prove that life in the Wired World is good. "I aim to prove that even though all my communication is limited to an Internet connection, for 88 days I can interact with the outside world on an international basis as well or better than through any other conventional channels of communication," he wrote on his Web page.

Scott Fraize, chief technologist at DimensionX, an Internet software company, says, "I'm a slave to my mailbox and calendar-scheduling program, and I would like to have voice mail forwarded to e-mail." Marianne LaFrance, a psychology professor at Boston College, says, "Changes are subtle and constant—people don't go from being a good human to an automaton overnight—it is a process of evolution."

These are hard-core netizens. Because of their obsession with being wired, they represent the future consumer. Their demographic profiles are future consumer profiles. Knowing what they want tells us what everyone will want in the next century. And given the big bucks waiting for ecash, smart cards, the Web, and value chain troopers, there is plenty of reason to study these early-adopter netizens. Who exactly shops in cyberspace? And what do they want?

There are four major sources of revenue in the Wired World:

- Subscriptions—user fees for gaining access.

- Advertising—billboards and product promotions.

- Products and services—what gets bought and sold.

- Transactions—taxing the flow of money.

SUBSCRIBING TO THE WIRED WORLD

Like the westward movement of 150 years ago, the migration to the Wild Web is moving at an astounding rate, headed for 250 to 300 million users within the next decade. With 45 million users in 1996, the Internet set a lower bound on revenues from subscribers. The first cash flowing from the Wired World is simply from cargo handlers who charge a fee to lead its pioneers to the Promised Land.

Revenues from subscriptions will approach $10 billion per year by the year 2000. In 1996 the largest on-line access provider was America Online, with revenues that exceeded $1 billion. AOL forecast revenues of $2 billion by 1998, and $4 billion by 2000. With over one-half of the paying customers in their installed base, AOL represents about one-half of the subscription base. Therefore, estimates of $8 to $10 billion appear to be reasonable.

Compared with the revenues generated by other kinds of media-like magazines, getting wired in the first place is a major business (see Table 5-1).

Media	Revenues, $ Billion
Home, Video	14.6
Recorded Music	11.2
Books	16.3
Magazines	7.7
Computer Software	2.6
Video Game Software (Retail)	6.0
Cable TV	20.6
Film at Theaters (Box Office)	6.0

Table 5–1. Consumer media spending circa 1993.

ADVERTISING

Forrester Research (www.forrester.com) says that early adopters of the Wired World medium generated advertising revenues of $74 million in 1996—a revenue stream that will rise to $4.8 billion by 2000. As a learning curve, this represents a 33% learning rate per year—about twice as fast as the computer industry in general. Throughout 1996–97, these estimates kept going up!

Compare the advertising revenue projections in the Wired World with other markets. By 2000, radio ad revenue will reach $2 billion, print ad revenue will hit $30 billion, and TV advertising will grow to $51 billion. Maybe $4.8 billion doesn't seem like a lot, but the Wired World has been in existence a mere decade. Not bad for a start-up!

Back in 1996, when things were just beginning to ramp up, monthly ad sales were hovering around $1 million per month per Web publisher. In early 1997 monthly revenues surpassed $3 million per month. There is no telling how high it could go, because predicting growth in the Wired World is like trying to hit a rapidly moving target.

In fact, the friction-free economy began operating in the Wired World almost as soon as it became a market space. Instead of the $15 to $50 per 1,000 viewers typically charged advertisers to run ads online, ad rates themselves began to plunge to commodity level. "Web ad prices are starting to tumble; advertising on Playboy's popular site, for example, costs just $3 per 1,000 readers, and other sites have accepted similar prices," observed Ollie Curme in 1996.[2]

Table 5-2 gives a snapshot of the top ten publishers along with the top ten advertisers in the Wired World as of January 1996. These numbers have changed radically since the early days, but they are a starting point in an attempt to quantify the size of the opportunity.

Unquestionably, the Wired World has become a place where you can reach customers. In fact, in the friction-free economy, a business cannot afford to ignore the Wired World. Failure to advertise in the Wired World would be like ignoring roadside billboard

Publisher	Ad Revenue ($000)	Advertiser	Amount Spent ($000)
Lycos	833	IBM	461
Yahoo	715	Microsoft	248
Netscape	650	AT&T	245
ESPNSports	467	NYNEX	198
InfoSeek	460	MCI	188
PathFinder	380	C|Net	178
HotWired	368	Internet Shopping Net	173
Excite	321	Excite	166
C|Net	295	Saturn Corp.	158

Table 5–2. Buyers and sellers of advertisements in the Wired World. January 1996 revenues are in thousands of dollars for each. (Source: *Internet World,* July 1996, p. 52.)

advertising in 1950. But the Wired World demands more sophistication than the Burma-Shave posters of the 1950s.

Because the friction-free economy drives everything to a commodity, ad space in the Wired World costs less than real estate in the physical world but requires more expensive means of production. For example, standard rates for TV ads ran about $170 per viewer in 1993. They ran about $240 per reader in the print media business. Compare this with less than $15 per on-line viewer in the Wired World. As the Wired World scaled its customer learning curve, this price dropped to less than a dollar—becoming a commodity.

On the other hand, an attractive advertisement in the Wired World requires an attractive Web page. The production costs of such a page can easily exceed $1 million. Furthermore, a Web site requires more attention than a Burma-Shave billboard. Marketing managers in the friction-free economy must learn the technology of Web page construction and the importance of a dynamic presence in the Wired World.

THE VALUE PROPOSITION

Of course, money means little in the friction-free economy. After all, money is just the symbol for where supply equals demand; and in the friction-free economy there is infinite supply, infinite demand, and zero manufacturing and distribution costs. The friction-free economy runs on value-add, not coins.

What is the value-add proposition for the Wired World? Where will wealth come from? Here is the fundamental rule:

> *Each level, stage, or phase of bringing a product, service, or idea to market in the friction-free economy must add value, if the wealth of the Wired World is to increase.*

Sounds like a restatement of Adam Smith's thesis that greed generates wealth. It is. But in the Wired World, greed is supplemented by learning curves, and currency generation is replaced by value-add generation.

The value proposition in the computer market space is this: if hardware manufacturers lower the consumer price barrier to lure consumers, then software and service vendors must share in the revenue stream generated by the entire value chain. Thus, a digital *keiretsu* is created whereby all vendors in the chain pull together. Value-add is more important than anything else in this approach.

CHANNEL DANCE

One of the most significant implications of the value proposition in retail channels is related to a form of flexible manufacturing called *channel assembly*. Channel assembly in the PC box business pushes customization beyond factory manufacturing. A company like Compaq, Apple, or IBM PC delivers bare-bones boxes to a reseller like MicroAge, where they are equipped with disk drives, monitors, memory, and other accessories. Jeffrey McKeever, CEO of MicroAge, says increased assembly in the channel reduces manufacturers' investments in new plants. But the true appeal of channel assembly is reduction of inventory costs. In an industry subject to the technology treadmill, inventory turnover cycles of a few weeks or days can save big bucks.

IBM's channel assembly program reduces inventory charges and increases fulfillment of customized systems. MicroAge and Inacom typically configure eight times as many systems as distributors and have fewer warehouses from which to ship machines, according to Pat O'Horo, vice president of Tech Data Corporation. Compaq Computer targets large buyers by off-loading customization and tailoring to its channels, which assemble PCs for large corporations.

This means of value chain integration creates flexibility and profits. Channel assembly is a dance that integrates the value chain. Each link in the chain adds value, yielding gains for everyone in the digital *keiretsu*.

THE WIRED WORLD VALUE CHAIN

The Wired World is a vast marketplace where products must plug into a larger matrix of interrelated products. The Wired World itself is a collection of modular products. Desktop PCs, cellular telephones, fax machines, network appliances, pagers, personal digital assistants, bridges, hubs, routers, cable modems, and so on are plugged together to form this infrastructure.

Thus, the original Internet has become a vast infrastructure consisting of best-of-breed components. Some parts will run on telephone lines, some on CATV cable, and even some fly through the air as part of a wireless network. This infrastructure connects all societies of the globe. In fact, it will eventually connect individuals to everything—whether traveling down the highway on your way to work, communicating while in a transcontinental flight, working in your home office, or videoconferencing from your office downtown.

There is no monolithic Wired World. Instead, the Wired World is an infrastructure for the friction-free economy that is made up of disintegrated products—components—which may be swapped in and out, and which fit together via standards which have evolved from day one of the Internet. A by-product of this seemingly ad hoc state of the Wired World has been the invention of even greater modularity in the products and services of the friction-free economy. (See Figure 5-1.)

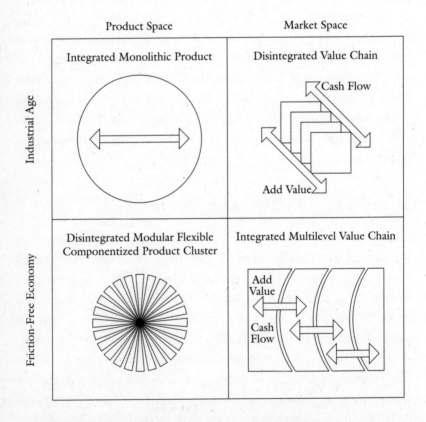

Figure 5–1. Monolithic products in product space are disintegrating, which in turn forces an integration of the value chain in the market space.

INTEGRATION OF THE VALUE CHAIN

As the product space undergoes the transformation from monolithic to componentized products, the market space undergoes just the opposite. Integration of the value chain is required because inverse economics wrings margins out of components. The value-add is imbedded in the way components are configured into systems, and then channeled through the value chain. This duality is shown in Figure 5-1.

The product/market space duality is a general trend in the friction-free economy. Note this: Integration of the value chain in the market space is closely related to the Japanese *keiretsu* and the co-evolution ideas of James Moore.[3]

DISINTEGRATION OF THE PC

Wei Yen is president and CEO of Jim Clark's latest brainchild, Navio Communications. Navio started life as a top-secret Netscape Communications skunk works called TVSoft. Its charter was to build a consumer device similar to WebTV. But like so many other start-ups in Silicon Valley, TVSoft soon learned that Wired World product spaces were rapidly disintegrating—faster than the ink could dry on their articles of incorporation. So TVSoft changed its name, direction, and product to join in the disintegration rather than fight it.

Navio's 1996 game plan was pure friction-free economy. The company would provide a platform for the network appliance and tax the value chain in return. Navio's system software would be licensed to hardware vendors who would pay a royalty on every box sold. Navio would also add value by providing the development tools to product developers. Thus, revenue would flow into Navio from several links in the value chain.

PRODUCT DISINTEGRATION IS UNIVERSAL

Does the value proposition proposed by Navio make sense? Is it really true that the PC product space is disintegrating? After all, if it is, then I should sell my Microsoft stock, because Microsoft has made its billions by integrating different technologies into a rather monolithic box.

For the first twenty years of the PC business, Apple Computer, Compaq, and other manufacturers attempted to produce all-in-one products. Apple Computer was especially good at it. The Macintosh needed absolutely no add-ons to be instantly useful. Apple was proud of the fact that a Macintosh could be taken out of the box on Christmas morning, and be printing letters and surfing the Internet by noon. Compare this with the Wintel approach, whereby a consumer would have to add a CD-ROM, sound card, video monitor card, network card, and mouse to "build" a complete system.

Apple had a good idea for the early years of a new industry. The problem with Apple's approach was the following: As the product space matured, the company could not keep up with all of the learning curves that go into producing the best-of-breed disk drive, network card, monitor, CD-ROM, and operating system software. The Macintosh began to lag the industry.

Contrast the monolithic Macintosh product space with the fragmented, flexible, disintegrated market space of Wintel products. While these products were more difficult to configure and tailor to particular niches, they responded much more quickly and with much more flexibility to market forces. As a consequence, they succeeded on a much larger scale than the Macintosh.

The disintegration of the PC product space is only beginning. In fact, the market for "Internet PCs," "Internet terminals," and "Internet TVs" is still a very small fraction of the market for complete PC systems. PC shipments are expected to top 70 million units in 2000, while Internet TV will barely reach 10 million units. However, ten years ago there was no such thing as differentiation in the PC product space. Now the space is disintegrating into at least three general categories.

What about software? In the mid-1980s several companies simultaneously came up with the idea of integrated application packages. These programs would do everything an office worker needed—word processing, spreadsheet, database, and e-mail. The monolithic or integrated software package failed. Why? Software disintegrated. Instead of an all-in-one solution, the market went for individual program suites that could pass data back and forth. The monolithic application package could not compete with a collection of best-of-breed stand-alone programs.

Indeed, the trend in software development is toward software *components* called *objects*, and away from large monolithic programs which are too inflexible, costly, and unmanageable. Once again, friction-free economy pressures forced software packages to disintegrate.

What about consumer electronics in general? Integrated TVs with built-in VCRs have had only mild success. TVs with built-in computers and computers with built-in TVs have not been successful, though a number of vendors have tried. Only the integrated boom box has made a dent in the consumer electronics space as a monolithic product.

Larger, older, and slower industries appear to thrive in an integrated product space. Boeing airplanes are monolithic products on the surface, but even Boeing does not make all of its parts. Underneath, Boeing is a systems integrator company. It takes parts from best-of-breed manufacturers like Northrop Aviation and Japanese aerospace companies and integrates them into a flying platform.

Products will continue to disintegrate in the friction-free economy. The disintegration will accelerate in the Wired World. To be a warrior in the Wired World, therefore, a business must master the idea of product space disintegration.

JOINT VENTURES BY ANY OTHER NAME

Notice that taxation of the value chain is a direct consequence of the disintegration of the product space. The Wired World space includes traditional TV, telephones, computer appliances, and the back offices where Internet servers serve up Web pages upon demand. At a deeper level, the Internet is itself made up of many products—routers, hubs, switches, and operating systems software. There are so many product fragments in the Wired World that it would take a CD-ROM to list them all.

As the product space disintegrates and heads towards commodity pricing, it becomes more and more difficult to make a profit. Only mainstream products thrive because they lock in their installed base of customers. But mainstreaming requires two things—speed and low prices. This means the entire food chain must contribute to the overall success of the market space. This forces competitors into a digital *keiretsu*.

In fact, market space integration and/or the implosion of the value chain around a digital *keiretsu* is happening all around us. We don't always recognize it for what it is. Consider only a few of the larger, more newsworthy joint partnerships, mergers, acquisitions, and other wheelings and dealings that took place during a space of a few months in 1996:

- America Online and CompuServe (competitors) agreed to use Microsoft's Web browser.

- DIRECTV—a unit of General Motors' Hughes Electronics Corporation, agreed to combine forces with Microsoft to deliver digital entertainment to PC users.

- NBC and Microsoft created a joint venture called MS-NBC to compete with CNN in the news broadcasting segment of TV.

- MCI and Microsoft agreed to develop an on-line service and promote Microsoft's Web browser.

- UUNet Technologies began working with Microsoft to build up its network infrastructure.

- Netscape Communications crawled under the covers with America Online, CompuServe, and Prodigy to push its Web browser into other chains.

- NETCOM On-Line Communications and PSINet agreed to work with Netscape to bolster its network infrastructure.

- AT&T, MCI, Pacific Bell, and GTE did deals with Netscape for various reasons.

- Netscape entered into trading deals with Sun Microsystems' JavaSoft division, which is working with archrival Microsoft.

- AT&T made its own deals with America Online and Oracle.

- Oracle made side deals with Sun Microsystems, VeriFone, and others.

This list doesn't even account for the electronic commerce deals these companies have in place or are constantly making. Joint ventures are a polite way of describing these value-chain integrating deals.

FIFTY MILLION CHANNELS

One of the most novel contributions to the Wired World was Internet TV, a technology created by three Apple Computer multimedia pioneers that made it possible for couch potatoes to use their televisions to travel in the Wired World with the comfort and convenience of a handheld TV control device, as well as communicate through electronic mail. The founders of WebTV Networks of Palo Alto, California—Steve Perlman, Bruce Leak, and Phil Goodman—figured out how to give away the razors and sell the razor blades by cleverly decoding the secret to mass merchandising in the Wired World. WebTV is also an example of how to disintegrate the product space and integrate the market space.

It is possible to change the world and make a buck only if consumer gadgets can be designed and handed out to consumers at extremely low prices. The WebTV founders understood that the boxes would have to become virtually free before consumers would flock to the idea of Internet TV. PCs were too expensive, and set-top boxes were too simple. An Internet TV had to be sophisticated, powerful, and cheap. How could WebTV build a product that essentially demanded to have its cake and eat it too? How does a business go about making a low-cost, high-powered product so easy to use that even a couch potato can get wired?

MILKING THE VALUE CHAIN

Of course, the answer lies in inverse economics and value chains. Drive the costs of the hardware and software to zero, and consumers will seek your field of dreams. While it is true that price-learning drives costs to zero, the Wired World moves in Internet Time—a compressed time constant that will not wait for technology to reduce manufacturing costs all by itself. Commoditization in the Wired World needs a little help from the value chain.

Sure, inverse economics was essential—in fact, the whole industry depended on it—but it was not enough back in 1996. What Perlman needed was a way to exploit inverse economics *and* the value chain. Perlman's solution was *doomonomics*—pure friction-free economics.

Internet TV would only mainstream if sold at a subsidized price point. Like the video game loss leader strategy, Internet TV boxes had to be priced artificially low. The money is in the value chain that reaches from the box builders, advertisers, WebTV, and everything in between, all the way to the consumer. Perlman and friends had to find a way to cut everyone in on the deal. They had to share in the revenues generated by subscribers, advertisers, content providers, and Internet service providers, in order to provide nearly free boxes and software to price-sensitive consumers.

MILKING COUCH POTATOES

The average American watches 1,000 hours of network TV and 400 hours of cable TV per year. Home videos, books, magazines, theater movies, and newspaper seat time all together barely add up to 300 hours per year. At 250 million strong, couch potatoes dominate the multimedia market with an astounding 250 billion hours of log-in time.

The money is in the 250 billion hours of TV viewing per year.

By 1997 WebTV had competitors. Everyone wanted in on the gold mine. But to mine this gold, box makers and service providers have to give away their wares in order to mainstream their product in Internet Time, establish a large enough installed base to attract advertisers and content providers, and lock in consumers. This is why Sony, Phillips, and Thompson planned to build Internet TV computers into their TVs.

REALLY FAST FOOD

If you think McDonald's perfected the art of fast food, then you haven't eaten at the World Wide Waiter in Los Altos, California. WW Waiter allows customers to place takeout and delivery orders from their computers via the Internet. Netizens access the service from www.waiter.com at no charge, no waiting in line, no pierced-ear minimum-wage irritants, no fuss, and no muss.

Michael Adelberg, vice president and cofounder of World Wide Waiter, is no burger flipper. He has a degree in electrical engineering from the Massachusetts Institute of Technology and an MBA from Stanford. After completing his MBA in 1993, Adelberg worked as a management consultant for LEK/Alcar Consulting in Los Angeles. Then, seeking more control over his life, he joined forces with childhood friend and classmate Craig Cohen to launch World Wide Waiter from his home.

World Wide Waiter is pure friction-free economy running on a flattened value chain. The on-line menu contains listings from 120 San Francisco Bay Area restaurants. The food is further customized through a set of options. Netizens can save their preferences in the system for reuse. Orders are electronically sent to the restaurants, which fill the orders in real time. Charges are billed to a credit card.

Adelberg and Cohen live off of the value chain they have created with the assistance of the Wired World. Customers pay nothing for the service, but the restaurant pays a "finder's fee" to Adelberg and Cohen. Business was increasing by 30–40% per month in the summer of 1996. "I would like to become the ATM of the food world," says Adelberg.[4]

What Adelberg and Cohen have done is flatten the value chain while taking a bite out of the middleman. Using the Internet, they have eliminated traditional human waiters. Elimination of a food server may not seem like much, but it illustrates how the friction-free economy reduces links in the value chain to rubble. WW Waiter is really fast food brought to you by really few people.

DEATH OF A SALESMAN

Value chains integrate market spaces, while product spaces become more and more disintegrated. That is a fundamental trend of the friction-free economy. As the pie gets divided among competitors, the competitors get more united along the value chain.

In the friction-free economy, value chains are under pressure to commoditize. Nobody can run and hide from the friction-free economy—it commoditizes even itself.

> *The friction-free economy commoditizes itself—it flattens value chains.*

A value chain is flattened by elimination of links. In the terminology of the old industrial economy, these links are called *middlemen*. They are often the go-betweens—distribution, warehousing, and brokering sales forces that lubricated the machine age. Many fortunes have been made by eliminating the middleman. Obvious examples are Wal-Mart stores, Fidelity Investments, Factory Outlet Stores, and Federal Express.

Middlemen existed because they could buy in volume, offer credit, expertise, and add value that the manufacturer couldn't or didn't want to. They existed because of imperfect knowledge and geographical constraints, where gathering knowledge was expensive in terms of both time and money.

But the Wired World reduces the cost of searching, gathering, and learning. Shoppers can post requirements on the Web and let 150 banks bid for their business. This changes almost everything. In particular, it changes the value proposition. Customers can deal directly with the producer of goods and services to gather, order, pay and gain after-the-sale support.

The elimination of steps in the value chain may be subtle in the friction-free economy. It may be as subtle as accessing your bank account from a PC at home, thereby reducing a step in the refinement of oil into gasoline. It may occur each time you order from a mail-order catalog, become a wholesale buyer of Nu Skin cosmetics, or buy your car over the Internet.

ADD VALUE OR DIE

The commoditization of value chains means that every link must add value or die. "Consumers are increasingly seeking out new sources for goods and services; this is no longer news," say Edith Weiner and Arnold Brown, writing in *The Futurist*.[5] "What is news is that [consumers] are bypassing traditional delivery channels—corner drugstores, doctor's offices, the mass media—in their search for quality, savings, convenience, and personal fit in all products and services." The Wired World integrates the value chain, and then shortens it as much as it can.

> *The friction-free economy squeezes out inefficiencies. It optimizes and commoditizes. It says, "Add value or die."*

Also writing in *The Futurist*, Nicholas Imparato and Oren Harari call this "disintermediation,"[6] and Samuel Bleecker claims that half of the retailers in business in the mid-1990s will be supplanted by virtual storefronts in the Wired World.[7]

Seattle-based DealerNet sells cars on-line through a virtual storefront that includes information from 250 dealers who want to move cars rather than pitch hard-sell stories to window shoppers. Customers from anywhere in the Wired World review literature, negotiate prices via e-mail, and place their orders—all from their armchairs at home. No muss, no fuss, no middleman. Dealers pay a one-time fee of $14,000 to be included in the Web site.

DealerNet simultaneously eliminates a middleman and adds value to a shortened chain that spans from seller to buyer. DealerNet thrives by taxing this new value chain—charging a one-time fee as well as cutting itself into the sales commission structure. The frictionless delivery mechanism of the Wired World makes it all possible—and profitable!

CYBERMALLS GO DIRECT

Early shopping malls in the Wired World—*cybermalls*, for short—tried to mimic physical shopping malls. They attempted to simulate streets, food courts, and storefronts. Time Warner's DreamShop featured Williams-Sonoma, Eddie Bauer, Sharper Image, and other "factory outlet" storefronts. There were some obvious advantages to this approach.

Because the Web has unlimited shelf space, cybermalls have much larger inventories. In fact, they have as much product as there *is* product, because they take the factory directly to the consumer. Cybermalls go direct. No middleman, no distributor, no retailer.

IBM's World Avenue and Microsoft's eShop were set up to help businesses eliminate the middleman. In exchange, IBM and Microsoft promise to help retailers set up shop in cybermalls—for a 5% cut of total retail sales. They know how to tax the value chain.

Robert May, CEO of Ikonic Interactive, operates one of the new breed of businesses that is thriving along the value chain of the Wired World. His company designs cybermalls for companies like Microsoft, Pacific Bell, and Virgin Records America. He knows the Wired World. "The idea is that you want to provide everything that an individual consumer wants," says May. "What [my clients are trying to do is] shatter their brand into pieces . . . and give each individual a mirror that perfectly reflects itself." May even understands Davidow's Law: "If it's not Levi's or The Gap, then it's going to be some guy in a garage who decides that he's going to sell blue jeans to the Czech Republic over the Internet."[8] He is right. Cybermalls fit the friction-free economy's goal of personalization and customization. They also fit the model of disintegrating product spaces—brands—and integrating value chains—from factory to outlet. Finally, if your business doesn't do it, another one will, rendering you obsolete in Internet Time.

ELECTRONIC WAREHOUSES

When a toy is purchased from Toys-R-Us, an automobile tire for your 1913 Hupmobile is bought from Sears, or a teeny-bikini scarfed up for your ten-year-old, it has to come from somewhere. Stores don't store much of anything. Rather, they order from a local warehouse.

Retailers and manufacturers compensate for poor forecasting by overstocking merchandise. This is called the *safety stock* or *buffered inventory*—fancy words for waste and inefficiency. In 1996 about $700 billion of the $2.3 trillion retail supply chain was in safety stock. That is, almost 30% was tied up due to waste and inefficiency.

The CFAR Internet protocol was codeveloped by Benchmark Partners and software vendor SAP AG in 1996 to eliminate the waste and inefficiency of safety stock. Wal-Mart and Warner-Lambert use the CFAR protocol to download their forecasting models (spreadsheets) directly to suppliers—bypassing the truckers and warehousers—thus cutting costs. The goods flow right from the factory into the consumer's shopping basket.

"It's actually a very simple Internet protocol that provides a standardized way for manufacturers and retailers to share information back and forth in order to agree on a sales order for a particular product," says Jim Kirkley, technology head of the CFAR project.[9] Of course, CFAR uses the Internet, which is cheaper than the proprietary network it replaced.

Warner-Lambert loads forecast data it receives from Wal-Mart into its demand planning software. The planning software automates—and eliminates—the process of estimating the size of an order. In addition, it takes advantage of volume discounts, delivery schedules, and it negotiates the lowest price.

This example demonstrates two key technologies that will be used in the friction-free economy of the Wired World to flatten the value chain:

- Electronic payment systems.

- Software that does the work of planning, shopping, and estimating for you.

This kind of software has various names, but it is often referred to as a *software agent*. Software agents will replace much of the outmoded distribution system traditionally associated with middlemen.

A PILE OF CRAP

Dan Lynch is founder and CEO of CyberCash, one of several businesses that intends to literally cash in on the Wired World. The whole idea behind Lynch's company is to convert paper money into electronic money. And the whole idea behind electronic money is to reduce friction in capitalism by eliminating the financial middleman. If CyberCash works, it could eliminate several links in the financial value chain and make Lynch a wealthier-than-you netizen.

Electronic money is to the banking system what gasoline is to cars and trucks. In fact, if Lynch succeeds in Microsoft style, CyberCash may eliminate banks altogether! Lynch led the ARPANet team that transformed the NCP (Network Communications Protocol) of the original Internet into the TCP/IP-based network of the modern Internet. He is an original Internet guy. Now he spends most of his time thinking out of the box, instead of in it.

When Lynch was asked what he thought about agents, he said,

"A pile of crap! They are way too general."[10] His emphatic reply convinced me that he was on to something. Agents must be the next big thing in electronic commerce. Disavowing any interest in them might be a way to throw off the competition. So exactly what is an agent, and what can it do for knock-down-and-drag-out cybershoppers?

If the Wired World is to become more than a low-cost alternative to the banking and distribution infrastructures of past ages, it must evolve toward electronic barter, communal groupware, virtual shopping malls, work-at-home, learn-at-home, vote-at-home, bank-at-home, and other unfathomable "at-home" products and services. Remember, the friction-free economy has an element of retro agrarianism to it. People want to get back to the land. They want to live where barter replaces price tags and virtual communities replace artificial industrial age "dis-communities." But consumers don't have time or knowledge enough to work the controls of the Wired World. What they need is a little help from software. They need agents.

A *software agent*, or simply *agent*, is a program that roams the cybermalls, cyberstreets and -alleys, and cyberbars looking for other software programs that it can interact with. Agents represent their human owners in on-line transactions—without constant attention from owners. Your fingers don't even have to do the walking when agents are used.

Agents have been written to search large information spaces and return results, watch and take action (monitor agents) when a condition such as "your balance has reached zero" occurs, deliver answers such as "who was George Washington's secretary of state?" and automatically send messages back and forth between colleagues—for example when e-mail is automatically answered in your absence.

GLOBAL SHOPPING, LOCAL RETAIL

For example, suppose real estate sellers unleash agents that look for buyers, and buyers unleash agents that look for sellers. The buyer agents hold data and instructions for selecting and negotiating the purchase of a house. The seller agents hold data about their house for sale, along with instructions for negotiating the sale. Third-party agents such as bankers, lawyers, and escrow accountants may also be involved in the ensuing transactions.

Buyers and sellers meet in cyberspace to negotiate, agree, and transfer value. Results of a sale may be reported back to the human owners, or forwarded on to the next transaction. When the agent does report back to its owner, most of the work is finished.

A four-bedroom French country farmhouse on eight acres near Gemozac, France—minutes from the beaches of Royan—was advertised in 1996 for $107,000 via the World Wide Web. "The Web has shrunk the global real estate market, bringing to desktops worldwide residential real estate opportunities," says Broderick Perkins in the real estate section of the *San Jose Mercury News.*[11]

The real estate market space illustrates a key ingredient of Wired World—it opens up global markets to local retailers. In the process of flattening global value chains, Wired World permits local access to products from around the world. After all, the Internet has infinite shelf space.

MICRO-CASH

Wal-Mart (www.wal-mart.com) discovered an interesting problem via its virtual storefront. As people became more comfortable with the wide selection, ease of use, and lower prices, they began to order less-expensive merchandise. Surprisingly, consumers wanted more small-ticket items such as toiletries, postcards, and socks. Some 4,000 e-mail messages after opening their virtual store, Wal-Mart faced the *micro-cash problem.*

In the industrial age it cost over $2 to cash a check or run a credit card through a cash register. Accordingly, it didn't make much sense, or profit, to use bank notes and credit cards to buy small-ticket items. This is why one rarely sees Coke machines with credit card–reading devices built into them.

But high-cost transaction processing won't work in the friction-free economy, because as the product space is disintegrated into smaller and smaller pieces, and the pieces become cheaper and cheaper, the banking system is nickel-and-dimed to death. The Wired World will not tolerate premium pricing on such transactions. And because most transactions in the world involve amounts below $20, there is gold to be mined in small-ticket commerce.

Micro-cash is needed to run the Wired World. But the industrial age charges too much for a transaction. So the future netizen needs a smart card.

SMART CARDS

Roland Moreno, a French journalist turned entrepreneur, was intrigued by a science fiction novel written by Barjavel, *Nuit des Temps*, which depicted an alien woman who could be communicated with only after decoding a ring containing all of her personal data. After reading the book in 1975, Moreno ran out into the streets of Paris and obtained patents on the concept of a *personal secure object*. Years later, when French companies like Schlumberger started making smart cards, Moreno sued and won over $100 million in license fees and royalties.

Moreno spent years in poverty while trying to develop a personal secure object device in his kitchen. Marc Lassus, CEO of Gemplus, "discovered" Moreno, who convinced Lassus to start Gemplus—a company that manufactures what became known as the smart card.

A smart card is a credit card–sized electronic device that has memory and a computer inside. Although the computer is very simple, it can add and subtract, compute a secret identification key, and perform simple routine tasks. It can keep track of what you buy, when and how much you spend, and what your buying preferences are. "A smart card can store data about customers, such as product preferences, spending history, and important information that can help provide improved personalized customer service," said Cliff Wilke, vice president of Mobil Oil Credit Corporation.[12]

Once the smart card becomes entrenched in the Wired World,

micro-cash will become practical. And once micro-cash mainstreams, billions of profits will derive from nickel-and-diming netizens from around the world at light speed. Think of it: 300 million consumers paying a nickel for a piece of your (segmented) product every day. Fifteen million dollars per day from nickels! But this revenue stream won't make a profit as long as it costs $2 to cash the check. When smart cards replace credit cards, and the Web replaces the banking system, a clever business can siphon millions from the Wired World.

A FINANCIAL *KEIRETSU*

The Wired World will bypass banks and other traditional financial institutions, unless they get smart. Americans—especially American bankers—were reluctant to get smart, at first. Finally realizing they had an opportunity to suck profit out of friction-free economy value chains through the use of smart cards, a smart card forum was created for the financial *keiretsu* of the Wired World in 1993. By 1996 this forum boasted 225 corporate and government members, including Chase Manhattan Bank, Citibank, MCI, MasterCard, Visa, Microsoft, Mobil, Delta Airlines, and the U.S. Postal Service, Federal Reserve, and U.S. Treasury Department! "Revenue from smart cards will reach $50 billion by the year 2000," says financial analyst Laurence Fong of Ferard, Klauer, Mattison of New York.[13]

Micro-cash equals lots of *ecash* in the Wired World. Plugging into the food chain of electronic commerce will guarantee this digital *keiretsu* plenty of revenues for hundreds of years. The opportunity is enormous. In 1994 the International Monetary Fund said there was at least $7.2 trillion—a sum equal to 20% of the world's annual economic output—sloshing around in short-term bank deposits. "These days, capital moves at the speed of light," says Michael Fradette, chairman of Deloitte Touche Tohmatsu International.[14] Like the safe stock in retail warehouses, this money is a buffer for doing business by wire.

The Wired World breaks down traditional barriers that have been created by big companies to lock out competition. But with access to ecash, anyone with a Web page can start collecting revenue via the Web. This opportunity is like turning every mom-and-pop store into Microsoft or IBM. It removes barriers—middlemen, large support staffs, and costly advertising campaigns—so that nearly anyone can compete. In short, it opens the flow of financial transactions to anyone. It levels the playing field.

LEVELING THE PLAYING FIELD

Brandon Inn is a tiny bed-and-breakfast hotel in Brandon, Vermont, owned and operated by Louis and Sarah Pattis. Like most small business operators, the Pattises could hardly afford the ads required to compete with the big chains operating in the Green Mountain State. Then, in October 1996, the co-owners established an elaborate ten-page Web site to tell their story. Soon the 210-year history of the National Historic Brandon Inn was blasted around the globe, and bookings started pouring in. Room rentals increased 15% and the bed-and-breakfast began signing up out-of-state weddings at $8,000 to $15,000 a whack.

Brandon Inn is a global company. It plays on a level field with the Hiltons and Marriotts. Its Web site attracts the thirty-some-thing crowd as well as the more traditional middle-aged vacationer.

In a Cahners Publishing Company survey of 400 businesses taken in 1997, 32% of companies with 1,000 or more employees viewed the Wired World as their biggest opportunity for market growth.[15] The smaller the business, the bigger the opportunity—42% of companies with 100 or fewer employees ranked a presence in the Wired World as their growth opportunity.

The Wired World expands business opportunity by leveling the playing field.

TRANSACTIONS IN THEM THAR WIRES

It has been clear for some time that wealth in the friction-free economy will come from taxing transactions. Every time someone somewhere buys or sells something, a small piece of money—micro-cash—can be collected and deposited into someone's account. It is no longer necessary that this flow be controlled by big banks or big companies. There will be no more traditional banks, no more traditional banking system, and no more traditional shopper. Instead, there will be frictionless, intangible, electronic micro-cash swirling around the world. At any point in time, billions of dollars will be suspended in wires. The problem is, collecting a transaction fee in the Wired World turns out to be more difficult than imagined. It will take a new group of entrepreneurial netizens to crack the code.

Who are these guys? Nobody knows yet, but in 1996 the players were companies with names like Open Market, DigiCash, ONSALE, CyberCash, VeriFone, and many others. They divided up early shares of the electronic transaction market.

A SMART CARD BANK

Open Market produced software for businesses to use to engage in direct commerce on the Internet. Their business-to-business software handles the back-office functions, data retrieval, security, merchant accounting, and customer/product analysis functions. Open Market processed credit cards in 1996, but its aim is to be your smart card vendor.

If everyone has a smart card and access to the Wired World, transaction costs can be commoditized. The reduction in transaction processing charges would open up the possibility of micro-cash transactions—direct commerce, as Open Market calls it—leading to a huge flow of money around the globe. Storefronts would pop up in the Wired World, opening the floodgates for marketers of all sizes. When you think about it like this, it brings back old times, for micro-cash returns us to a barter system.

ELECTRONIC BARTER IN THE WIRED WORLD

Jerry Kaplan, former CEO of Go! Corporation, which pioneered pen computing in the early 1990s, created ONSALE Inc. to bring auctions to the Wired World. ONSALE re-creates the experience of bidding at an auction, where prices and availability change in real time. ONSALE is returning society to the agrarian age of barter. For example, a personal computer can be purchased from ONSALE by bidding, watching, responding, and buying. This creates an exciting and entertaining atmosphere for consumers. ONSALE combines the thrill of Las Vegas with the boredom of shopping for toothpaste at Wal-Mart. Merchants who want to auction their products through ONSALE begin by sending a description to ONSALE via e-mail at auction@onsale.com. Customers browse and buy at their own leisure, but don't wait too long—someone else will bid the price up or buy the last item in stock! Airplane tickets, antiques, art, cars, coins, computers—you name it—are on sale in ONSALE. In late 1996 ONSALE foot traffic exceeded 15,000 customers per day. Kaplan was raking in $700,000 per week in sales, and projecting a leap from $35 million in annual sales to over $1 billion real soon now.

CHARGING YOUR ECASH CARD

David Chaum developed the secure payment algorithms used by DigiCash to guarantee safe and secure buying and selling in cyberspace. Founded in 1990, DigiCash invented the term *ecash*, and the technology for processing ecash tokens in the Wired World. Their first product was a road-toll system developed for the Dutch government and later for the Japanese market. By late 1996, 30,000 people were spending ecash. MasterCard was an early adopter of ecash—to be used in their smart card. The consumer "charges up" their smart card by withdrawing money from a bank account. The smart card stores the money until it is used at any virtual mall that accepts ecash. One side benefit: Buyers retain their anonymity. The merchant never needs to know who you are.

CYBERWALLETS FOR CYBERCOINS

CyberCash was founded by Bill Melton and Dan Lynch in 1994. CyberCash Wallet works as an on-line form that the consumer fills out to buy something. When the PAY button is mouse-clicked, the customer's account is decreased by the amount of the purchase. In 1996 CyberCash had 400,000 electronic wallets installed on personal computers across the Wired World, and connections to 80% of the banks in the U.S. In 1996 CyberCash released CyberCoin to handle micro-cash, i.e., charges as small as 25 cents.

Here is how it works. A product-hungry shopper sitting at his or her PC sees something they want while browsing the Wired World. They launch the CyberCash Wallet program and select a method of payment—credit card or checking account. The transaction goes to the cybermall, where the order is processed by the merchant. The merchant forwards the payment information to CyberCash, which in turn takes care of the electronic funds transfer—either from the purchaser's bank account or credit card company—and returns an "Okay/Not Okay" message back to the merchant. The merchant then tells the consumer whether the transaction succeeded or not, and if it has, ships the product.

CyberCash wants to muscle into the banking system. They want to get a cut of the transaction. But why does CyberCash need the banks? Why the middlemen? Why not simply bypass them? The answer today is spelled F-L-O-A-T. CyberCash does not have enough money in the bank to finance the float. But give it a few years, and CyberCash could own its own banks.

SMART TRANSACTIONS

Other companies, like VeriFone, are competing in this field of dreams. Build a better bank, and depositors will come. VeriFone, for example, shipped over 5 million electronic commerce systems to 100 countries by 1996. They also added Microsoft to their digital *keiretsu* for the purpose of capturing the point-of-sale market. Sterling Software entered the market in 1996 to leverage its installed base of 40,000 customers in sixty countries. Everyone, it seemed in 1996, wanted to siphon off a little cash from moving transactions through wires.

VeriFone's idea is to build a community of consumers who pack their own automated teller machines in the form of personal smart cards. Their P-ATM—personal ATM machine—plugs into telephones so you can drain money from your account into your P-ATM card, pack it around like a debit card, and discharge it into a reader whenever the urge to buy overcomes you. Cash is digitally recorded inside of the P-ATM, and can be discharged only with a secret password that only the owner knows. Thus, a P-ATM is safer than cash. It might even be safer than a bank vault.

Wells Fargo Bank of California rents out the P-ATM card for about $3 per month. Wells Fargo and VeriFone will provide card readers to physical world retailers, but the real target is the wired netizen. This includes Net-crazed consumers who shop from a home PC, upscale buyers who carry a smart phone everywhere they go, and Internet TV couch potatoes.

VeriFone's business model is completely in tune with the friction-free economy. The company wants to integrate the value chain by combining links. Because everyone in the chain stands to gain, everyone must foot the bill. "In other words, everyone from insurance companies to car rental companies may be willing to help subsidize the cost of smart card networks, lowering the fees charged to consumers."[16]

Whether MasterCard, Visa, or American Express ends up sucking profit out of the Wired World transactions, or it goes to new companies like VeriFone and CyberCash, the bottom line is this: There is gold in them thar wires, and someone is going to mine it. The $5 trillion economy of the U.S. alone could generate a tidy sum of $50 billion on the back of a 1% transaction fee.

WHO WILL BUY?

By June 1996, 33 million (18%) out of 181 million adults in the U.S. were hooked on the Wired World. These netizens were at the top of the economic ozone layer. At least 88% owned a home computer, had a college degree, and a household income of at least

$80,000 per year. More than twice as many households with income over $100,000 a year surfed the Web per capita than did less wealthy households. As household income went up, so did the rate of Wired World consumption. Because of their relative wealth and education, netizens represented the vanguard of twenty-first-century consumers.

Younger (under thirty) and older (over fifty) netizens spend much more time socializing than buying. They were the chat line consumers who often spent over $100 per month just for the opportunity to chat with other people from distant places. They fed the on-line services industry—companies like America Online—through subscriptions and connect time. They also purchased music CDs and software.

Middle-aged netizens (thirty-five to forty-four) were more focused, spending most of their on-line time looking for specific information. This was the largest segment of Wired World netizens in 1995–96 (see Figure 5-2). They bought books, made travel reservations, and purchased food.

On the merchant side, the Wired World companies were middle-sized in 1996. The largest segment—44%—had fifty to ninety-nine employees. The larger the company, the smaller the likelihood that the company had a Web page. Clearly, the Wired World was dominated by forward-looking small and medium-sized businesses during its early years.

We conclude that making money in the friction-free economy of the Wired World is in its infancy. The technology is raw, the distribution channels are uncharted, and the demographics of its consumers are narrow. Larry Ellison, CEO of Oracle, when asked if the Wired World would make it, said, "It's the most bizarre question I've heard in my life. Everything will be digital, everything will be intelligent, but we will have smart TVs, computers, telephones, burglar alarms, and light bulbs. A variety of different smart devices will be attached to the information superhighway."[17]

The Wired World is perfect for flattening the value chain, eliminating the middleman, and targeting the well-heeled early adopters.

Like gunpowder to a gun, the Wired World is about to ignite a flurry of activity in the friction-free economy. But first, making money in the Wired World must get beyond the ozone fringe of the well-to-do consumer.

BEYOND THE FRINGE

The Wired World is many things, not all of them evident to Net cruisers who shuttle up and down the World Wide Web. It is license to porno peddlers, golden opportunity to commerce, dating super-service, social lubricant to the verbose, heir-apparent to TV's waste-land, and magnet to intellectuals in hot pursuit of the world's knowl-edge at their fingertips. Wired World is the new shopping mall in multimedia colors, venture capitalist dance craze of the 90s, political mantra of the ultra left, right, and middle-of-the-road. It is home of

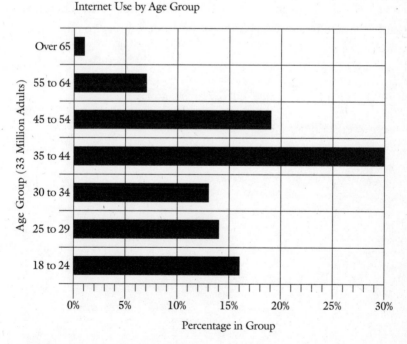

Figure 5–2. Age group breakdown among Internet users in June 1996.

the technically elite yet socially inept, corralled by the cyberpunk cowboy of the computer age, and yes, most carefully defined by the clan of Gates, McCaw, Case, and House of Netscape.

The Wired World is more than just another channel on TV. It is the largest distribution channel ever conceived by humans. While I doubt very much that Bart Simpson will shoot his TV and buy a Blockbuster Video vending machine, Internet TV is inevitable— no, necessary—to the friction-free economy. The megadistribution channel is simultaneously undergoing product space disintegration and market space integration. This phenomenon defines what works and does not work in the Wired World. It defines the marketing approach of every business that wants to succeed in the friction-free economy.

The stampede to the Wired World is an entirely new phenomenon, which cannot be judged by comparison with earlier technology. But one thing is for sure: The friction-free economy runs best on the light waves of the global network. Therefore, I think it is safe to say, everyone will be a netizen in the next century.

6

Exploiting the Market-of-One

BURNING MAN

Somewhere in a 400-mile-square region of the Southwest, 8,000 software engineers and artists amass to watch the Burning Man ritual. Winnebagos disguised as huge elephants, motorcycles dressed up to look like giant furry rodents, and mud-soaked gray earthlings mingle in the rays of the setting sun. One woman, wearing large ram's horns on her head, says she is a software engineer from Silicon Valley. "I don't know why I am here, but I am having fun." A chained robocop in leather headset obediently follows behind a woman dressed as Princess Leia from *Star Wars*.

The sun goes down over the makeshift village as flashlights, candles, and headlights cast shadows on the surrounding hills. Then an eerie neon glow engulfs a statue in the center of the tribal gathering. The statue is Burning Man—a steel monolith about ten feet high. The art nouveau tribute to high-tech bursts into flames, and then into a fireworks display! Likewise, the crowd bursts into celebration. Chaos reins throughout the night.

It is tribal. It is a dominant force of the friction-free economy.

SOFTWARE ENGINEERS IN THE DESERT

Similarly, in an African village 10,000 miles away, a clan gathers around a village campfire to tell stories and perform age-old rituals. Here culture, art, myth, religion, technology, economy, and survival meld into one. They cannot be compartmentalized, separated, or shelved in anticipation of some future need. No, tribalism defines the clan's very existence—here and now. Ritual is the social glue that binds these people. The Burning Man ritual celebrated by software engineers in the desert is no different.

Though their cultural roots are worlds and years apart, the modern Burning Man ritual and the ancient tribal ritual represent the same thing: the need for ritual and connectedness. This is the paradox of the modern human condition.

HUMANO VERSUS TECHNO

During the agrarian age, tribalism and ritual defined every aspect of society. The hard work of survival stripped away all facades, all ulterior motives, all pretense. Fundamental needs, desires, and motivations were not only known by everyone in the clan, they were celebrated around the bonfire. Lacking technology, tribal agrarianism operated at a very basic level—the Fundamental Human level. This was the Humano period.

But then, the rise of technology in the machine age separated humans from their humanity. It compartmentalized art, myth, religion, technology, economy, and means of survival—reducing everything to its elemental parts. *Reductionism* marked the rise of the industrial and postindustrial stages of civilization and the decline of the Humano period.

Now reductionism has just about played out. It is no longer necessary to pursue a lopsided reductionist reality, because the software age makes it possible to once again embrace personalization, customization, and individualization via technical products and services. This return to the Humano scale of interaction thrives on ritual. It works best when technical products and services empower the Fundamental Human in us all.

The friction-free economy rewards retro cultures that yearn to return to agrarian tribalism.

Our Humano needs require that we organize ourselves into communities simply to increase survivability, whereas our Techno needs derive strictly from the advantage that technology provides to go beyond time and distance in an effort to build communities.

They are different sides of the same coin compelling humans to communicate. Curiously, the friction-free economy thrives on integrating all forms of communication—not just face-to-face and individual, but all levels, from individual netizen to the entire Web community. Apparently, humans have the urge to talk.

In the friction-free economy, efficient managerial and organizational analysis can be replaced by computerized access, search, inference, and filtering. This frees humans to be creative. It frees them to participate in ritual. This theme can be observed in operation in the friction-free economy over and over again. Through community-building, on-line chat, and relationship-oriented selling in the Wired World, human culture is becoming increasingly retro.

Technology is now able to provide for both—the Humano factor of tribal agrarianism, and the Techno factor that thrives in a technological society. Their goals are the same. Society wants both comfort and the humanity that coincided with the agrarian age. To the extent that technology can improve tribalism and human interaction, technology will thrive. Otherwise, technology is nothing more than a sidetrack. It may even divert society from its pursuit of comfort and humanity.

The friction-free economy takes society back to the agrarian tribe through individual barter, one-on-one interaction, personalized, individualized, and customized products and services. It uses virtual communities to simulate, if you will, the agrarian tribalism of our ancestors. It is definitely tribal and is definitely a dominant force of the friction-free economy. Companies that want to do well in the friction-free economy must take note of this fundamental shift.

THE PICN FACTOR

The friction-free economy is making it possible to combine the Humano and Techno achievements of the past 2,000 years through the *PICN factor*—personalization, individualization, customization, and narrowcasting. When technology is used to increase PICN, it accelerates the friction-free economy. It also makes businesses very successful.

The PICN factor has a specific meaning in the friction-free economy. *Personalization* means the product fits like a glove; *customization* means the customer can tailor the product himself or herself; and *individualization* means the product is designed for the lifestyle of a particular person. Because products, services, and ideas are becoming individualized, marketing them is also becoming individualized. Thus, individualization implies narrowcasting. *Narrowcasting* means the customer is reached by searching out markets-of-one. Together, these are the PICN factor.

> *In the friction-free economy, personalization replaces efficiency, individualization replaces mass production, customization replaces customer support, and narrowcasting replaces mass marketing.*

THE TRIBAL TECHNO-SHAMAN

"This latest crop of programming engineers acts more like the ancient tribal shaman—the tribes being Microsoft, IBM, Adobe, and the like. The program is presented as a commodity that will allow the user to rule the world, or at least that sector of his cubicle," writes J. W. Zook.[1] While Zook's remarks were meant to condemn technology, they do a better job of summing up why there are software engineers in the desert.

The Burning Man ritual is simultaneously meaningless and meaningful. It is meaningless because it is simply fun. Sure, riding around the desert in a ram's horn hat is good entertainment. It is meaningful because it rejoins people with their fundamental humanity. What better way to meet people than around the Burning Man campfire? The construction and subsequent destruction of Burning Man represents the simultaneous rise of Techno and resurgence of Humano.

The return to tribal agrarianism is not an antitechnology trend. It is not a neo-Luddite movement, nor is it a condemnation of progress. Unlike the Luddites before them, technologists in the friction-free economy *use* technology to return to the land of cyberspace. They know that modern society yearns to return to agrarian tribalism—even more than it wants to expand technology. Therefore, progress is defined as how well a new technology fits in with the resurgent Humano movement—a movement which I call *tribal agrarianism*. In this context, ritual becomes almost an obsession. Even more important, selling becomes ritual.

Selling in the friction-free economy becomes ritual. The greater the ritual, the greater the financial reward.

WHEN RITUAL BECOMES AN OBSESSION

What sells in a compartmentalized, impersonal, highly technical and efficiently automated society? The answer: personalization, individualization, and customization—PIC. This is why software engineers, schoolteachers, and cocker spaniels are motivated by products that add value through greater personalization, individualization, and customization. Basically, consumers want products that fit them, not the other way around.

Making products fit consumers instead of the other way around creates communities of people who wear the same size gloves. These communities may be real or virtual. They may be next door or on the other side of the globe. They may speak different languages, drive on the wrong side of the road, and dress funny, but they all wear the same glove. By simply using the same product, these people are joined together in a common ritual. In this respect, they belong to the same tribe.

Tribes stay together. They are loyal. They subscribe to the same mythology—the same rituals—the same habits. In other words, tribal behavior is a lot like brand behavior—once you belong, you rarely stray. This leads to lock-in, and nothing is more powerful in the friction-free economy than a locked-in base of customers.

When ritual becomes obsession, a business has lock-in.

ATASCADERO FOR CHOCOLATE

On my way back to Monterey from Silicon Valley, I pass through the Garlic Capital of the World, Gilroy. I often swerve from Highway 101 onto Leavesley Road and then into the parking lot of In-N-Out Burgers. There is usually a line at the window—not because of the wafting garlic, but because many people belong to the In-N-Out Burger family. Why do we swerve off of 101 to enjoy a bit of beef? Clearly, we are engaging in a bit of 1950s-style retro behavior.

I am not as smitten as some waiting in line. Mike Kemmerrer drives for more than three hours to satisfy his urge for In-N-Out. "I discovered they had opened a store in Gilroy. That was an answer to my dream," swallowed Kemmerrer. Mike is not the only one. J. T. Tananuu drives his semi truck right past the factory outlet stores, McDonald's, and Burger King, making a beeline for his favorite lunch. Jim Walker has been hooked for twenty years.

The four of us told bigger and bigger stories as meat eaters pressed their way into the tiny fast food joint on opening day. Kemmerrer's friend Margaret Lukens lamented, "Personally, I would only drive to Atascadero for chocolate." She has a point. In a world dominated by McDonald's, Burger King, and Wendy's, who in their right mind would open another burger stand? But In-N-Out burgers are selling like hotcakes. Why? "They do burgers the way I would at home," said Tananuu. The Animal Burger has extra pickles, onions, lettuce, and tomatoes. The mustard is fried into the meat. "I've been eating them all of my life, and they are by far the best. It's a hormonal thing," burped Walker.

In-N-Out takes you back to the 1950s. The family-owned business has red and white tables and booths, white tiles with red palm trees painted on them, and servers wearing red and white uniforms. Since 1948 In-N-Out has grown from a neighborhood stand in southern California to over 100 restaurants. The secret to success? Tribal marketing.

The tribe, in this case, is obviously carnivorous nostalgiacs who love fresh-cooked hamburgers made out of fresh ingredients. Friendly service tops it off. In-N-Out customers are a community. A tribe. An outpost of gastronomic delight in a desert of low-fat political correctness.

TAKE AIM

Efficiency, cost-effectiveness, optimal solutions, and right sizing are contrary to the friction-free economy. Sure, efficiency was the mantra of postindustrial business, but no more. As Nicholas Negroponte says, "Independence of space and time is the single most valuable service and product we can provide humankind."[2] The Techno/Humano blend of today craves a high standard of living within a highly personal, up-close, villager lifestyle. This urge shifts product design towards personalization, individualization, and customization. It also shifts marketing towards narrowcasting instead of broadcasting, i.e., *targeting*.

The PICN factor forces manufacturing to go beyond the point of sale. Instead of monolithic, generic mass produced, inflexible products and services, the friction-free economy churns out products and services that can be modified after they are produced. They can be customized years after they come off of the assembly line. This has important ramifications, especially as it pertains to marketing:

> *Market targeting is to the friction-free economy what the*
> *assembly line was to Henry Ford.*

Like mass production in earlier times, targeting makes it possible to deliver products that satisfy the PICN factor. It is yet another mechanism that delivers better products at lower prices. But unlike earlier times, "better" today means "customized."

INSOMNIACS ASYLUM

Insomniacs Asylum is a fashionable Web site for Generation X nightcrawlers who stay glued to their America Online browser long after the rest of us have dozed off. It was designed and produced by Warner Brothers Online—a division of the movie company headed by Jim Moloshok.

Warner Online noticed a spike in traffic between 10 P.M. and 2 A.M. Honing in on this bulge in viewers, Warner employees listened in on the chat and began to throw out topics for discussion. In a sense, they planted people in the audience. These plants turned ordinary conversation into entertainment.

Warner discovered what kept everyone up so late. They concluded that "what people want is a community that is uniquely theirs."[3] Making cyberspace uniquely theirs was equivalent to making a community. As a consequence, Insomniacs Asylum—on from 10 P.M. to 8 A.M.—focuses on five topics that the audience plants found were of the greatest interest to viewers: romance, comedy, news, arts, and supernatural phenomena.

The site was receiving 30,000 messages per night and growing at 40% per month in late 1996. Viewers also spent about twice as much time (8 minutes) at the site as the average AOL viewer (4.25 minutes). AOL and Warner Online are cleaning up in the Wired World simply by returning viewers to the ancient ritual of campfire talk.

In typical friction-free economy style, Warner Online receives a percentage of the fees collected by AOL from foot traffic, as well as a slice of the advertising revenue pie. They are integrating the value chain, and making money for themselves and AOL. But without targeting the narrow market space of AOL's subscribers, there wouldn't be anything to split between Warner Online and AOL. Targeting a tribe is what makes Insomniacs Asylum so sane.

TRIBAL VALUE MULTIPLIERS

Targeting is simple math. Every link in the value chain multiplies value passed to it from the previous link. Therefore, the value proposition of any market space is this: Add value or die. This proposition applies to burger stands, software vendors, and airplane manufacturers alike. It is a universal truth in the friction-free economy.

The size of a value multiplier is determined mostly by the price of a product (price), number of customers reached (traffic), advertising and promotion costs (ad costs), response rate (hit rate), and closing rate (how many people actually buy). These factors, and more, all contribute to the success (or failure) of each link in the value chain. Each factor must be carefully managed, to get the most bang for a buck.

How much bang does a link provide?

The size of a value multiplier is directly proportional to the response rate, closing rate, and price, and inversely proportional to the ad cost.

Given a fixed price point for a product that sells through a value chain, a business should increase response rate and closing rate, while decreasing the ad cost. Since the response and closing rate are directly linked to the narrowness of the audience, one should target as narrowly as possible. Remember, the rules in the wired friction-free economy are different. It is possible to target a very narrow segment of the general population and still reach millions of potential buyers. This is what the Wired World is all about. In fact, it is more profitable to narrowcast than broadcast:

Value-add goes up as a market space is narrowed.

STRATEGY OF THE WEAK

Narrowcasting—focusing a market space like a laser—can be more profitable than broadcasting. Why? Because the return on advertising investment can be higher. But more important, it is a strategy of the weak.

Targeting is a maximum strategy of the weak.

Say a business first targets a relatively narrow community of customers to gain a foothold. This foothold is expanded as the product begins to mainstream. Gains in market share follow the mainstreaming rule, which says that existing market share begins to take over as customers get locked in. Once this happens, the product has crossed the Chasm and is on its way to market leadership.

The effectiveness of targeting declines as the product gains market share. Eventually the rate of change caused by the narrowcasting effect drops to zero. By then the business will have achieved a monopoly, or near monopoly, and the game ends. Thus, targeting is a strategy of the weak and not the strong.

A WEAKNESS OF THE STRONG

The best strategy of the weak is a weakness of the strong. Got it? Once a business gains 74% or more of its market, its ability to gain more market share is weakened. A start-up typically grows at rates of 40% to 50% in its early years, simply because its market share is small and the mainstreaming phenomenon thrives on a large remaining market share. This is a mathematical fact—not a reflection of the business that employs this fact. Hot young companies may seem hot because of rapid relative changes in share, but the truth is less glamorous—they are simply riding a mathematical formula to success.

Strong (market-leading) companies cannot benefit from targeting as much as weaker (start-up) companies can. A market-leading company becomes vulnerable to new companies that can effectively target their installed base. Thus, a highly successful business creates its own vulnerability—it develops its own weakness and can be ruined by another company that targets its tribe.

A PUPPY WITH BIG FEET

The more narrowly a product, service, or idea targets a community, the more likely it is to mainstream. But if a niche product mainstreams, how can it remain a niche product? What happens when a niche product blossoms into a mainstream (mass) product?

Ellen Pack and Nancy Rhine found plenty of technical lingo and arcane science and medical discussions on the Net in 1991, but nothing specifically aimed at women. So they created Women's Wire—a dial-up service where subscribers could send e-mail and chat with like-minded women. More than 1,500 women—and many men—signed up. Then Pack and Rhine took their community to the Web (www.women.com). Two years later Women's Wire was getting 7.5 million hits per month and was ranked among the top ten favorite sites in 1996!

"We wanted to build a collaborative community and central clearinghouse of information related to women."[4] And they did. Their niche turned out to hold the attention of lots of people. It is still focused on women's issues, but it is no longer small.

From this niche, Women's Wire has become a mainstream product. But Women's Wire is like a puppy with big feet, according to CEO Marleen McDaniel—growing, but awkward. In fact, the site grew too fast and made some major mistakes. In 1996, when it closed down its bulletin board service and urged subscribers to join a women's forum on CompuServe, one third of the subscribers were enraged. The tribe had come to think of Women's Wire as their special place in cyberspace.

This illustrates a common trait of a successful business in the friction-free economy. It starts out as a one-product company with a mission—to satisfy a market-of-one client. If it does its job well, the niche grows until it becomes a mainstream market space. Then the business must cope with challenges to its fundamental reason for existing.

The strategy of the weak is to target the narrowest possible market segment, and then go after dominance in that segment. Companies such as Cisco Systems have elevated this scheme to an art form. Using this idea, Cisco Systems grew from a few million per year in revenue to over $6 billion within a span of about four to five years.

But targeting very narrow markets does not imply that a company remains a niche player. In fact, the opposite is true: A business that can successfully target, and then dominate, a narrow market segment, can target and dominate a mainstream market space. Segmenting and targeting is simply how a business learns to walk before it runs in the Wired World.

FLEXIBLE MANUFACTURING

What is the narrowest possible target? It is a single person. That is, the biggest marketing bang for the buck is obtained by reaching the individual who is looking for exactly the product you sell. Market-of-one selling maximizes the value multiplier; hence, it maximizes the value chain.

Serving a market of one seems ridiculous. It seems extreme. Suppose Henry Ford had made Model Ts to order. A customer comes in, orders a custom T, waits a month, and drives away with a one-of-a-kind automobile. What is wrong with this picture?

First, a Ford would have cost as much as a Rolls-Royce. Second, Ford's factory was not designed to make just anything, so a new factory would had been needed to build each car. This too would have added to the price of each Ford. Third, because customers didn't know what they wanted anyhow, Ford had to tell them, "You can have any color, as long as it is black." This is not exactly what makes a product unique. Educating the consumer would have added another few thousand dollars to the retail price.

Ford may have been a genius of assembly-line mass production, but he didn't even think of *flexible manufacturing*. It was technically unthinkable in 1905. Is it technologically unthinkable in the friction-free economy? Indeed, flexible factories in the Wired World add fuel to the friction-free economy. Not only are they possible, they are smart business.

In the friction-free economy, flexible manufacturing provides low-cost, high-quality, near-perfect goods and services for almost nothing. Therefore, the distinguishing feature of a product or service is almost always how well it fits a single person. In fact, individualized products sell for more than mass-produced products, not because they cost more to make, but because they fit better.

Flexible manufacturing makes it possible to build products for individuals. This is a means of locking in a tribe. In fact, it is another principle of the friction-free economy.

Personalization and individualization maximize the value multiplier.

NO SIMPLE VILLAGERS

The perfume is garlic along Monterey Road in Gilroy, California, across town from In-N-Out Burgers. The air is also split by the sound of roaring motorcycles. Gilroy is the home of California Motorcycle Company, the second-largest motorcycle manufacturer in the U.S. CMC may be in second place, but they are far behind Harley-Davidson. In fact, CMC revenues are less than 1% of Harley-Davidson's sales. So with Harley-Davidson's enormous size and market share, why did Ray Sotelo, Richard Zahm, and Rett Schmidt get into building motorcycles? What did they know that Harley-Davidson didn't?

Women make up 32% of the market, according to Zahm. "They want to ride their own bike rather than hang on for dear life on the back."[5] But Zahm claims women have more buying power than bikers might think. "If a woman gets on a bike, there is a good chance her boyfriend will get a bike." The women's model is lower in front and has a full-sized gas tank so they won't have to stop frequently and make everyone wait while they refuel.

These guys are no simple villagers. Sotelo has been making motorcycles for eighteen years. Zahm has two university degrees— one in business and the other in law. They know how to target bikers with spending cash. The company is doing very well in the $16,000 to $29,000 retail price segment. They sold 400 bikes in their first year of business, and expect to sell 1,700 bikes their second year, 1997. CMC's Web page gets 2,000 hits per week (www.calmocycle.com). The trend is definitely upward.

CMC knows this: They can thrive in the shadow of legendary Harley-Davidson simply by employing flexible manufacturing techniques made possible by technology. As a result, CMC makes motorcycles that fit individual consumers better than Harley-Davidson does. CMC's flexible manufacturing aims to deliver a bike "your way." Tailored seat, foot bags, handlebars, and the rake of the front fork— matched exactly as the buyer wants. When an order comes in, CMC takes less than six weeks to respond precisely to the market-of-one.

CUSTOM NEWSPAPERS

What is the difference between individualized products and customized products? How can a business make money by distinguishing between the two? Individualization makes products fit, perfectly. Customization makes products that customers can make fit, perfectly. In other words, customers become part of the manufacturing process when a product is designed to be customized. Think of customization as manufacturing after the point of sale.

BroadVision's Web site (www.theangle.com) manufactures a tailored personal newspaper right before your eyes. But first you must tell it what topics interest you the most and how you want your electronic paper to look. This is equivalent to telling cub reporters what news to look for, and then telling the production artists how to lay out the finished product. You get to personalize the content, of course, but you also get to customize its appearance.

A menu of format selections ask how you want to get your news: fact-based, opinion-based, reserved, alternative, brief, deep, many topics, focused, artistic, funny, trendy, and/or unique. You decide. Then you select the topics of greatest interest on a scale of one to eight—from arts and entertainment; home and lifestyle; Internet and technology; travel, sports and fitness; business and money; news; and/or government and community. Again, you decide by rating each category.

After a brief pause while the Web server collects and formats your customized newspaper, a colorful page appears with graphics and text that fit perfectly. No printing presses, no layout artists, no copyreaders, no delays. Instant news is tailored to your tastes. In other words, it's a customized newspaper.

By the way, unlike uniquely manufactured Rolls-Royce autos, this uniquely manufactured product is free! Who says it costs too much to flexibly manufacture products built for one?

CUSTOM MONEY MACHINE

BroadVision's custom printing presses don't cost much to produce, but how does the company make any money? After all, anyone can connect to the Wired World, enter their preferences, and get a free newspaper. What gives?

Newspapers take in more than $13 billion annually from ads, says the Newspaper Association of America.[6] Over one-third comes from recruitment ads, another third from used and new car ads, and the remaining one-third is evenly split between real estate and miscellaneous advertisements. This revenue accounts for most of a newspaper's operating margin. The NAA estimates that a decline of 25% in ad revenue would reduce operating margins to 9%.

BroadVision's custom newspaper is a money machine. By giving it away, BroadVision creates foot traffic that in turn creates demand for its ad space. Because the Wired World has near-zero manufacturing costs and near-zero distribution costs, giving away the news is highly profitable! The profit is in the value multiplier, which in turn is paid for by every advertiser that runs display ads in the customized newspaper.

COMMUNES IN CYBERSPACE

In late 1996 virtual community pioneer Howard Rheingold created Well Engaged, a Web page that provides tools to help Web publishers build communities. "The name of the game is not content," said Maria Wilhelm, president of The Well (www.well.com) and Well Engaged. "It is a rich sense of community. Sites have to have a persistent audience. Conferencing encourages return visits by building a sense of belonging, a sense of community and at the same time enhances the web site's content value."[7]

The Well, Rheingold's original commune in cyberspace, was flooded with Deadheads (members of The Grateful Dead rock band tribe) following the death of Jerry Garcia in August 1995. Communes in cyberspace are proliferating. Michael Jackson's first appearance in cyberspace (www.sony.com/Music/MichaelJackson) on August 17, 1995, generated keyboard-only standing room on America Online, CompuServe, and Prodigy—all at once.

By 1997 the idea of virtual communities and communes in cyberspace had become a major thrust in the social Web segment of online services. The most popular social Web sites were Time Warner's Pathfinder (www.pathfinder.com), Cyborganic (www.cyborganic.com), Geek Cereal (www.geekcereal.com), Electric Minds (www.minds.com), Forum One, HotWired, Utne Online, and The Well. Cyborganic, for example, includes a soap opera in addition to chat. Steve Silberman, senior editor at HotWired, says, "This is not a fad that will go away." Jonathan Steuer, president and CEO of Cyborganic, says, "It starts with individuals and community."[8]

TRIBES IN THE WIRED WORLD

John McAfee—the same pioneer who created computer virus pro-
tection software and the company that now bears his name—understands the importance of communes in cyberspace. He even owns
the Wired World domain name—*tribe*. In 1996 McAfee unleashed
PowWow for free at www.tribe.com. PowWow is for tribal chat.
Anyone can use this software to create an on-line chat forum on the
fly. It requires no server, no corporation, no permissions—nothing
except a computer with a browser—to hold mediated conferences
in the Wired World. It is software that lets communities gather
around the tribal campfire and chew the fat.

PowWow supports any number of moderated conferences in
which one window of your computer is controlled by a conference
coordinator and another window is out of control—it is a free-for-
all, where anyone in the tribe can butt in and contribute commen-
tary. In addition, members of the tribe can split off into private discussions—powwows—where only a subset of viewers is allowed to
participate.

One of the innovative features of PowWow is the Web cruise
capability. Here users can latch onto a leader who steers the group
through cyberspace. As the leader navigates by clicking on links to
other locations, everyone in the group follows. Everyone sees the
same Web pages, together. The follow-the-leader mode is much
like a chieftain leading his tribe into battle.

The "communal thing" is more than a return to the 1960s. It
is a deep trend in the friction-free economy, because it returns people to their tribal agrarian roots. And like the tribal urge to con-
form, it plays on our herd instincts.

HERD INSTINCTS

Psychology, sociology, and anthropology are all increasingly important in the friction-free economy because products will become
increasingly tailored. And tailoring is not just a property of the Wired

World. For example, ZIBA Design of Portland, Oregon, hires anthropologists, sociologists, and others to design award-winning products for the computer, auto, food, and service industries.

ZIBA was employed by McDonald's to figure out how to serve hamburgers faster, by General Mills to determine how to sell more cereal, and by FedEx to speed up company deliveries. Why do these big companies reply on ZIBA instead of their own people?

ZIBA searches for herd instincts.

ZIBA hired Mark Dawson soon after he completed his master's degree in anthropology from the University of South Carolina, because Dawson understood group behavior. He joined a team of other ZIBA consultants to develop an integrated fax/copy/printer machine for a high-tech Japanese company. Using focus groups, plant tours, interviews, and studying videotapes of consumers, Dawson and his team work hard to find the market-of-one for the new product. Once the market-of-one niche is found, it must be turned outward—to appeal to entire groups of like-minded consumers. This is where training in herd instinct comes in. This is where anthropology and sociology meet technology.

STAMPEDING CELEBRATION

Sociology meets technology every day in Celebration—a town where a marching band struts down the spotless street, as above-average children clap, parents smile, and Mickey Mouse dances. The observing crowd collects along the street not only to watch, but also to perform. Every night is a celebration. It is tribal. It is Disney.

Five miles south of the Magic Kingdom near Orlando, Florida, lies Celebration—built by Walt Disney Inc. for people who want to go back in time. Celebration is a nineteenth-century town for the twenty-first century. Its public school, post office, town hall, golf course, health center, and 20,000 residents form a community that yearns to hearken back to the days of lemonade stands, zero crime, and orderliness.

The first 350 units of the $2.5 billion city went on sale in 1996 on November 18—Mickey Mouse's birthday. Property ranged in price from $127,000 to $750,000. Interest was so great that the company had to raffle off property. Who wants in? Not everyone, and that is the point. Celebration is targeted at a narrow segment of society—those who want to return to community, neighborhood, and cartoon characters.

Celebration signifies a general trend:

Products and services in the friction-free economy must simultaneously fit a single person and yet appeal to an entire tribe.

ONE TOUGH MOTHER

Tribalism is the key to successful business in the friction-free economy, because it gives meaning to the term "personalization." But personalization is in the eye of the consumer. One woman's work of art is another woman's tattoo. One man's meat loaf is another man's steak. The trick is to get everyone with the same tastes corralled into the same community. This is a job for one tough mother.

Take "Gritty Gert" Boyle as an example. Twenty-six years ago she buried her husband on Monday and took over the business on Tuesday. After eight years of struggle, she had saved Columbia Sportswear from bankruptcy, turned her son into a TV ad star, and earned the title "tough mother." The company recently outgrew its east side Willamette River headquarters near the St. Johns Bridge and had to move to new and larger quarters in North Portland, Oregon.

Selling sportswear to picky individuals has made Gritty Gert rich. Creating a community of consumers has made her famous. TV ads depict her as an overbearing, eagle-eyed matriarch who loves to make her son do all of the dirty work. Gert's spiked hairdo imitates the Statue of Liberty in one ad. She shows off her Born To Nag tattoo in another ad. Gert and son challenge harsh winds, cliff-hangers, and virtual polar bears in order to sell real Columbia Sportswear parkas.

Her business started from selling a very narrowly focused product in 1960. You might say that she was an early pioneer of narrowcasting. Gert's husband Neal drafted her into designing a multipocketed fishing vest for his fishing buddies. Mr. Boyle advised Gert to put a pocket here, another one there—anywhere the boys wanted it. The fishing vest had to exactly fit each of his buddies. This was housewife Gert's first product designed-for-one. Three million vests later, former Presidents Carter and Bush rave about the company's multipocketed vests.

Columbia became the world's largest outerwear manufacturer in 1995, with $316 million in sales. The company is reaching for $1 billion in revenue by 2000. At this rate, Columbia will threaten cross-town specialty shoe maker Nike for the title of most successful Oregon corporation.

Personalization paid off. Targeting paid off. Tribalism paid off even bigger. Competitor Steve Rogerson of rival Patagonia says, "Ma Boyle's almost this mythical figure."[9] Columbia Sportswear is more than a business—it is the focal point for a community, with one tough mother as tribal leader.

This tough mother invented a product that simultaneously fit a single person and yet appealed to a much larger community. She then locked in consumers with ads that created a mythology. Columbia Sportswear is doubly a business of the friction-free economy and the firebrand of a tribe.

PLATFORM ZEALOTS

Products that are a focal point for a community achieve the ultimate goal of lock-in. The tribe simply refuses to buy alternative products. Loyalty to the tribe, and by inference, to the product, keeps them buying no matter what happens. The Apple Macintosh is a glaring example.

The Church of the Mac Evangelist is a semihumorous Web site for the Mac tribe—the millions of users of the Apple Macintosh computer. Using graphics, video, and audio sermons on the virtues of the Macintosh, the site beseeches viewers to stay in the fold. Here misguided souls are delivered from "Wintel Hell." True believers are admonished to resist the widespread, conspiratorial assault on their digital deity.

Platform zealots may joke about their devotion to an operating system or platform, but they are locked in to the platform in the worst way. Take, for example, Carl Franklin, an engineer for NASA's Johnson Space Center in Houston. "I don't like PCs, and I'm a pain in the butt."[10] Franklin rallied over 100 NASA employees, who protested standardization with Microsoft Windows. The protest halted the Windows migration pending a review of NASA's situation.

NASA is not unique. Valuable workers have quit over changes like this. Bill Howey quit Avco Financial Services of Irvine, California, when the company decided to switch to Windows NT from OS/2. Greg Cifu threatened to quit a Southern California aerospace company that announced it was replacing 500 Macs with Windows machines. "I plan to quit by the end of the year—I am a dead man walking and have nothing to lose."[11]

Whether it is the Mac tribe, OS/2 clan, or Windows commune, lock-in becomes personal when the product is highly personalized. The humanlike qualities of these products evoke emotional as well as analytical responses. "It has to do with the DNA of the Mac from the very start," says Guy Kawasaki, Apple Computer evangelist. "From the time it boots up and smiles at you, there's something special going on."[12]

This is exactly what PC manufacturers want. Highly personalized products lock in the installed base. But highly personalized buying is even better. How does a business like yours lock in consumers by personalizing the buying experience?

FREQUENT SHOPPERS

Lock-in may be the goal of creating a tribe, but it has to be earned in the modern age. Simple product branding is not enough. In the

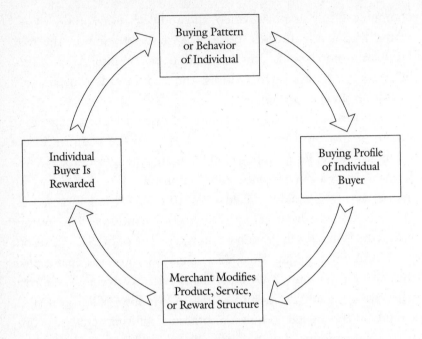

Figure 6–1. The learning feedback loop of targeted marketing using data collected on individual shoppers.

friction-free economy, customers must be rewarded for their loyalty. This is why United Airlines has a frequent-traveler club and grocery stores have frequent-shopper discounts.

Businesses in the friction-free economy shape their customers' behavior by rewarding buying patterns. This is done by learning the personal preferences of individual buyers, and then using these preferences to promote customer loyalty and future purchasing. As personal preferences are taken into consideration, buyers change their behavior. Targeting is an iterative process whereby a business tracks individual buyers, feeds this data into a computer (which recommends how to target the individual buyer), and changes buying habits in response (see Figure 6-1).

The measure-reward-measure cycle continues as the merchant learns more and the consumer changes. Buyers are guided into specific buying directions as merchants modify buyers' behavior patterns. For example, if a merchant wants to quickly unload a certain brand of beans before a new shipment arrives, a quick computer run can pick out every buyer who purchased beans within the past month. A special mailing or newspaper insert can be sent to only the people on the hit list.

Many Las Vegas casinos issue courtesy cards to their guests for buying food, renting horses, playing the slot machines, and going to the shows. As it turns out, these cards are smart enough to remember everything you did. A month after returning home, junk mail pours in. Offers of four-day weekends with free horse rides go out to the people who spent all of their time on horseback, and other offers of free admissions to stage shows go out to the lounge lizards.

In the friction-free economy, keeping customers is more important than optimizing profits. If a business locks in its installed base, it can always recover from a bad quarter. But if the same business loses its loyal customers, it may never be able to recover.

Keeping a customer adds more value to a business in the friction-free economy than getting a new customer.

FOOD LIONS

U.S. companies lose roughly one-half of their customers every five years. To make things worse, it costs much more to solicit a new customer than it does to hold on to an existing one. To remedy this, businesses use powerful computers and software to reward repeat customers. They do this by building electronic relationships with individual shoppers.

At Food Lion in North Carolina, shoppers join the store's MVP club to save money, but what they are really doing is joining a loyal tribe. Here is how it works. The more you spend, the greater your discount. MVP-tagged items are discounted by 5% if the total purchase is under $20, 10% if between $20 and $50, and 20% if more than $50 worth of merchandise is bought. Non-MVP shoppers don't get any discounts. If you want to save money, you have to join the tribe.

Even narrower targeting is possible by stores that track customer purchases on an individual basis. One Midwestern grocery store uses kiosks where frequent shoppers insert personal ID cards to get a list of items that match their previous buys. This is more than convenient—the kiosk-addicted shopper is rewarded with additional discounts. Such stores reward their big spenders and lure small spenders into spending more. In addition, the *store* suggests what to buy, instead of you!

LOOK-ALIKES

In the preindustrial agrarian age, merchants knew every intimate detail of the customer's life. Consumers had even less privacy than they do today. Such intimacy was impossible during the mass merchandising machine age. A lot of people know Sam Walton, but Sam Walton doesn't know a lot of people. Thus, buyer and seller became estranged.

The retro software age operates much like the agrarian age, except acquaintances are stored in a computer database. In the software age, computers and specialized software make it as easy as it was in medieval times to know your customer. Or at least to know the electronic profile of your customer. Software age merchants track individual consumers in great detail so that they can find everyone else who looks just like you!

Businesses with computer databases target new customers by looking for *demographic look-alikes*—potentially new customers that are exactly like existing customers. The look-alike profiles are used to go prospecting for additional people who might be coaxed into the store. Through the behavior modification cycles described above, noncustomers are transformed into club members who become consistent shoppers. After all, how is a tribe to propagate itself?

In the friction-free economy, it is easier to grow by adding customers who look exactly like the ones you already have.

DATA WAREHOUSES

In the friction-free economy, product storage warehouses are eliminated along with the middlemen who own them. Businesses erect data warehouses in their place. These warehouses, and the software that goes along with them, are called *decision support software*. DSS is used to extract additional revenue from communal groupings in the Wired World. This is called *database marketing*.

A data warehouse is where extensive data about individual members of the tribe are amassed and analyzed for all sorts of economic information. In fact, businesses store *massive* amounts of data on their customers' purchasing profiles, personal habit profiles, and other demographic categories.

Decision support software sifts through the data warehouse looking for trends or clues to customer segmentation. For example, it might locate the most loyal customers, or identify which customers are likely to abandon a particular product and switch to another one. Using predictive sampling techniques, this kind of software can accelerate the learning process of a business by automating pinpoint market-of-one opportunities. The purpose is to automate the learning process that can propel a business to mainstream market domination. Learning in this fashion is called *adaptive response*.

ADAPTIVE RESPONSE

The Reader's Digest Association Inc. turned to sophisticated adaptive response software to tailor Web content to specific users. Using BroadVision software tools, Reader's Digest targets numerous markets-of-one. "We have all of this data on people and we have an ability to predict what people will do with our products," says Sarah Hammann, director of new business development. "We will be able to develop one-on-one marketing programs."

BroadVision's One-to-One software lets Wired World customers create their own customized radio programming on NetRadio's cybermall (www.netradio.net). Customers enter music preferences and other demographic information into the Web browser and the software creates a personalized play list based on their preferences. The software also suggests related Web pages that match interests— jazz, country, or rock—and then recommends products and services from its on-line store. "Electronic commerce has us going from mass distribution and mass marketing to targeting markets of one," says Geoffrey Bock of Seybold Group in Boston.[13]

Here are some additional examples of adaptive response:

- PhotoDisc of Seattle generates about $200,000 a month from its cybermall (www.photodisc.com), using CONNECT's OneServer adaptive response software. PhotoDisc provides thousands of images to commercial artists over the Net. But it does more than this. Users are asked to describe their interests as they search for images. PhotoDisc gathers information about its customers, and in return, customers get free images delivered directly to their desktops. "We have the ability to change the interaction from the moment they enter a site to the moment they leave," says Bart Foster, vice president of CONNECT. This permits PhotoDisc to "target a group of people who are just like a particular user."

- SaveSmart (www.savesmart.com) was the first business to combine the power of shopping via the Wired World with the fun of buying locally—at discounted prices. A customer joins the SaveSmart shopping club via the Web, and then receives a plastic identification card through surface mail. A wired netizen shops in cyberspace with a virtual shopping cart in tow. As products are added to the virtual shopping cart, the consumer is rewarded with discounts. But customers must go to the physical store to complete the transaction.

At the physical store, the customer's plastic identification card is swiped through a reader so that the customer can collect the reward—a discount for shopping in the Wired World. This idea is based on the fact that 85% of purchases are made within fifteen miles of home.

But discounts and convenience are only a small part of the SaveSmart business plan. What SaveSmart really wants is to know you better. They want to create a database on your preferences, desires, and quirks. Over time, SaveSmart's computers learn quite a bit about you by "watching" your shopping habits. Their computers create and maintain a database on everyone who gets a discount. If you buy cat food, a SaveSmart merchant may offer you—and you alone—discounted kitty litter.

"People come to this site because they are going to get very specific, definite value," says Ashok Narasimhan, founder, chairman, and CEO of SaveSmart.[14] The Wired World storefront can personalize the shopping experience more precisely than a real world mall. In addition, database marketing provides greater adaptive response. "We're using the Internet to make that experience far more rewarding and practical."

ADS THAT CLICK

Businesses go to elaborate extremes to get customers, hold on to them, and then coax them into spending ever more money on highly personalized, customized, individualized products. But the magnet that draws people into the tribe, and keeps them there, is not automatic. "It's great if you can get a transaction, but if you can't compel people to come to your site, then they're not going to buy anything," complains Sandra Vaughan of BroadVision.

Seth Godin has a solution to this problem: He pays people to read ads! Godin is president of Yoyodyne Entertainment—one of the new businesses that uses targeting to increase the value of advertising in the Wired World. Godin pays people to watch Internet TV. In fact, Godin pays $100,000 to lucky Net surfers who parlay luck and visits to advertised Web sites to win Yoyodyne's Get Rich Click contest. This contest attracts consumers to sponsors' ads like newlyweds attract in-laws. Here is how Get Rich Click works:

Surfers, sifters, and strolling netizens are automatically entered into the Get Rich Click raffle each time they click on an ad paid for by one of Yoyodyne's sponsoring companies. For example, if Yoyodyne sells Microsoft ad space on its Get Rich Click cybermall and I click on it, I automatically get registered for the grand prize of $100,000! If I click on the same ad in another page, I get extra credit—leading to possibly bigger prizes. It is entertainment for greedy netizens.

Here is the friction-free economy rationale. Yoyodyne charges 50 cents per click, or hit, and guarantees lots of hits—say 70,000 hits for $35,000. This is $500 per thousand—a much higher rate than the usual Internet ad rate. So how does Godin get away with such high prices? He guarantees viewers.

CYBERSPACE IN YOUR FACE

Christopher Hassett started writing software for Digital Equipment when he was sixteen years old. He rapidly climbed the corporate ladder of responsibility with jaunts at Adobe Systems and BluePoint Technologies, and finally became CEO of his own company in 1994 when PointCast was started. PointCast builds electronic communities by customizing and personalizing desktop news. What makes PointCast different is how the company's product gets in your face.

Partner Jim Reilly had a brilliant idea: Why not tailor information to individuals and then blast it onto the screen of the individual's computer? Now PointCast's vice president of corporate strategy, Reilly invented a better screen saver. A PointCast screen saver filters news and other information from the Wired World and automatically displays it on the screen of your computer whenever it is idle. Workers are confronted with a PointCast ad when returning from a coffee break.

PointCast screen savers "learn" the preferences of individual users. These preferences are used to filter the information that is blasted onto the PC screen after it has been idle for a period of time. Sports scores, stock prices, and newsreels are automatically collected, filtered, formatted, and sent to the right screen.

Here is the clever part. Market-of-one products pop up as animations! "We've found that you can deliver advertising to targeted users that are passive," says Reilly. In other words, desktop PC users are one-third couch potato, one-third big spender, and one-third information hungry.

PointCast was charging advertisers $50,000 per month for ad space on its screen saver just a few short months after opening its doors. The business started with two people—Hassett (whose brother was added later) and Reilly—grew to 160 people in two years, and was doubling every six months by late 1996. PointCast may become the first personalized information service provider to mainstream its product in the Wired World. GE Capital Corporation, Knight-Ridder, Times Mirror Company, Adobe Systems, and Compaq Computer liked the company so much, they invested $36 million in the start-up.

CHANNELING

Pinpoint targeting to the body electric in the Wired World is equivalent to targeting programs played over channels in TV land. But unlike the thirty to fifty television channels under the control of a few media moguls, the Wired World has 50 million channels. This changes everything.

The 50 million channels of the Wired World must blend content with advertising, and advertising with content, to attract viewers. Without seamless mixing of content with ads, community breaks down, and people surf to the next channel. The Wired World is much more segmented, focused, and tribal.

Robert Levitan, vice president of marketing at America Online–backed iVillage Inc., used the concept of very narrow channels to sell ad space to MGM, Polaroid, Toyota, Starbucks, Fisher-

Price, Compaq, and Sandoz—the big ones. How? Levitan doubled the hit rate of ads by blending content with advertising and adding community. iVillage charges $150,000 for annual sponsorship plus $44 per thousand hits. Instead of the industry standard 1% to 3% *click-through rate* (this is what Wired World marketers call the response rate), iVillage achieves 5% to 10% rates, bringing in $750,000 ad commitments from sponsors.[15]

Excite Inc. created www.tours.excite.com, consisting of over 200 virtual tours through the Wired World to attract viewers. In essence, Exciteseeing Tours are TV channels—200 of them to be precise—that target narrow audiences. Topics range from fixing your credit rating to prescribing medical advice to parents. In 1996 Excite had plans to develop thousands of different topic-specific tours, according to Steve Childs, Excite's director of communities.[16]

THE PUSH MODEL

A channel in the Wired World is an aggregation of content plus the tribe that subscribes to it. But it is even more than this, because until products like PointCast came along, the Internet followed predominantly a "pull model," meaning that consumers had to pull information from the Web. Like TV, the push model pushes information from the broadcast station to the consumer. According to the Hassett brothers, "We are to the Internet what ABC and CBS are to the airwaves. We are building a road between the producers of content and their customers."

The push model is much different. Here the merchant pushes information from the server to the client. Information flows out to the desktop through a channel. In fact, it flows through 50 million channels! Push is replacing pull as the mode of operation in the Wired World.

PointCast, Marimba, and BroadVision are examples of companies whose products are redefining the mode of operation in the Wired World, converting it from a pull to a push model. This has major implications.

With 50 million channels, the Wired World can segment greater, specialize deeper, and target much smaller communities than any TV channel. With inverse economics at full tilt, just about anyone can own and operate their own channel. This raises the question of how communities create wealth in the friction-free economy.

VIRTUAL VINEYARDS

Arthur Armstrong and John Hagel, writing in the *Harvard Business Review*,[17] list four kinds of wealth-creating communities in the Wired World:

- Transaction communities.

- Interest communities.

- Relationship communities.

- Fantasy communities.

These may overlap, according to the authors. Of course, transaction communities generate revenues through buying things in the Wired World. Interest communities generate revenues by providing product information and referrals; relationship communities produce chat revenue (subscriptions and connect time); and finally, fantasy communities play games.

Virtual Vineyards, for example, is a Web site that sells wines. Therefore, it is a community of transactions, because the compelling content is cheap pricing of expensive wines. In addition, Virtual Vineyards has infinite shelf space, so it can list wines from the smallest to the largest vintner. Add together huge inventory with low prices, and the cash flow is not hard to swallow.

GardenWeb, on the other hand, is a community of interest. Consumers are bound together by a common interest in gardening. Viewers share ideas and suggestions with one another through forums and bulletin boards. Products get sold indirectly, by word of mouth.

There are other interest communities. The Motley Fool on

America Online focuses on the stock market. Pope John Paul II can be found in the Wired World at www.vatican.va. Although the variety of topics covers just about everything, each community is focused on a single topic—none of them engages viewers in discussions of their personal lives. Personal relationship communities fall into another category.

In communities of relationship, viewers focus on divorce, widowhood, infertility, and dating. Here the viewers themselves provide both entertainment and content. After all, what can be more entertaining than finding someone with a broken heart just like yours?

How does a relationship community generate revenue for the on-line service provider? For one thing, the on-line time is billed to the consumer. America Online makes more money when lovers meet in the Wired World than when business people send simple e-mail to one another. But there is more. When consumers shop for goods and services, they often seek advice from others before they buy. They often seek advice from people looking for relationships. A community of relationship essentially blends the needs of the viewers with the sales ambitions of sponsors. Such Web sites make excellent billboards.

Communities of fantasy create entirely new environments—*virtual worlds*—where viewers can take on different personae. On-line interactive games attract members to fantasy communes. For example, a 3D replication of Yellowstone Park can be viewed at www.worlds.net. The Red Dragon Inn on America Online lets a viewer pretend to be a medieval baron. ESPNet, a sports site, lets viewers create their own sports teams that compete against teams created by other viewers. Virtual habitats spring up like shantytowns in cyberspace as netizens move into alien worlds created to satisfy personal tastes, tribal impulse, and software age ritual.

PSYCHOGRAPHICS

Professionals, military personnel, technical workers, and students use the Web nearly twice as much per capita as does the general population. People under thirty years of age and older (fifty years and up) spend much of their time socializing with others via e-mail. More users access the Net from home than work. Middle-aged users make up the bulk of on-line shoppers. What do all of these statistics mean?

Statistics are powerful segmenting tools, but they are not always detailed enough for the friction-free economy. Why? Because they do not tie in with what makes humans tick. They do not discern what gives people the urge to splurge. They are not narrow enough.

For example, what is the impact of the Wired World on TV viewing among children? Children twelve and under directly or indirectly influenced $615 billion in purchases in 1995, according to professor James U. McNeal of Texas A&M University. So knowing how the Wired World and TV interact could mean big bucks. As it turns out, businesses are emerging to collect and sell such specialized information. They will tell you that girls spend more time in front of computers than boys from preschool age to about the sixth grade. Then the trend reverses—boys spend more hours in front of computers than girls. Both groups trade time in front of the TV for time in front of a computer, given the option.

Why?

The combination of sociological/psychological motivations and market demographics is a field of study called *psychographics*, based on the techniques pioneered in the 1970s by SRI International of Palo Alto, California. It is perfect for elucidating the friction-free economy, because it combines the knowledge of who can buy a product or service with why they should buy it. It is a technique that can be used by any business to adapt products and services to consumers.

The SRI International system—called VALS*—divides a population into eight segments according to resources and motivators. At the top of the economic heap are people with lots of resources—

---

*VALS is short for "values and lifestyles."

education, money, and opportunity. At the bottom are people with few resources. Within each resource level, people are motivated by various personality and psychological factors.

In a June 1996 survey of 1,700 U.S. households, SRI found that 18% of the U.S. population, or 33 million adult consumers, used the Web. They were highly educated, affluent, and under time pressure. There were more actualizers, achievers, and fulfilleds than the population at large among Web users. Actualizers are characterized as upscale, active, adventurous, and in the prime of life. But because they are under time pressure, they use the Web to become more productive. However, this segment was already approaching saturation by 1996. How much more revenue can be squeezed from them?

Achievers are stable, family-oriented, hardworking management or sales-oriented consumers. They represented the greatest uptick in growth in 1996. They were moving up from 20% of all Web users—representing the best place to target new users.

Fulfilleds were Web skeptics in 1996. They represent the kind of buyer who wants to know everything about a car before buying it. Fulfilleds are older, information-anxious consumers in the thirty-five to forty-five age group, who often find the Web frustrating and difficult to use. They were waiting for the market to mature. Products like Internet TV appeal to them.

The people in the other psychographic segments were left out as of 1996. They were the experiencers and strivers who do not have the resources—money or skills—to get plugged into the Wired World. It will be some time before they become netizens.

Figure 6-2 summarizes the marketing opportunity remaining to be addressed by merchants in the Wired World. It shows the ratio of Web users to the population as a whole in the United States in 1996. A ratio of 120%, for example, means that more actualizers use the Web than should for the number of actualizers in the overall population. Similarly, a negative ratio means fewer people in the psychographic category use the Web than overall. The negative ratio categories are where new customers will come from.

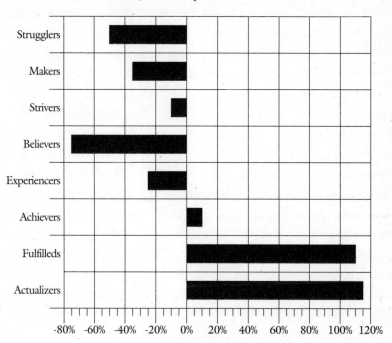

Ratio Web Users / U.S.A. Population

Figure 6–2. Psychographics of netizens of the Wired World in the United States.

PERSONALITY TRANSPLANTS

Products and services in the friction-free economy must have personality—that quality or look and feel that appeals to the Humano factor. Personality may be hard to define, but products that have it have market share.

Sales of typewriters peaked at $1.4 billion in 1988. By 1994 sales revenues had dropped to $500 million, and the possibility of extinction loomed large on the horizon. Still, it is curious that typewriter sales were greater than zero a decade into the PC era. When asked why she continues to use her 1920s vintage Remington, Elizabeth Stafford, twenty-six, says, "A typewriter is personal."[18] Personal products never die.

Typewriters are a throwback to an earlier era. They represent the retro nature of the friction-free economy. They also slam-dunk the importance of the PIC factor in the friction-free economy. No matter how sophisticated and technologically superior our products become, people want personal, individual, and customizable products and services.

The Wired World is about communities and one-on-one interactions. It is paving the cybermalls, and creating a new wired metropolis. Plug into www.bev.net/ and check out one such wired metropolis. Blacksburg, Virginia, is living in Internet Time and using technology to create community, called Blacksburg Electronic Village—BEV, for short. BEV plug-ins include the regional hospital, city library, restaurants and taverns, and 700 homes with ISDN connections. BEV's biggest problem is software support: "[T]he Presby-net lady grew frantic until the Blacksburg Electronic Village fixed a software problem that prohibited her from contacting church members electronically."[19] Even grandmothers are shopping in the Wired World. Why not—their market-of-one awaits them.

7

How to Kill
a Giant

THE VOICE OF GOD

I was in midsentence when the voice of IBM's president boomed into every office, lab, manufacturing cell, hallway, and restroom of the Boulder, Colorado, facility one fine morning in 1977. Everyone froze as the speaker blasted the Voice of God across the IBM empire. This is how news was delivered to the half-million employees of the megalithic giant of computing. The bad news mesmerized everyone. It also changed the course of computing.

IBM reigned supreme over computerdom as mainframes roamed the Fortune 1000 corporate landscape. Personal computers were considered mere hobby toys, and the Internet was but a gleam in a few visionary eyes—it would be two decades before it reached the mainstream. IBM was so powerful that the entire computer industry was referred to as "IBM and the seven dwarfs"— suggesting that only IBM registered on the industry's radar screen. IBM's leadership was exactly what the New Lanchester Strategy said it should be—74% market share. The game was over. The only trouble was, nobody told IBM's competitors.

The Voice of God spoke to everyone at IBM that day. It spoke the dreaded words of change. IBM's radical next-generation "801

Project" was dead. Employees were told that there would be no more leapfrogging innovation in the computer industry. Instead, the industry would gradually evolve along the master plan that IBM had charted two decades earlier. After all, IBM's plan had propelled it to the top. Why change? Why take a risk? Why render your own products obsolete when you don't have to?

BEFORE RADICAL WAS CHIC

Bruce Shriver, Wayne Anderson, and I trucked from the flatlands of Louisiana to the hills of Colorado each summer to lend IBM a hand. We figured even monopolies needed encouragement, cheerleading, perhaps adulation. Through brilliant lectures, insightful prognostications, and bad jokes, we cajoled career veterans of the mainframe maker into thinking radical product thoughts—like making IBM personal computers, entering consumer markets, and revisiting the fundamentals of computer architecture. We were bold, brash, and radical, relative to the staid, thin-tie-over-white-shirt IBMers. Who were these young Turks to tell the dominant force of free-world computing anything new?

Although we did not know it at the time, IBM was halfway through the 801 Project, a highly secret exercise. It was more radical than us bearded professors, because of its technology, and also because of its implications for the typical information technology organization. For one thing, it would have rendered IBM's market-dominating technology obsolete because it advocated a changeover from *Complex Instruction Set Computer* (CISC) architecture to *Reduced Instruction Set Computer* (RISC) architecture. None of IBM's existing software would run on the new RISC processors. For another thing, it advocated the elimination of far-flung computer operators, and centralized the management of computing around database servers. This idea preceded the maintenance-free NC (network computer) that Oracle, Sun, and IBM itself would praise two decades later as the savior of information management.

Project 801 was simply too risky. What if locked-in customers considered other vendors, because if they had to retrain people anyway, why not retrain them on someone else's equipment? What if customers refused to buy? Why take the chance?

IBM lived and died by Davidow's Law before Davidow discovered it.

Project 801 anticipated the future about fifteen years before it occurred. Most of what IBM's research engineers had expected actually happened. RISC processors are mainstreaming, and the client/server architecture is consuming information technology data centers. In hindsight, Project 801 was exactly the next big thing for IBM to do. Unfortunately, most of the ideas were exploited by IBM's competitors—not IBM.

IBM's 801 futuristic whiz-bang project was so grand that IBM couldn't bring itself to believe in it. The company's managers were not bold or brash enough to follow through on their own vision. As a consequence, IBM invited competitors to challenge its domination. In a near-textbook demonstration of the New Lanchester Strategy, IBM's lead began to erode as the rules of the game changed, but IBM did not. IBM's competitors entered niche markets that were poorly served by IBM, and then grew these niche markets into major industries.

Up until this point in history, IBM had been a risk-taking innovator. In the late 1950s it risked all to give birth to the System 360—the system of hardware and software that defined mainframe computing. But IBM's 1950s to 1960s high-stakes adventure paid off handsomely for the third-ranked accounting and tabulating machine company. IBM's innovative engineering and marketing of the 360 mainstreamed the entire company. Within a decade of unleashing the System 360 family of machines, IBM ranked number one in the world. Everyone else faded from the race. IBM was the god and goddess of computerdom.

Never before had any computer company taken on such a big development project. In fact, the software development effort for the System 360 was itself as big an undertaking as NASA's *Apollo* project for landing a man on the moon.

Only a risk-taking, innovative IBM would have attempted the System 360 project. Why was the 801 Project different? Maybe IBM's managers thought that once was enough. Maybe they thought the world would never change. In the 1960s, when radical was chic, IBM suddenly got cold feet. It lost its edge. It began a decade-long decline that resulted in its loss of leadership.

THE TIME SCALE OF DECLINE

IBM was a classical industrial age organization in the 1950s, 60s, and 70s. Top-down, button-down, and rigid in its 1950s style of management, the company naturally obeyed industrial age rules of decay. Meltdown took a long time. In 1960 the time scale of decay was measured in decades.

In fact, IBM began to fail in 1977, but the consequences of its decline did not show up on the balance sheet until a decade later. By the late 1980s the company was on the ropes. In 1987–88 its stock went from $160 to less than $50. The company was forced to lay off hundreds of thousands of workers, and its reputation as an industry leader was forever tarnished.

In the industrial age, companies took forever to fail. Premier companies went from leaders to laggards just like companies in previous eras, but it took decades. IBM was not the only famous company to experience this. Table 7-1 lists the top ten Silicon Valley companies in 1985 versus the top ten a decade later. Forty percent dropped out of the top ten. Worse still, more than 60% of the top 100 companies of 1985 disappeared from the list within a decade. Life was brief in the postindustrial-age jungle. Life is even more abbreviated for businesses that fail to master the fundamentals of the friction-free economy.

In the old economy, failure took a decade. In the friction-free economy, failure occurs in Internet Time. If a failing company does not turn around within eighteen months, it will become toast in twenty-four.

Company	1985 Sales ($B)	Company	1994 Sales ($B)
Hewlett-Packard	6.5	Hewlett-Packard	24.9
Apple Computer	1.9	Intel	11.5
Consolidated Freightways	1.8	Apple Computer	9.2
National Semiconductor	1.7	Sun Microsystems	4.7
Intel	1.4	Consolidated Freightways	4.7
Saga	1.3	Seagate Technology	3.5
Syntex	.98	Conner Peripherals	2.4
Varian Associates	.97	National Semiconductor	2.3
Advanced Micro	.86	Advanced Micro	2.1
Raychem	.68	Quantum	2.1

Table 7–1. Top ten Silicon Valley companies in 1985 and 1994.

LESS BUTT, MORE TEETH

One of my favorite advertisements promotes Cyberspace Public Relations. The flashy PR company uses an analogy with evolution to describe what happens when a business evolves from small start-up to megalith—and back down again. The friction-free economy is the age of *digital Darwinism*, according to CPR, and digital Darwinism can work in your favor as well as against you. CPR's notion of digital Darwinism goes something like this:*

---

*Darwin measured the passage of time in eons. His cousin, Digital, measures time in microseconds.

Young and aggressive businesses start out with a very low *teeth-to-butt ratio*. These young wolves aspire to become lions by chewing their way across the Chasm on the way to mainstreaming. Being of limited teeth, wolves hunt in packs and bring down their prey by outrunning and outnumbering them. They have less butt, and less teeth—not too much of either one—but they are on their way to getting more of both.

Lions, of course, have a perfect teeth-to-butt ratio, because they can both eat and run. They do not need to hunt in packs, occasionally taking down an antelope on their own, and so can afford to stay off of the savannah for a period of time without starving to death. The problem with lions is that they want to become elephants.

Elephants are big, smart, and capable of squashing the competition, when inclined. They are the real kings of the jungle, because they have it made. Unfortunately, elephants are vegetarians, they cannot move very fast, and they make big targets. Elephants are lion food.

This is the law of the jungle: Wolves work their way up the food chain through speed and numbers. Lions have a big bite and great speed, but they lust to become elephants. Elephants rule the jungle, but only for a time. The law of the jungle is to eat and be eaten. This cycle cannot be broken without smart management. And smart management has learned the lessons of the friction-free economy.

The answer, according to Cyberspace Public Relations, is for small companies to grow more teeth and large companies to go on a diet. Wolves need more teeth and elephants need less butt.

LESS TEK, MORE HP

Tektronix of Beaverton, Oregon, illustrates the law of the jungle. In 1980 Tektronix led its market segment, electronic test equipment, with sales of almost $3 billion. It was the big guy in its market segment. It had achieved the status of an elephant. Remarkable as it may be in hindsight, it was actually larger than competitor Hewlett-Packard—a company that is a legend today. What happened to this elephant?

Fifteen years later, HP has become a $30 billion company—ten times its former self—while Tektronix has struggled to remain in business. Tektronix became a helpless backwater company. The elephant was eaten by the lion. I doubt that many readers today even know what a Tektronix is. Hewlett-Packard, on the other hand, is a household word.

The reason? Too much butt and not enough teeth. Instead of retaining a sleek leonine silhouette, Tektronix morphed into a house pet. It is a sad example of what happens when management fails to understand the friction-free economy.

IBM, Tektronix, and many other companies have proven the truth of the New Lanchester Strategy: Once a company reaches a monopoly position, it is ripe for a downfall. Like an elephant in a jungle, monopolies become large, slow, and inviting targets for lions and wolves. The question for an elephant is, "How can I protect myself?" The question for a lion is, "Where can I find the tastiest meal?"

Strategy	Challenge	Some Methods
Brute Force Play	High Learning Rate	1. Beat price-learning curve (low risk) 2. Branding (low risk) 3. Tailoring (low risk) 4. Volume manufacture (low risk) 5. Execute Davidow's Law (medium risk)
Momentum Play	Gain Momentum	1. High, but not chaotic, learning (low risk) 2. Joint ventures, consortia (low risk) 3. Mergers & acquisitions (medium risk)
Anti-Monopoly Play	Kill a Giant	1. Change the rules (low risk) 2. Target the weak (low risk) 3. Lobby Congress (medium risk) 4. Litigate (medium risk) 5. Introduce chaos (high risk)
Pure Play	Consistent Execution	1. Hit shooting range targets (low risk) 2. Introduce chaotic fluctuations (high risk)

Table 7–2. Strategies for defeating a market-leading competitor.

BRUTE FORCE PLAY

Table 7-2 lists some strategies, and their methods, for displacing market leaders. Each strategy requires exquisite execution, of course. Assuming perfect execution, a challenger can be hugely successful—or a huge failure.

The *brute force play* is the most common method of winning in the friction-free economy. It requires very high learning rates, and perfect execution of the techniques repeated throughout this book, including both low- and medium-risk techniques.

Low-risk methods require rapid descent of the price-learning curve, use of branding, and tailoring of products through personalization, individualization, and customization. And of course, one mustn't forget to ride on the wings of inverse economics through volume manufacturing, or to apply Davidow's Law—or let Davidow's Law take its toll on competitors.

The brute force play is a favorite for any businesses. Consider the tale of two companies, where one business mainstreams its product faster than any other high-tech company in history. In this brute force play, one company kills a giant while the other misses an obvious opportunity.

A TALE OF TWO BUSINESSES

SyQuest and Iomega Corporation battled each other for many years during the 1980s. Both companies were innovators in removable disk drive technology. Users could eject a SyQuest or Iomega cartridge from their computers, throw it into a suitcase, and take it with them without sacrificing storage capacity for mobility. The $500 Bernoulli box made by Iomega, for example, held a hundred times as much data as a floppy but took up only four times as much space.

SyQuest was named after founder Syed Iftikar, who was no novice engineer. He had helped found Seagate Technology and designed many of Seagate's products. But when Seagate ignored the market potential of removable disk drives in 1982, Iftikar took his stock options, left Seagate, and began building removable drives for a niche market—the Apple Macintosh. Seagate expanded beyond the niche like any good business should, and by 1994 the company was the world leader in removable disk drives and cartridges for personal computers. SyQuest was the only elephant in the removable disk drive jungle.

Iomega had been founded a few years earlier to do the same thing. But unlike SyQuest, the Roy, Utah, company sank to the bottom of its niche market by 1993. Iomega lost $18 million, and sales were drying up like the Great Salt Lake. To make a short story even shorter, Iomega was a toothless wolf—all butt and no teeth. The company had to change, or prepare to be eaten by other wolves.

These two competitors worked in the backwoods of disk drive technology, so their products went largely unnoticed for a decade as attention was showered on floppy drives, CD-ROM drives, and tape backup systems. Even in good years, SyQuest and Iomega were not exactly trendsetters. Removable cartridge drives offering lots of storage capacity weren't exciting to consumers, and mainstream disk drive buyers didn't like the high price of these products.

For both companies it was the worst of times, and the best of times, because they would both see their roles reversed. In 1994 one company (SyQuest) was on top of the world and the other company (Iomega) was on the ropes. Within eighteen months SyQuest would take a nosedive, and Iomega would look like the next Microsoft.

NEGATIVE LEARNING

SyQuest began to fail as soon as it became the market leader. To add insult, SyQuest's failure occurred in the friction-free economy, where time passes in Internet years. Instead of taking a decade to fail, businesses in the friction-free economy fail in eighteen months. SyQuest's eighteen months began in 1994—just as it reached its peak. By 1996 SyQuest would report massive losses, and its rival,

Iomega, would report massive profits. In fact, Iomega would set the land speed record for double-time mainstreaming of a high-tech product.

The SyQuest versus Iomega saga demonstrates the effect of negative learning—the process of failing that occurs when a business learns too slowly to keep up with its industry. Negative learning is the flip side of Davidow's Law. It is what toppled IBM, Tektronix, and dozens of other victims.

ZIP'ITY DOO-DAH

After thirteen years of slow backwoods growth Iomega's sales were in such a steep decline that its very existence was threatened. Things got so bad that the company hired a new CEO in January 1994 to turn the starving wolf into a prowling lion. The hiring tactic worked. Things began to look up soon after marketing veteran Kim Edwards signed on as CEO.

Edwards previously had been at General Electric and battery maker Gates Energy Products. These were consumer product companies, not computer companies. They were also classical information age companies. Nonetheless, Edwards had learned the lessons of customer-driven learning. These lessons would be just what Iomega needed.

Edwards immediately recognized Iomega's need to learn more about its customers. So he brought Tim Hill into the company as vice president to find out what customers *really* wanted. Not only Iomega but the entire removable disk drive market needed to learn more about what motivated people to buy removable storage devices. Only after an analysis of customers' motivations could Iomega build a winning strategy.

The idea took root with Hill, who hired the Portland, Oregon, market research firm Market Strategies to help Iomega invent the removable disk market all over again. The company conducted 1,000 person-to-person interviews and held 100 focus group meetings to answer the question, "What do users really want in a data storage product?" The answer defined Iomega's turnaround product—the Zip drive.

Both SyQuest and Iomega had been locked into preconceived ideas of what a removable disk drive should be. Their preconceptions derived from Seagate's Winchester drive technology. It did not derive from customer needs. While SyQuest pursued technology that would advance Winchester technology, Iomega learned that customers could care less about advancing technology for technology's sake. What customers really wanted in a storage device was an easy-to-use, inexpensive way to transport their data. The fact that Iomega discovered this before SyQuest even asked the question is what led to Iomega's dominance in this market segment.

Iomega's $200 (100 MB) Zip drive became one of the hottest products in the history of high tech. It sold over 1 million units before its first anniversary, 2 million in fifteen months, and 3 million before its second anniversary. In addition, Iomega sold ten times as many cartridges as it did drives.

By comparison, sales of SyQuest's higher-priced, larger, and more limited EZ135 barely reached 80,000 units. Within only a few months of the introduction of Iomega's Zip drive, SyQuest was gasping for breath. Iomega was riding the crest of a mainstreaming wave that leveraged inverse economics to the hilt.

The Zip caught on because it offered a simple way to back up information stored on an internal Winchester disk, or to transfer massive files. And because Iomega created a marketing buzz around removable backup storage—historically a sleepy product category—their drives zipped to the top. Zip drives no longer tried to become removable Winchester drives. They became celebrities instead.

Iomega's Zip drives were touted to an audience that probably did not know what a removable drive was. The mainstream press— *USA Today*, *Business Week*, and most popular trade magazines— awarded best-product prizes to the Zip drive throughout 1995. Suddenly there was talk about Iomega as a standard setter. Iomega's stock soared from less than $5 to over $50. Simultaneously, SyQuest's stock plunged from $28 to $8. As sales reality and PR perception reversed, so did the fortunes of the companies.

In 1996 Iomega purchased a factory in Penang, Malaysia, to build its new $500 Jaz drive, which stores a billion characters on each removable disk cartridge costing $100. Zip and Jaz technology have become an industry. Most Iomega Zip drives are now made under contract by Seiko Epson, and many other companies are making Zip and Jaz drives under license from Iomega. Is there no end in sight?

When a business achieves a monopoly in its market space, it is susceptible to competition and decline. A negative learning curve always lurks in the shadows behind a market leader—even an occasional monopoly. Now that Iomega is the giant of its segment, it must continuously look over its shoulder for the next technological breakthrough that might reverse its fortunes. Could it be CD-RW?* Could it be the flash memory card?† Who knows what evil lurks in the shadows?

In early 1997 Iomega remained true to its new culture—it introduced an even smaller, cheaper, and more exciting miniature disk drive for network appliances. So far, Iomega's learning curve is positive. As long as the company can stay ahead of its competition, it will never succumb to a brute force play.

MOMENTUM PLAY

The fundamental idea underlying every *momentum play* is to accelerate past the competition by simply crushing them. This takes two

---

*CD-RW means Compact Disk-Read/Write. These are optical CD-ROM disks that can be used like magnetic disks—data can be recorded and played back. A 4.5 gigabyte CD-RW disk costs ten times less than a Zip cartridge and stores ten times as much data!

†Flash memory is like RAM—made from semiconductor material (transistors), but able to store data and hold on to it even when disconnected from a computer. Credit-card-sized flash cards can hold 16 MBits of data for about $500, but by the year 2000 the cost could be low enough to make flash cards an alternative to floppies.

things: speed and market share. A company can learn faster than the players, as Iomega did, or increase its momentum by joining up with other players. Joint ventures, standards consortia, mergers and acquisitions, and other ways of combining forces are used to execute a momentum play.

The best examples of momentum plays can be found in the struggle of anti-Microsoft companies against the software giant itself. This is a complex story of thrust, counterthrust, plot, counterplot, and outright mischief. It may not be pretty, but it is instructive.

In the following soap opera, you can watch Corel Corporation use high, but not chaotic, price-learning curves as a weapon against Microsoft's Office Suite product. You will observe Netscape, Sun Microsystems, Oracle, and other members of the software elite form consortia, joint ventures, and mergers to gain enough momentum to take on all of Microsoft. By 1997 the outcome was not clear as the skirmish continued. But the tactical plays of momentum-building consortia, joint ventures, and bold-faced public relations illustrate the point.

Momentum plays are big plays, typically involving clever strategy and skillful use of the press. Skirmishes seem to change the balance of power on a day-by-day basis, leaving customers confused and the players themselves in a tangle of relationships, contracts, and contradictory positions. The fog of war may be impenetrable even to the referees—often the antitrust department of the U.S. Department of Justice. Nonetheless, momentum plays are second only to brute force plays in popularity, perhaps because they require such diabolical thinking.

DRIVING MR. BILL

Larry Ellison, CEO of Oracle Systems, cuts a wide swath among the anti-Microsoft forces. Ellison is a proponent of resetting the computer industry, using non-Microsoft standards, non-Microsoft products, and anti-Microsoft rhetoric. His basic approach is to restart the entire computer industry from scratch. Eliminate the PC and you eliminate Microsoft. You see, in 1995–97 Ellison was in the midst of a Holy Jihad—a momentum play so grand that it thrust nearly the entire computer industry into upheaval.

Perhaps the mother of all momentum plays first occurred to Ellison when he and other executives from Silicon Valley escorted President Bill Clinton around on Net Day.* Semibearded Ellison, always perfectly dressed in a Grieves & Hawkes suit, may have felt a bit out of place with the left-leaning President on that muggy day when he suggested that the computer industry build a computer for everyone—a machine at one-tenth the cost of a PC. Such a machine would allow even ghetto schools to jack into the Wired World. No longer would the information age leave the poor and uneducated masses on the scrap heap of society. Rather, the $500 computer would liberate everyone, lift them into high-paying jobs, and get Mr. Bill re-elected.

Ellison's pitch struck a chord. "I proposed that the President challenge the computer industry to build a machine that would sell for no more than $500," recalls Ellison.[1] What a populist idea! The two men hit it off. Clinton invited Ellison to ride in the presidential limo to discuss the idea further—not just one geek's ride with Bill, but a giant ride for all geeks.

Two years earlier Ellison had secretly tried to buy Apple Computer—the whole company. Along with Philips Electronics, Samsung Electronics, and Michael Milken (yes, the infamous financier), Oracle offered $3 to $4 billion for the Apple of Steve Jobs's eye. Ellison planned to use Apple Computer technology to build the $500 consumer computer. Surely this would overthrow the Microsoft/Intel monopoly. Ellison was serious. He filed trademark papers on NC™, the Network Computer.

Maybe the limo ride with Mr. President energized Ellison, maybe not. Maybe the NC was a pipe dream, maybe not. But some-

---

*Net Day is a California thing. Everyone gets together one day per year to volunteer advice, donate equipment, and work like dogs to install Internet connections in schools.

thing drove him to pursue the idea against the advice of his lieu-
tenants. Whatever it was, it grew into an obsession—a rebellion that
became the industry rallying cry of a movement.

The momentum began to build as the rebellion spread. Then
one day, words that could not be spoken burst into headlines like an
E. coli epidemic. "It's my job to try to topple Microsoft," crowed
Ellison.[2] There it was. Someone had said it. No longer did the netizens of the Wired World have to whisper such heresy under their
breath. Heresy turned into controversy, controversy turned into
action.

DOG FOOD

Ellison became a media star when he declared "The PC is dead" in
a speech at a conference in Paris. The PC would be replaced by the
NC. The NC was cheaper, simpler, and easier to maintain. The PC
was a "ridiculous device," Ellison said later on.

These were fighting words. They had to be answered. Cameron
Myhrvold, vice president of Microsoft, followed Ellison to the
podium and called the NC a "dorky idea." Bill Gates took a poke at
Ellison's NC and roundly bashed the general idea. All in all,
Microsoft employees had a good time. (A year later, Microsoft
would join the movement and offer an NC with partner Intel—a
defensive move intended to *soak in* while deciding what to do
about the NC.)

Ellison was personally insulted by the Microsoft tribe. Rather
than get mad, he decided to get even. Returning to home base, he
promptly demanded that his team make the NC a reality. The battle lines were set. If Microsoft wanted war, it would get war. But it
would be a momentum war—one that Ellison of Oracle, Clark of
Netscape, Gerstner of IBM, and McNealy of Sun Microsystems dic-
tated. It would not be waged on Microsoft's playing field.

In 1996 the NC alliance became yet another branch of the anti-
Wintel gang: Oracle, Apple, IBM, Sun, and Netscape were charter
members. They set ambitious goals for themselves. First, a refer-

ence design was openly shown to anyone who might want to build boxes. This was intended to break the Wintel stranglehold on hardware. Next, a software platform was quickly pieced together that blatantly excluded Microsoft operating systems, languages, and applications. This was designed to break the Wintel lock-in held by Microsoft.

Nineteen ninety-seven was targeted as the big launch year. Sun, Oracle, and others would flood the market with announcements—indeed, a rash of announcements. These anti-Microsoft giant-killers had to build momentum. They had to learn faster and drive the prices down so low that Wintel could not compete. They had to work together to change the formula that Intel and Microsoft had so carefully crafted over the previous fifteen years.

The payoff would be big. By the year 2000 they expected to own 20% of the world PC market. Instead of buying Wintel PCs, 20% of the 200 million PC owners would purchase NCs. They would access Internets and Intranets using Netscape Web browsers running on non-Wintel platforms. The NC, and other appliance computers, would muscle their way past Wintel in about ten years, and that would put an end to Microsoft.

As Lou Gerstner, president of IBM, said a few months into the momentum play, "One of the ways we're telling if we're on track is are the dogs eating the dog food."[3] Nobody is sure whether he was referring to customers or partners, but the industry suddenly became energized by Ellison's idea. Maybe it was possible to topple Microsoft and Intel after all. This question, and the nagging thought that Gerstner had mixed his metaphors, provided work for computer industry reporters well into the spring of 1997.

INVASION OF THE PC MUTANTS

To gain the upper hand in a momentum play, a competitor must first kill the other company's momentum. Rather than overtake a speeding bullet, might it be easier to erect a brick wall in front of the bullet? With Microsoft stopped in its tracks for a short period, perhaps everyone would have a chance to pick themselves up and start at the beginning of a new race.

Therefore, an important strategy for a momentum player is to change the rules. A new set of rules might act like a brick wall and stop Microsoft in its tracks—for a time. Then, if Microsoft had to play by different rules, everyone could embark on a new learning curve together.

Old-timers like Ellison had seen Darwinism work before— dinosaur mainframes died off when fleet-of-foot PC mutants entered the food chain. Why not knock off PCs with something even smaller, cheaper, faster, and simpler? The NC was designed to render PCs obsolete, just as PCs had rendered IBM mainframes obsolete. The PC mutant would be killed off by another muta-tion—the NC.

Again, Lou Gerstner said it best: "One player who doesn't like the set of outcomes" might be left behind if the rules suddenly change.[4] Other netizens, such as Netscape's CEO James Barksdale, soon began to put an anti-Microsoft spin on the sea change brought on by the NC. Netscape's part would be to paint Microsoft products as proprietary, closed solutions. According to Barksdale, Microsoft software is "like a houseboat—it ain't a great house, and it ain't a good boat."[5] This was supposed to scare off customers.

The invasion of the mutants picked up more supporters as 1996 ended. Going into 1997, the NC looked like a mainstream prod-uct. But Microsoft and Intel still held on to their monopolies. The scare tactic was not working. Momentum was not building in favor of the anti-Microsoft forces.

PREDATORY PRICING

Predatory pricing got John D. Rockefeller into trouble when he used it to grow Standard Oil into a monopoly. It almost worked until muckraker Ida Tarbell demonstrated how Rockefeller and the Standard Oil company had driven her brother's employer out of the petroleum business by lowering prices to eliminate competition.

Selling product below cost destroyed Standard Oil's competitors—a technique that was subsequently outlawed by the U.S. government. After the competition had died off, Standard Oil would raise prices so that it could reap huge profits as a monopoly.

Enter the friction-free economy. Predatory pricing, in the form of free software delivered over the Web, is in full force. Only this time, the outmoded, sluggish industrial age legal system is not up to the task of regulating monopolies. Without an effective deterrent, software companies can get away with almost anything.* Might predatory pricing be a good game plan for momentum players?

As Jean Belanger, CEO of Metrowerks Inc., said in reference to the Wintel monopoly, "The critical factor for success in beating dominant market players is attacking their monopolistic cash flow, not their position in business."[6] What Belanger meant was that an army can be defeated by wiping out its supply lines. It was not necessary—in fact, it was suicide—to attempt to destroy the opponent's guns. Microsoft simply had too many guns in 1996 to attempt a frontal attack. So the anti-Wintel predators set about to kill a giant by starving it to death. And what better way to cut off its food supply than to give away competing products?

Change the rules and cut off supplies. That was the plan of attack in late 1996. Exactly how could this be done? First, by rendering Microsoft's operating systems inconsequential. In 1996 Microsoft operating systems accounted for 60% of the company's $8 billion revenue. Netscape, Sun, and others took on the task of reducing the importance of Windows 95 and Windows NT. They would do this with a browser that worked on anything, and a programming language that ran on anything.

The next step toward moving the platform from Windows to HTML/HTTP and the Internet would be to render Microsoft operating systems completely inconsequential. If these contrarians had their way, the Internet—and its standards—would become the

---

*Well, not quite anything. A predatory business must still show that some form of competition remains, even if it is only an irritant.

platform of choice for developers, instead of the Wintel platform.

Sun Microsystems president and CEO Scott McNealy announced that the Sun NC—JavaStations—would not run Microsoft software. When the new product was unveiled in October 1996, he suggested that JavaStations might even be given away with every purchase of a Sun server. Score another point for the predators.

The momentum play would not become a major force in the computer industry until 1997, however, when Microsoft's supply lines came under direct attack. To strike at the heart of the Empire, it would be necessary to dive deeper into the depths of technology.

THE AUTO-OIL EMPIRE OF WINTEL

What exactly did Microsoft and Intel have that held such a lock on the computer industry? It was Microsoft's API (Application Program Interface) and Intel's microprocessor. In simple terms, Microsoft's software and Intel's hardware grip on the computer industry created a lock that might be compared with an auto-oil empire consisting of all automobile and petroleum companies of the world rolled into one giant company.

THE HARDWARE MONOPOLY

The resounding success of the original IBM PC had been only a short-term victory for IBM, because the simplicity of the machine soon allowed other manufacturers to make exact duplicates. The IBM PC design, and hence IBM's PC business, soon escaped from IBM's control. All anyone needed to clone the design was an Intel microprocessor and the boldness of a wolf pack, and they were in business. IBM was left with virtually no advantage over competitors while clone manufacturers like Compaq became wildly successful selling "IBM PCs."

IBM may have lost its monopoly, but Intel continued to gain new customers. Each time a clone manufacturer opened shop, Intel gained a bigger piece of the pie. Intel locked in 80% of the industry.

Intel may have become the first accidental monopoly in the universe soon after IBM selected its x86 processor in 1981 for its IBM PC.

IBM may have been slow to respond, but in the early 1990s the company started its comeback. IBM executives completed a deal to supply disk drives to traditional rival Apple Computer. If IBM and Apple could cooperate on disk drives, why not cooperate in other areas? The two companies decided to cook up a challenge to Intel. If IBM could make processors that outperformed Intel chips, Apple would be mighty interested.

Apple would need millions of chips, so a second source of supply was required. The largest surviving chip manufacturers after a decade-long war with the Japanese semiconductor manufacturers were Motorola and Intel. But Intel was the enemy, so Motorola was invited to the party. With IBM, Motorola, and Apple combined, it might be possible to make a second run against Intel. The PowerPC product line and the PowerPC consortium were born.

The PowerPC consortium would have to pull out all stops in order to compete with Intel. Their technology would have to leapfrog the leader. It would have to use an academically interesting, but untried, RISC technology, which could reset the entire semiconductor industry by breaking the Intel monopoly on processors.

Twenty years after Project 801 was canceled, IBM, Motorola, and Apple Computer rejuvenated the radical idea of purposely obsolescing their own older CISC designs, replacing them with the PowerPC RISC chip. Rather than let Intel take over their customers, the PowerPC consortium would hit and run—obsolesce their installed base, but quickly provide an alternate solution before Intel could react.

When the PowerPC came out, and Apple Computer began shipping them inside of millions of Macintosh computers, Intel reacted like a wounded animal. It fought hard to preserve its lock-in. The company changed its schedule of new product releases. It modified prices to herd its customers into next-generation chips at critical moments. It used hand-to-hand combat marketing techniques to blunt the PowerPC consortium.

At the same time, the PowerPC consortium fell behind schedule. It looked for a while like Motorola and IBM were on a negative learning curve. The partners did not deliver on optimistic predictions of high speed and low cost. While they understood the rules, they could not play by them as well as Intel. After a few years it became obvious that Intel still ruled Silicon Valley. The PowerPC consortium had stalled, at least for the time being.

THE SOFTWARE MONOPOLY

By 1994 the Microsoft API had been practically memorized by all software developers, because it was essential to making an application program run on various Microsoft operating systems. This API defined the parts of the operating system used by programmers to write application programs (e.g., menus, windows, forms, and character fonts). The Windows API had lock-in. Without it, programs could not run on most of the world's computers. Software developers fed Microsoft more elephant food each time they developed software for Microsoft operating systems. And the elephant grew.

By 1995 Microsoft's software monopoly was complete. The company had the largest share of almost every market segment it entered. It began throwing its weight around, telling standards groups what to do, and acting like an industry-leading business. But not everyone appreciated the company's leadership. In fact, some claimed that its domination of the industry was dangerous. It was alarming, they said. Yet, there was little that anyone could do. Then Java came along.

JAVA GROUPIES UNITE!

Java is merely a language. But it took on the quality of a religion as soon as people realized that it might be a weapon against Microsoft and Intel. In many minds, Java was a Wintel killer. The reason: Java programs could theoretically run on anything, so it promised to render particular operating systems and microprocessors irrelevant. "We don't think about the Mac or Windows platform; we think about the Java platform, and so the number of potential users is enormous," said Karl Jacob, founder and president of DimensionX, a San Francisco software company.[7]

Java groupies were energized in late 1996, when Java product development was starting to lag. Venture capitalists Kleiner Perkins Caufield & Byers raised $100 million and signed up ten major anti-Microsoft companies to form the Java Fund to help start-up companies develop products based on Java. "It's a tremendous validation of Java as a platform," said Kim Polese, CEO of Marimba Inc., after cashing her check for $4 million from the fund. Marimba was founded by Polese and Arthur van Hoff, two developers who had worked on the creation of the Java language while ensconced in SunLabs.

The Java Fund includes only ten of the forty-seven early licensees of Java. Microsoft, of course, is not a member, even though it licensed Java as part of its "embrace and extend" strategy. These companies might be considered hard-core netheads, but they were most likely interested in making a significantly high return on investment. Java companies were a hot investment.

Why are Java Fund companies betting against Microsoft? According to venture capitalist Roger McNamee, Microsoft cannot sustain a $6 to $10 billion enterprise on revenues derived from a saturated operating systems and office suite market. "The ability of Microsoft and Intel to dominate the agenda of our industry may be peaking," says McNamee, who is a partner in Interval Capital Partners.[8] In order to grow, Microsoft must enter some other market. The only ones big enough to generate $6 to $10 billion are Internets and Intranets. And as everyone knows, Intranets—the application of Internet technology to internal networking of corporations—are far more lucrative than Internets—the consumer publishing half of the Wired World. Therefore, Microsoft must compete on the Intranet battlefield. And Intranets require Java.

ANTIMONOPOLY PLAY

Litigation is a valid ploy in any anti-Monopoly play (see Table 7-2). In fact, litigation is almost a necessary sideshow, intended to distract the prey, but never seriously considered a contest-deciding blow. After all, the industrial age legal system is virtually ineffective in the friction-free economy. Still, Netscape Communications played this card in 1996 when it realized that Microsoft's competitor to Netscape Navigator—Internet Explorer—was about to run Netscape's browser business out of town.

Netscape's 83% market share of the browser segment irritated Microsoft so much that the Redmond, Washington, megalomaniac began targeting Netscape. In 1996 and 1997 it appeared that Microsoft was willing to do almost anything to gain back the initiative it had lost when the rise of the Internet occurred without its permission. Microsoft started its attack by giving away its Internet Explorer browser and radically decreasing the price of its server. On July 30, 1996, Microsoft formally asked Netscape to "cease and desist" promoting its Web server software for use on Microsoft's Windows NT workstation product. Then, on August 13, 1996, Microsoft announced agreements with the top seven Web sites and offered them incentives to use Microsoft's browser instead of Netscape's. Microsoft went further. It made allegedly illegal deals with AT&T, America Online, and many PC manufacturers—deals that these companies could not refuse.

Netscape filed papers with the U.S. Department of Justice to halt Microsoft's alleged predatory pricing and bundling practices. Netscape accused Microsoft of twisting its licensees' arms and its other value-added resellers' body parts to coerce them into selling Internet Explorer instead of Netscape Navigator. Gary Reback, Netscape's counsel, charged that Microsoft offered clandestine payments, discounts, and other financial favors to companies that stopped selling Navigator and started selling Explorer. He said, "Microsoft tactics include manipulating the disclosure of APIs, and the bundling of products such as FrontPage, Internet Explorer, and Microsoft's

Internet Server with Microsoft's monopoly operating systems."[9]

In a return salvo, Microsoft replied that vendors were free to ship any software they chose and to place icons for non-Windows software on the Windows 95 screen. "Microsoft doesn't do anything Netscape doesn't do in rewarding providers that lead new customers to its browsers," said a statement issued by Microsoft.[10]

In this case, Netscape was David and Microsoft was Goliath. Microsoft knows that it is possible to kill a giant through an anti-monopoly play. Both competitors take litigation seriously. Like two alley cats fighting in the night, Netscape and Microsoft each defended their territory. What does Netscape have to lose, and what does Microsoft have to gain?

Clearly, Netscape Communications could lose its life. This was a struggle for survival by Netscape, whose revenues amounted to petty cash when compared to Microsoft's cash flow. Microsoft struck at the heart of Netscape's supply lines—its browser business.

By the year 2000 the market for browsers could reach an installed base of 300 million.* At $35 each, this constitutes $10 billion in business—more money than Microsoft makes each year selling all of its applications software combined. Add to this the $250 each for the 50 million servers needed to complement browsers, and Microsoft's coffers could swell by another $12.5 billion. This would once again double Microsoft's application software revenues.

It appeared that Microsoft was winning the browser wars in late 1996. Realizing this, Netscape responded by shifting its emphasis from the client to the server, and moving from desktop to the enterprise market space. "Netscape will have to rely on server software for a growing percentage of both its revenues and profits," said a report from Summit Strategies Inc.[11]

The antimonopoly play by Netscape failed to kill a giant. It rarely does. Competitors in the friction-free economy must rely

---

*Of course, Microsoft's operating systems sell in the millions of units. But Microsoft's best-selling application, Office, only had 22 million users when this was written.

instead on more substantial methods. They must find the Achilles' heel of the giant.

Litigation is ineffective for anything other than slowing down a competitor in the friction-free economy. It won't kill a giant.

THE PURE PLAY

Consistent execution of a pure play strategy is perhaps the best defense for a market leader like Microsoft. In this approach, company managers have a clear vision of where they are going, what the objectives are, and how to hit their targets. There are two variations of the pure play: finding a shooting range and taking aim, and introducing chaotic fluctuations into the market space. The first approach is much safer and typically used by large companies, while the second is very risky and therefore a strategy of the weak. When a company has little to lose, it can risk a lot.

Microsoft is obviously a master of the low-risk pure play. It has demonstrated a keen ability to respond to challenges to its market leadership. In effect, Microsoft is a dancing elephant that has been picking up loose change left lying on the dance floor. Capitalism may abhor a (Microsoft) monopoly, but it also abhors a vacuum. Microsoft has successfully filled many empty spaces left unprotected by its competitors.

CAPITALISM ABHORS A VACUUM

Microserf* Russ Siegelman convinced Bill Gates that Microsoft should build its own on-line service.[12] It would be called MSN—Microsoft Network—and blow away America Online, Prodigy, and CompuServe. Bolstered with a big wad of money and Bill Gates's

---

*Microserf is the name given to Microsoft employees who till the digital vineyards and sit behind plowing workstations.

blessing, Siegelman set out to construct a proprietary on-line service and fill the vacuum.

About the same time, other microserfs within the Redmond, Washington, company touted the Internet as the way to go. Proprietary products were a bad idea, they protested. To them it was obvious that the global Internet was where the action was. But Microsoft's management was oblivious to the rapid mainstreaming of the Web that gathered steam in 1993. Bill Gates himself reportedly called one microserf a communist for suggesting that Microsoft give away its Internet Explorer browser over the Internet.

A year later the Microsoft Network was dead, and Microsoft was struggling to catch Netscape and others in a race to dominate the Wired World. This slight hesitation in 1993 cost Microsoft the leadership position in the Internet browser boom that swept the industry in 1995–96. If Gates had not tried to fill the on-line services vacuum with his own MSN, perhaps he would have immediately achieved a dominant position in the Internet market space. Instead, Gates found his company playing catch-up.

The MSN failure taught Microsoft a lesson. Look before you leap. In fact, the MSN debacle honed the company's wits and sharpened its competitiveness. It would be the only mistake the company would make as it adopted a pure play strategy that would foil many thrusts of the anti-Microsoft forces.

MICROSOFT'S ACHILLES' HEEL

No matter how hard they tried, Microsoft's challengers failed to slow the juggernaut into 1997. Microsoft's revenues continued to climb even though the rate of increase slowed throughout the 1990s. By 1996 quarterly revenues were running in excess of $2.2 billion. Any business that grows at the rate of 25% to 35% per year on a base of $8 billion has a right to be feared.

In fact, Microsoft is in good shape. But there were indications that the company was becoming weaker as far back as 1996. Microsoft began to look more and more vulnerable as its products became more dominant. And its domination was fragile mostly because its product line became overly concentrated. By 1995 it was almost a two-product company—operating systems and Microsoft Office—its cash cows and its Achilles' heel, respectively.

The task of crimping Microsoft's supply lines was made much easier because of this concentration. Another anti-Microsoft strategy soon emerged: Replace Microsoft Office with something that was much simpler and yet could run on everything. This new attack could bring the company to its financial knees, reset the entire industry, and save capitalism for the whole world. Could it work? Several challengers rose to the occasion.

But Microsoft could not be toppled by a well-known company like Sun, Oracle, IBM, or Netscape. No, many had tried and failed. If there was ever going to be a Late, Great Microsoft, it would require a David. The most likely David to Microsoft's Goliath had to be a small, aggressive, little-known company with a flamboyant CEO. Such a company would have little to lose, and much to gain, if it could stop a company as famous as Microsoft.

BRAVEHEART

A small company in Canada was attracted by the vulnerability of Microsoft's application suite. Corel of Ottawa took it upon itself to singlehandedly defeat Microsoft. It fit the role perfectly. It was small, aggressive, and unknown. It had a daring CEO. It could only win—even if it lost.

Corel devised a one-two punch to take out Microsoft Office. It went something like this:

- Buy WordPerfect from Novell, add the Quattro Pro spreadsheet, Corel's drawing program, Borland's Paradox database program, bundle it with Netscape Navigator, and sell it cheap.

- Rewrite everything in platform-independent Java, flood the Internet with it, and again, lowball the price so that buyers have to think twice before they spend much more on Microsoft Office.

In late 1996 Corel started rolling out its product and strategy. Step one was doing very well, with Corel PerfectOffice outselling Microsoft Office 50% versus 45% in the retail distribution channel. The Corel product packed a punch. It included 5,400 clip-art images, 200 photos, 67 sounds, 187 textures, and 150 type fonts, in addition to the PerfectOffice main course.

Corel pushed even harder. It forged bundling deals with hardware and software developers. It was reported that Corel bundled PerfectOffice for $10 per copy—less in some cases. Packard Bell agreed to ship 6 million copies with its computers. "Corel has been pretty aggressive at retail and accomplished what they set out to do," said Jeff Silverstein, editor of *Software Industry Bulletin* of Stamford, Connecticut. In one fast quarter, Corel Office doubled its market share, and started its journey up the mainstreaming curve.

Microsoft was stunned, and forced to fight fire with fire.[13] Microsoft quickly bundled Office through hardware deals just like the ones made by Corel. In response to the Corel–Packard Bell bundling deal, Microsoft turned to old rival Apple Computer to test the idea of bundling Microsoft Office for the first time in history. In 1997 Power Macs were sold in Europe with a copy of Microsoft Office preinstalled on their disks. The company even threw in WordArt—a competitor to CorelDRAW—to sweeten the deal. "To prevent further erosion of its dominant share, Microsoft will add WordArt, a drawing package, to Office 97." Microsoft's vice president Steve Ballmer was reportedly breathing heavily and heard saying in a muffled voice, "We're gonna get Corel."[14]

Corel's strategy introduced chaos into the Office market segment by dramatically lowering the price of its high-quality product and then targeting a narrow segment of the distribution channel—retail. Thus Corel has adopted a high-risk pure play. Only a small, aggressive company run by a brash CEO would attempt to kill a giant using this approach.

The waves of this chaos might quickly reach the shores of Lake Washington (Microsoft is near this lake) and induce instability in Microsoft's monopoly. If it does, it will be another demonstration of mathematical chaos in action. If it does not, Corel will simply be yet another bug that Microsoft stepped on en route to conquest.

Corel is the only Braveheart to attempt such a high-risk strategy. What kind of an upstart is this company? Who is its flamboyant CEO?

POSTER BOY IN OREM

Fast-talking, fast-walking, and fast-traveling Michael Cowpland became the poster boy of Orem, Utah, when his company saved Novell's WordPerfect division from extinction at the hands of Microsoft. On a snowy day in January 1996, Cowpland and several other executives from Corel rode into town to boost the spirits of WordPerfect employees, who listened to their new boss speak in the company cafeteria. Corel had just paid $170 million for WordPerfect—down from $1 billion paid by Novell just two years earlier. At least someone came to WordPerfect's rescue. But what was Corel going to do with the world's second most popular word processor? Understandably, WordPerfect employees were a bit worried.

"Standing at a makeshift podium in the cafeteria, Cowpland, president and CEO, looked pleased with himself and his shiny, new WordPerfect. A consummate showman, he oozed confidence, predicting that under Corel's care, WordPerfect would capture a staggering 50% of the office suite market within three years, up from around 5% at the time of the acquisition. There is nothing, according to Cowpland's merchandising ethos, that cannot be recycled, repackaged, and tossed back onto the market," wrote software analyst Paul Kedrosky.[15] This ethos permeates Corel, and now it would permeate WordPerfect.

WordPerfect had fallen a long way from being the number one word-processing vendor in the world. But would the brash CEO help or hurt the culturally sedate WordPerfect? The Utah company had deep roots in the Mormon community and Cowpland's roots were peroxide. Not exactly a perfect match. Cultural mismatches are not uncommon in mergers and acquisitions, but the marriage of Corel with WordPerfect stretches the limits. In fact, the acquisition was considered incendiary by the pundits in 1996. For one thing, WordPerfect is not exactly a braveheart. For another thing, Corel is not exactly a faintheart. Cowpland's platinum-blond wife Marilyn owns a clothing store and gets publicity the Hollywood way—by posing in a tight red Spandex Santa-suit for the cover of *Ottawa Magazine.* Her Porsche is pink and his is silver. The neighborhood went downhill, according to the local press, when the couple tore down a quaint brick Victorian and built a gaudy 20,000-square-foot mansion in its place—in the oldest and most expensive suburb of Ottawa. Good taste is not part of Corel's culture; it surely won't become part of WordPerfect's.

Cowpland, born in England, was educated in electrical engineering. He first formed Mike and Terry's Lawnmowers—Mitel, for short—to manufacture PBX switches with partner Terry Matthews. Mitel sales reached $500 million by the late 1970s. Cashing out and moving on, Cowpland looked for bigger fish to fry.

Corel's strategy is a mixture of brute force and pure play. It lowballs prices, and turns over revisions on a short cycle. "Corel then sets prices as low as half of the competitors, bundling CorelDRAW with a boatload of extras. Then, rather than retiring old product versions when new ones arrive, Cowpland leaves them on the market and discounts them further, creating instant product families. Corel completes the merchandising mix by hitting the trade media with a wave of vertiginously garish advertising."[16]

Corel's strategy is based on jolting the dug-in market segment dominated by Microsoft. Sudden changes in market share could cause ripples. Vendors might cut and run from the Microsoft fold. Look at Packard Bell. Others will follow.

The question lingers: Can Corel kill the Microsoft giant? In 1996 Corel was the fastest-growing company in the software industry's top ten. Figure 7-1(a) contrasts forecasts of CorelDRAW market share (in the graphics segment) with annual growth rates of all of Microsoft. Figure 7-1(b) forecasts sales revenues of the two companies based on mainstreaming curves, but using revenue growth rate estimates. Draw your own conclusions.

THE WHOLE COW

Corel's PerfectOffice jolt was just for openers. PerfectOffice warmed up retailers, but Cowpland knew that he had to bomb Microsoft's supply lines—Fortune 1000 corporations. The IT (Information Technology) managers of big companies don't buy their cereal in a box—they order directly from Kellogg. So Cowpland's next move was aimed at the big corporate buyer: the 1997 launching of Office for Java.

Office for Java was designed to convince IT managers to jump the Microsoft mother ship once and for all. Because Java runs on everything, Office for Java runs on everything. "When IT managers go to resellers they are given a clear choice: either buy a package of programs that run on one type of machine or buy programs that run everywhere," says Amy Wohl, editor of *TrendsLetter*, a computer industry report.[17]

Will the Java jolt pry IT managers away from comfortable Microsoft Office? After all, nobody fires an IT manager for buying Microsoft products. If a manager is going to risk his or her job, then Office for Java had better offer a significant improvement over Microsoft Office.

To get a foot in the door, Corel had to move PerfectOffice through the distribution channel. So much for Corel's razor blades. But to keep up the momentum, Corel had to start selling the razors. Office for Java is Corel's razor.

Corel, along with nearly everyone in the anti-Microsoft camp, is betting that buyers no longer want the whole cow when they can get by with just part of it. According to W. D. Riley, "The time when a big corporation can sell you an expensive monster application just so you can do mailing labels is almost over. Applications are getting so big that we have to develop new operating systems without conventional memory just to run them. Take Microsoft Office, for example. A nice piece of software, but it's about a zillion times more stuff than most people ever need."[18]

Contrast Microsoft Office with Office for Java. Corel's product runs from a server. It does not need to be installed on individual machines. Instead, pieces of it are downloaded as needed, used, and then erased from the desktop machine. This simplifies maintenance, upgrades, and training. It might also take a big bite out of Microsoft Office sales. "Microsoft is doing a great job of adding value to Office, but they are at risk of losing market share if they continue to develop a fat client," said Eric Brown of Forrester Research—a market research firm.[19]

Figure 7–1. Comparison of Corel Corp. with Microsoft Corp. (a). Market share growth of CorelDraw and year-to-year change in total revenues of Microsoft. (b). Revenue growth curves for Microsoft's Office division versus all of Corel.

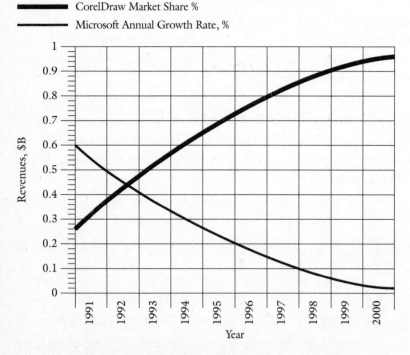

(a). Corel's drawing product CorelDraw is expected to gain market share while the growth rate of Microsoft (measured in terms of change in total revenues) is expected to slow.

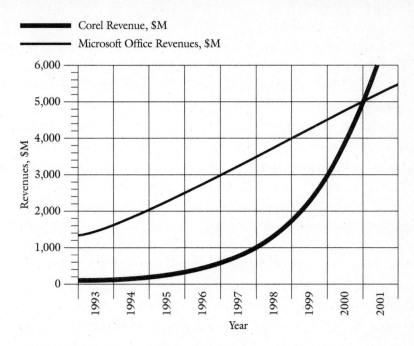

━━━━━━ Corel Revenue, $M

────── Microsoft Office Revenues, $M

(b). **Projected revenues of Corel WordPerfect versus Microsoft's Offiice product, based on Corel's early retail channel sales in 1996.**

The Wintel foes wanted to reset the industry. Corel wanted to reset the Office suite segment of the industry. This was a perfect marriage.

WILLIE SUTTON OF SOFTWARE

Has any company ever beaten Microsoft? Intuit has. The Palo Alto company was a Microsoft buyout target in 1994, barely escaping capture when the U.S. Department of Justice frowned on the acquisition idea. Intuit makes Quicken, the world's most popular personal finance software product, used by 10 million people and thousands of banks.

Perhaps Microsoft could not bear to be a distant second in this race. Or maybe it was simply the money. When Willie Sutton was asked why he robbed banks, he explained, "Because that is where the money is." Microsoft's competing product, Money, wasn't where the money was. Quicken was.

Intuit was the first truly consumer-oriented software company. Its business goal has always been to make consumers happy. When Microsoft ran into competition from Quicken, it simply could not cut it. But Microsoft liked Intuit's cash flow so much, it tried to buy the competition.

After the acquisition floundered, Intuit continued on as a profitable but troubled independent company. However, it may be the only company to stand up to Microsoft and live to talk about it. Years later, Intuit's 10 million customers amount to 80% of the personal finance market—Microsoft Money could claim only 17%.

Yet, Microsoft has not given up. Intuit executives must watch their flank as Microsoft continues a low-level attack on the company. After launching version 7.0 of Quicken early in 1997, Intuit complained that Microsoft rumormongers were spreading "not too cool misinformation" about Quicken users. According to Intuit, Microsoft claimed that Quicken users were switching to Microsoft Money, suggesting that the Quicken faithful would soon be orphans. So Intuit sent copies of Money to fifty of its own Quicken users to see how tempted they might be. Nobody wanted to switch.

Intuit beat Microsoft the old-fashioned way—it simply had a better product. It delivered value and service with dignity and a minimum of hype that is rare in the friction-free economy. Maybe Intuit will never become the next Microsoft, but this little company in a residential section of Palo Alto outclassed big and brash Microsoft. Intuit scores 100 points for style.

AN ENEMY OF MINE IS A FRIEND

The computer industry entered a new phase in 1997 when the network computer, network appliance, and Internet TV were introduced. These devices challenge the industry status quo, because they are an order of magnitude cheaper, and in some cases an order of magnitude more powerful, than their predecessors. Price-learning curves that plunge prices by a factor of ten almost always cause revolutions. Thus, 1997 marked the beginning of yet another revolution in the friction-free economy.

Microsoft has somehow achieved the status of industry nemesis in this revolution. Perhaps it deserves this label, perhaps not. But one thing is clear: Microsoft has created an environment where competitors have banded together to ward off monopolistic behavior on the part of Microsoft. The computer industry chant seems to be, "An enemy of my enemy is my friend."

The anti-Microsoft portion of the software industry is an example of the enemy-of-my-enemy groupings that have led to flights of fantasy over who will destroy the giant Microsoft. These anybody-but-Microsoft competitors—Sun, Oracle, Apple, IBM, Netscape, and Novell—have spun a web of partnerships, consortia, and forums pitted against the Wintel monopoly. In one fantasy scenario, IBM beats Microsoft by purchasing just about everyone left in the industry. According to J. Gerry Purdy, editor of *Mobile Letter* in Cupertino, California, IBM should buy Lotus (done—for Notes), Novell (for networking), and Apple Computer (for the MacOS).[20] This would give IBM enough technology and market presence to topple the Wintel monopoly. Stranger things have happened in the friction-free economy.

THE LATE GREAT MICROSOFT

Microsoft is a well-known success story. It has captured the imagination of entrepreneurs everywhere, and made Bill Gates rich and famous. But the company is not invincible. In fact, it is not even the largest software company. In 1996 IBM's software division generated about 50% more revenue than all of Microsoft. IBM's research bill is more than Microsoft's annual revenue. Even so, Microsoft is perceived as the king of the jungle.

It is not easy to kill a giant. It takes strategy, determination, hard work, and probably a lot of luck. Even then the outcome is not predictable. In the rapidly changing environment that every business competes in, it is not inconceivable that elephantine companies will fail while wolves and lions rise to positions of domination. It is not inconceivable that the law of the jungle will be obeyed.

8

Surviving and Thriving in the Friction-Free Economy

DRINK PEPSI, GET SOFTWARE

USA Today, the nationally distributed newspaper started in 1982, did not reach its break-even point until 1996. The Wired World equivalent, *USA Today Online*, became profitable in a matter of months—nearly ten times as fast as its printed version. This illustrates a fundamental principle of surviving the friction-free economy: Things happen fast.

The face of business will look very different in the friction-free economy. The postindustrial age is dying, and the friction-free economy of the software age is blossoming. The final years of the twentieth century find us in between these two major eras. Sometimes postindustrial rules govern, while other times the friction-free economy rules. Strange things are happening to businesses.

For example, in late 1996 Microsoft and Pepsi-Cola Bottling Company together spent $20 million to convince consumers to drink Pepsi and get software. This would have been an extremely unlikely alliance in any other era. But in the friction-free economy, such alliances make perfect sense. Microsoft wants to become mainstream, and Pepsi wants to become hip. They both want brand recognition. Ruthann Lorentzen, director of marketing at Microsoft, said, "Because the personal computer was becoming more of a mainstream household appliance, it made more sense for high-technology companies to do joint promotions with leading consumer brands."[1]

Pepsi and Microsoft conspired in 1996 to further carve their brands into the consciousness of consumers, leverage their partnership, and increase sales, by plastering 200 million cans with images of animated characters taken from a Microsoft CD-ROM series. In return, Pepsi's Web page (www.pepsi.com) hosts a sweepstakes raffle, and lets consumers send greeting cards to each other. Microsoft is reaching millions of lips, while Pepsi is reaching millions of eyeballs.

Meanwhile, Microsoft's old nemesis IBM was trying to reach an agreement with Microsoft. IBM's proposal was to sell Microsoft software to run on IBM hardware. One week IBM's CEO was bad-mouthing Microsoft's CEO, the next week they were in love. In another part of the country, Texas Instruments and Samsung hung up their daggers and swords after a year of litigation over licensing royalties, and agreed to work together. The accord ended a squabble over royalty payments on RAM chips, but more important, it began a partnership that transcended legal differences between the competitors. Strange times make for strange bedfellows. In the transition between the postindustrial age and the friction-free economy, my enemy's enemy is my friend.

Finally, a tiny start-up in Menlo Park, California, Be Inc., held the fate of giant PC maker Apple Computer in the palm of its hand when its operating system—BeOS—became Apple's best hope of playing catch-up with Microsoft. The BeOS was being bundled with Mac clones, thereby displacing Apple's MacOS at the same time that BeOS gave new hope for a Macintosh resurgence.* On the one hand, Apple Computer was being held hostage to an upstart competitor; on the other, Apple was about to be saved. If Apple won't obsolesce its products, then Be will! Even the most alert companies rediscover Davidow's Law.

What do these odd pairings mean? They are symptoms of the friction-free economy. Rapid change, mainstreaming to gain lock-in, learning curves, emergent behavior, branding, inverse economics, markets-of-one, value chain integration, and tribalism are the drivers of this new economic order.

> *The era of Adam Smith, Karl Marx, and John Maynard Keynes has passed. The era of mathematical chaos and positive feedback has arrived. This is the friction-free economy.*

How do we survive?

CORPORATE JESTER

At the risk of sounding like a wild-eyed futurist, I claim that everyone in the friction-free economy must be a crystal ball gazer. It has worked for past businesses—big businesses like Shell Oil, IBM, and others. It works even better in the friction-free economy, because there is simply not enough time to plan.

A business must learn to compete in the friction-free economy by doing, by busily gaining market share while everyone else plans. There is no time to contemplate the requirements, the market, the consumer's tastes. A business must dream—in the form of *scenarios*—make-believe walks through possible futures. How might development of scenarios help your business survive in the friction-free economy?

---

*The high drama lasted for only a few months. Apple reversed itself and paid $400 million for NeXT instead.

Peter Schwartz is cofounder and president of Global Business Network of Emeryville, California. He made millions for Shell Oil by foretelling the collapse of oil prices in the early 1980s, the downfall of communism in the former Soviet Union, and the rise of "teenagers running around with automatic weapons."[2] "I was a corporate jester, telling the kings what they didn't want to hear, but in an entertaining fashion so that it would help," explains Schwartz, a gray-bearded forty-nine-year-old with intense eyes and wry humor. Schwartz is one of many soothsayers who have become a necessary part of the friction-free economy.

Thirty years before starting his consulting company, Schwartz was a member of *Students for a Democratic Society*. He demonstrated against the "establishment"—meaning corporate America—like many other 60s radicals. Now on the other side of the fence, Schwartz has made a business out of selling advice to oil companies like Shell.

Future-thinking prognosticators like Schwartz construct scenarios—imaginary skits showing how the future might play out, or what might happen if there is a sudden change in megatrends. For example, Schwartz urged Shell Oil to buy up failing oil companies after the big oil price shakeout—a consequence of the breakup of OPEC. Shell did so, and within a few years sped past Exxon to become the largest oil company in the world. The former Soviet Union was sitting on huge oil reserves when things began to head south for the communists. Again, Schwartz encouraged his company's executives to position themselves for conquest. When the Wall fell, Shell was in the right place at the right time.

Such accurate forecasting requires out-of-the-box thinking, a skill that few button-down corporations from the industrial age cultivate. Many companies buy such creativity from consultants. Being outside observers, consultants can identify the "outliers"—exceptions and low-probability scenarios—that might hold the key to new markets or competitive advantage. The purpose: to head off technological and sociological surprise attack. Every business needs more of what Schwartz did for Shell. To survive in the friction-free economy, businesses must be able to anticipate the future.

Prognosticating is more than just gazing into a crystal ball. It is a technically sophisticated science. A number of high-tech companies have cropped up expressly for this purpose. Take Thinking Tools Inc. of Monterey, California. Founder and chief technologist John Hiles has been in the business-simulation business for over a decade. He designed simulations for Maxis (SimCity, SimTower, etc.) in the early 1990s, and then formed Thinking Tools to focus on serious businesses.

Thinking Tools uses extremely advanced technology to build scenarios that look for outliers. Genetic algorithms, software agents, and emergent behavior algorithms are employed to simulate placement of distribution points throughout the globe, generate scenarios of competitive environments in various businesses, and jolt management with surprising outcomes to common business processes. For a price, John Hiles can build a computer model of your business that will illustrate the non-Keynesian behavior of the chaotic friction-free economy at work in your neighborhood.

Making scenarios, extrapolating data, and building computer models are as important to survival as cranking out widgets on a frictionless production line. Because the friction-free economy is an economy of rapid change, anticipating that change gives any business the necessary edge.

FUTURE SHOCKS

It is becoming increasingly clear that surviving the friction-free economy is equivalent to exploiting future shock. In fact, more than one idea advanced by Alvin Toffler (*Future Shock*, 1970) has found its way into this book. But the friction-free economy demands more. It demands forward thinking.

Companies have found that forward thinking can be quantified and computerized in the form of a computer-based scenario—a simulation. Scenarios help a business to make plans in Internet Time. They also help technologists design, also in Internet Time. And herein lies the power of computer-based scenario generation:

It allows competitors to get a jump on laggards, by integrating planning and product design.

Scenarios are turned into active models—simulations—for the purpose of planning and advanced product designing. Therefore, simulation and modeling have become essential business tools for even low-tech businesses in the friction-free economy. Given a set of assumptions and trend data, a computer model is constructed that represents an imagined future world where products, services, and ideas can be explored in "what if" scenarios. When activated or "executed," models become dynamic representations of reality.

THE NEXT BIG THING

In order to survive in the friction-free economy, there must always be a Next Big Thing—a challenger to the status quo. Businesses depend on innovation, obsolescence, and change in the friction-free economy. This is a natural consequence of living in Internet Time and Davidow's Law. Over 50% of the revenues of a business must be derived from products that are less than eighteen months old. Old products simply cannot compete with new ones.

The Wired World is an extreme case of a Next Big Thing. It thrives on a Next Big Thing mentality. Webzines, customer support, shopping, and downloaded products from the Wired World must be updated on a nearly continuous basis. Product life cycles are even shorter, because they occur in Internet Time.

The Next Big Thing has been particularly harsh on governments. Tape recorders were partially responsible for the overthrow of the Shah of Iran because they were the only way the people could listen to the speeches of the Ayatollah Khomeini. Radio broadcasts and computers contributed to the fall of the Soviet Empire. The fax machine became a powerful weapon in the hands of students during the 1989 Tiananmen Square rebellion in China.

There is a lesson in these examples: The rate of technical, social, and cultural change will create surprises and dangers. As a consequence, survival will depend on how well a business forecasts.

Prognostication is a necessary tool in the friction-free economy. Every business must have a Chief Scientist or Head Futurist, whose job is to read tea leaves, make predictions, and question the wisdom of management, in order to anticipate the Next Big Thing.

TECHNO BREAKDOWN

Ed Christie is director of SRI Consulting, a for-profit spin-off of nonprofit SRI International, located in the suburbs of Menlo Park, California. Consultants in the friction-free economy need to be wise as well as fast, like Christie. Ed's job is to tell businesses what lies ahead. He is the archtypical prognosticator, the modern scientific soothsayer, and a constant beacon to marketers.

Christie's office is perched atop one of the lowest-bidder buildings in the SRI International complex on Ravenswood Avenue. Here is where his team plots the rise and fall of businesses. Here is where the shakers and movers gather to listen to the team explain why the Next Big Thing won't work. The day I sat in on discussions, Christie and team were lecturing a group of high-powered corporate visitors on why video-on-demand (VOD) failed, and why the transition of the Internet from techie nirvana to mainstream consumerland might also fail. Christie's scenario went something like this:

Joe Lunchbucket comes home from a hard day at the widget factory to "lean back" and relax. He grabs a beer, turns on the TV, and flakes out. Now a CATV operator tries to sell him interactive TV–VOD. Joe can punch in numbers, select content, and pay through the nose for boxing matches and more beer, according to the CATV pitch. Joe can point and click, just like he does all day at work. He and his wife Josephine can type on their wireless keyboard, again just like they do all day at work. The more Joe and Josephine think about it, the more VOD looks and feels like more work! After a few days in front of VOD, the Lunchbuckets cancel their subscription. As a consequence, CATV operators lose millions and become the consumerland Laugh-in of TV.

Christie's nightmare scenario came true. Today VOD is dead.

Not everyone agreed with the SRI prognostication. In 1993–94 Motorola did a study of VOD that showed how consumerland would embrace VOD by 1995 or 1996.[3] They determined it was going to be the Next Big Thing. How could it miss when so much money was being spent by so many important companies to make it happen? Ameritech, Bell Atlantic, NYNEX, SNET, and Time Warner had deployed trials in Illinois, Wisconsin, Ohio, Indiana, Michigan, Virginia, New Jersey, Massachusetts, Rhode Island, Connecticut, and Florida. Over a million homes were involved in these trials. Americans would soon be wired to the teeth with more TV content—but it would be delivered when they wanted it, instead of when the network pushed it down their throats.

Some of these trials used telephone connections, but most used CATV technology. Christie and team were early to recognize that VOD through CATV technology would never work. It simply failed a number of tests that the SRI Consulting team felt must be met. Sure, they were swimming against the tide in 1993 when everyone else was preparing to reap the harvest. But the VOD vision was blind to a number of obstacles to success.

VOD was technologically possible, but improbable. It was ripe for *Techno breakdown*—a situation where technology fails even though it is theoretically possible. Techno breakdown can happen when a good idea lacks all the right ingredients to succeed. The technology may not be quite ripe, or the social and economic environment may be rotten. Timing is an important factor in mainstreaming a new technology, too. For whatever reasons, Techno breakdown can put the brakes on a new product, service, or idea faster than a venture capitalist can take an unprofitable start-up public.

Techno breakdown killed VOD because of lack of consumer demand, pricing, regulatory stranglehold, limited bandwidth, and lack of standards for interoperability. What interested SRI Consulting most of all, however, was the lack of consumer demand. Why would consumers pay an extra $40 per month to "lean forward" in their living rooms? In Christie's view, interactive TV demanded too much from the viewer. It demanded a brain, and a TV viewer's main motivation for watching TV is to check their brain at the entrance to the living room. Their motivation is to relax and enjoy the "lean back" experience.

VOD failed because it did not appeal to human motivations. It did not humanize the experience. It came up short on the Humano scale. It also demonstrated an important lesson in surviving the friction-free economy:

Most new technologies disappoint customers. To survive, a business must use technology to personalize, customize, individualize, and return its customers to a form of tribalism.

THE BIGGEST MACHINE IN THE WORLD

The Seven Wonders of the World were catalogued twenty-three centuries ago. But things have changed somewhat since then. Perhaps it is time to update the list. After all, even civil engineering has advanced since designer stones. The IEEE (Institute of Electronic and Electrical Engineers) recently selected a new list of wonders: FLAG (Fiber-optic Link Around the Globe—a telecommunications cable that runs from Europe to Japan), the Twin Towers of the Kuala Lumpur City Center in Malaysia, Hong Kong's Chek Lap Kok Airport, the Boeing 777 Jetliner, the Swiss rail reconstruction project, the International Space Station, and the human genome project.[4]

What's missing from this list? The biggest machine in the world—in all of human existence—the Internet. It is by far more powerful, complex, heavy, and expansive than any pyramid, fiber-optic cable, or aircraft. The First Wonder of the World is now the Internet. It connects nearly all of humanity, contains most of what we know, and is in everyone's face twenty-four hours per day. Never before has such a machine made such an impact on society.

The Internet is the biggest machine ever built, and will get bigger over the next century. It is a force to be reckoned with, although we can only guess at what this means. To stay competitive in the friction-free economy, every business in the world must learn to navigate in the Wired World. This will require constant vigilance and a willingness to change. It will require a presence on the Internet.

All businesses must reckon with the Internet: Get wired, live long, and prosper. Otherwise, prepare to die.

DRIVE MY (WORLD) CAR

Paul Mehring spent years convincing board members of Daimler-Benz AG, Germany's largest corporation and parent of Mercedes-Benz, to sponsor an outpost in California. Then he spent nearly as much time trying to find office space in the heart of Silicon Valley. Millions of D-mark later he made it to America, set up shop on Page Mill Road in Palo Alto, California, and started scouting for technology. This was no small accomplishment in a year when Daimler-Benz lost $4.5 billion.

Why would a megacorporation like Daimler-Benz place such a high priority on being near Silicon Valley? Actually, DBAG has outposts all over the world. As Mehring knows, even large European companies must think locally to sell globally. Mehring is in charge of the Silicon Valley office, but others like him have spread around the globe to learn the local culture, pick up technology, and generally improve prospects for selling their products around the entire world.

Take the experimental Mercedes-Benz in the driveway at DBAG's Research and Technology Center–North America, for example. It has a fully equipped Internet server in the trunk, a wireless connection to the Web, and video consoles on the dashboard and back seats. The kids in the back can be surfing the Web while the parents are reading maps and navigating through real space. Using GPS (Global Positioning System) and a built-in inertial guidance system, the E420 can find the nearest restaurant, movie theater, or rest area better than a cabbie in downtown Manhattan during rush hour.

Mehring's group combined Germany's preferred method of transportation with the Internet to come up with a smart car. His researchers plan to marry the globally standard communications system of the Internet with local tastes, and come up with a product that people all over the world will want. Perhaps the future Mercedes-Benz will be conversant in twelve languages and know its way around any city in the world. Perhaps not. But Mehring's plan is completely in line with the ambitions of a business hoping to remain in business into the next century:

> *Human interests—both personal and institutional—will be globalized. So businesses must design and build for local markets, but sell globally.*

SALAD SHOOTERS FOR $9.95

Chen Jingwen, thirty-three, has an American-made Ab-Rotor, American-branded warm-up suit and running shoes, and imported Miracle Mop, but no telephone or credit card. He is one of millions of Chinese whose rising affluence is fueling the Asian Century. "My next plan is I want to buy a jogging machine or a stationary bicycle, if the price is fair," said Chen from his two-bedroom apartment in Beijing.[5]

With a population of 1.2 billion, which is spending more cash than ever before, China has become a merchant target of Western imperialists. Ideology has been pushed aside as consumer goods manufacturers look for ways to penetrate the inscrutable mainland. Even retired general Colin Powell says, in reference to the emerging free market system in China, "There is no way communism can compete with a salad shooter for $9.95."[6]

The problem is, China, and Asia in general, are not Manhattan. In order to sell local products in Asian markets, Western merchants have to learn how to think locally and sell globally. Maybe China has 250 million TV sets, but they don't have telephones and credit cards. This problem will require friction-free economy ingenuity to solve.

Even though Chen Jingwen lives far away from the designers, factories, and marketers of sweat suits and Ab-Rotors, his desires are amazingly similar to consumers everywhere. He likes to jog and watch TV. He has an apartment to furnish and a dog to feed. Nonetheless, Chen belongs to a community with its own lifestyle, politics, ethnicity, and interests. This requires businesses in the friction-free economy to learn the local culture in order to respond to targeted community consumerism.

While they seem to contradict each other, localization and globalization actually complement each other. Localization means fitting the product to the consumer regardless of where he or she lives. Globalization means distributing localized products to anyone, anywhere. The key is to pinpoint the buyer—not his or her location on the face of the globe.

Communities are organized according to lifestyle, politics, ethnicity, and interests. Personalize, individualize, and customize products and services that allow people to belong to a community. Put a face on your products, localize, and target.

VIRTUAL PLACE

The idea that community no longer means location also permeates Western civilization. The absence of place and time has particularly interesting ramifications for work.

By 1994, 43 million Americans maintained an office in their homes and cars. Furthermore, the number of SOHOs (Small Office–Home Offices) shot up 77% from 1988—corresponding with the rise of PCs and networks. But even more significant, the number

of full- or part-time corporate workers—SOHO and non-SOHO—
has been steadily climbing as the friction-free economy kicks in.
Figure 8-1 shows an upward trend that appears to reach the full workforce by the second decade of the twenty-first century. Pretty soon we
may all live and work out of our homes, cars, and cyberspace cubicles.

Telecommuters is what they are called, because they commute
by wire. "The strength of working out of home is not having to
deal with traffic," says Ray Estrada, who left the Marines to join
American Express, and now runs his sales territory out of his home
in Katy, Texas. Estrada says his home office has everything, including a Doberman and a pit bull as assistants.[7]

Businesses can redirect the money they save from not having
employees in offices to buy equipment for the home. At-home personal computers, faxes, on-line services, teleconferencing cameras,
and car phones are far less expensive than at-work equipment sur-
rounded by walls, heat and light, with janitorial services, and resid-
ing in expensive buildings.

If pure accounting principles don't convince a business to
introduce telecommuting, then consider the inevitable improvement in productivity. The U.S. Department of Transportation
found that telecommuters were 15% more productive than office
workers. Pacific Bell reported a 20% increase in productivity. Blue
Cross/Blue Shield claimed 50% increases! What is going on here?

Technology has not only made it practical to reach out and
touch someone from anywhere in the world, it has also made it possible to work *asynchronously*. Asynchronous access to colleagues is
the main contributor to increased productivity. It is the most
important benefit of telecommuting.

Asynchronous access—say, through e-mail, voice mail, and
groupware—enables groups to communicate with one another at
any time. For example, e-mail increases productivity simply by eliminating face-to-face meetings.* Instead of wasting time trying to

---

*The length of a meeting quadruples as the number of people doubles—
Lewis's Law of Wasted Time.

schedule a common time when everyone can get together, and then wasting even more time actually meeting in a room face-to-face, e-mail meetings take place anytime, anywhere. Sure, the conversations take place out of sequence, but they can occur randomly and without scheduling conflicts. Asynchronous meetings take place twenty-four hours per day, 365 days per year, from car, home, airplane, or hospital bed. Herein lies the hidden power of technology as it applies to human intercourse.

Time zones are meaningless; the world has become asynchronous. Exploit technology's ability to deliver goods and services "just in time," i.e., anywhere, anytime.

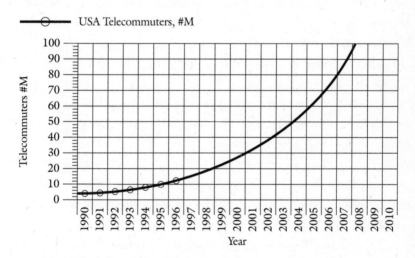

Figure 8–1. Full and part-time telecommuting workers. The number of telecommuters will double between 1995 and 2000.

TOY STORY

"Jump five to ten years down the road and you're going to see movies that look exactly like live-action films, but the production process will be almost entirely digital," said Carl Rosendahl, president and founder of Pacific Data Images in Sunnyvale, California. "Directors won't need elaborate sets; we can do that in the computer. Stunts can be done with safety wires and then the wires can be deleted in the computer. Even lighting can be enhanced in the computer."[8]

The resounding success of *Toy Story*, a completely artificial movie, has signaled the beginning of a new era of moviemaking. *Toy Story* has no human actors, no real-world sets, and takes up very little space in the real world.

The physical world is slowly being replaced by the virtual world. Is the Next Big Thing in movies complete immersion? Will consumers want to be injected into their own artificial reality? Total immersion. Total stimulation. Total consumption.

If this seems far-fetched, then perhaps cold hard cash will make virtual reality seem more real. Multimedia Realty Inc. of Beverly Hills is selling *real estate* in cyberspace. Maybe it should be called *virtual estate* instead. The domain name of www.wallstreet.org goes for $375,000; www.gratefuldead.org for $175,000; and www.videodating.com, a mere $30,000. There is gold in the Wired World, whether the real estate is real or imagined.[9]

Already travel services are moving out of real space into virtual space. When 345 travel managers were asked in 1995, "How do you think travel arrangements will be made in five years?" 49% said by computers. One-fourth said more faxes will be used to make reservations. Over one-third predicted the collapse of travel agencies altogether—or at least massive consolidation.

In 1995 the banking industry laid off 300,000 workers. The reason: automation. Fewer people are needed because banks do most of their work in virtual vaults. Banking is getting wired, and the consumer is getting on-line. Fewer walk-ins mean fewer human tellers.

Virtuality is replacing reality. Virtual cyberspace reduces the need for physical space. Opportunities will increase for products that permit people to live, work, buy, sell, and socialize at home and in the car. Products that simulate, model, or immerse people in virtual worlds will diminish the need for tangible products.

PROSUMERS IN THE WIRED WORLD

If the real world is vanishing like the lost world of Atlantis, then how will businesses make money? Who will buy, and who will sell? The friction-free economy is evolving into a market of *prosumers*— people who are both producers and consumers. The idea of a prosumer goes all the way back to Toffler's *Future Shock*, but only since the rise of the friction-free economy has it become practical.

Perhaps the best illustration of how this works is the new wave of multilevel-marketing (MLM) companies that have revolutionized the cosmetic and personal health industry. Companies like Amway ($6 billion), Nu Skin ($1 billion), Mary Kay ($1 billion), and HerbaLife (almost $1 billion) depend on a form of prosumerism to make their MLM system work. MLM is still in its infancy, but because it fits the Wired World model so well, it is fast becoming a mainstream marketing technique in the friction-free economy.

GEOMETRIC MARKETING

Charles King, professor of marketing at the University of Chicago, offered perhaps the first college-level course on MLM. He is a proponent of the so-called Wave Three version of the marketing technique, which he defines as one-on-one, word-of-mouth, person-to-person, selling-through-a-network organization.*

Here is how it works: Everyone who buys, for example, a bottle of skin lotion is both consumer and producer. Each consumer buys more than he or she can use. The excess merchandise is sold to someone else, and the seller keeps some of the commission and passes some of it up the chain to a higher-level prosumer in the form of cost-of-merchandise. In turn, the next-level-down buyer can sell his or her excess for a profit. This can go on for many levels.

---

*Wave One was the pioneering era when Amway, Shaklee, and HerbaLife started; Wave Two was the era of establishing legitimacy (Amway was taken to court and won); and Wave Three is the technological era whereby MLM is merging with computers and streamlined distribution systems.

Each seller gets a commission, so everyone saves, or even earns, money.

This method of selling is very efficient because every customer is also a sales representative. The payback to the top of the pyramid (the first one to sell to someone) can be enormous, because the number of buyers mushrooms as the number of levels increases. This means all sales commissions generated by the geometric increase in number of buyers flow back to the top dog! Thus, income expands geometrically, because the market expands geometrically.

MLM is to marketing what the microprocessor was to high-tech. The geometrically increasing speed of microprocessors has made nearly everything in high-tech possible. The geometrically expanding market size of an MLM market space makes everything in Wave Three marketing possible. There is, however, a dark side to MLM. As prosumers descend the ladder of the MLM hierarchy, they get smaller and smaller returns. In fact, their return diminishes at a geometric rate.

The geometric rate of expansion, and contraction, of the MLM technique has already earned it a bad name. Even though MLM has been accused of being a Ponzi scheme or pyramid scam, it has survived many legal challenges. In 1979 the Federal Trade Commission ruled that Amway was a legitimate business, not a pyramid scam. That ended Wave One. Wave Two kicked off great activity after that ruling. But it turned out that Wave Two was too complicated. Prosumers had to know how to stock lots of merchandise, handle billing and advertising, and run a business.

Wave Three has taken the order entry, warehousing, shipping and billing, and computer operations out of the prosumer's hands, and places the "back office" functions in a corporation such as Nu Skin. In Wave Three, prosumers need only use the product, and by word of mouth, recommend it to others. These leads are then handled by the Wave Three enterprise.

The MLM system is ripe for the Wired World, where buying and selling can easily be automated. In addition, MLM is person-to-person, one-on-one, and tribal. But tribalism is exactly what on-line chat is all about. The market-of-one trend in the friction-free economy plus the tribalism that exists in the Wired World are perfect for MLM. Combining MLM with Internet Time will become big business in the next century as barter becomes the principal mode of electronic commerce.*

Surviving in the friction-free economy will require clever marketing techniques such as MLM. It will demand customer satisfaction at the same time it commoditizes the very process of selling. To get both, novel marketing will become essential.

The Wired World will commoditize buying and selling, and will leverage prosumerism and electronic barter, and its derivatives, to reduce marketing costs and increase customer satisfaction.

INTERFACE IS THE PRODUCT

Diba (a contraction of Dibachi—the name of the two brothers who founded the company) is a conglomeration of people from Oracle and Apple Computer who were looking for a faster track.†
Their impatience led them to build a start-up. "We want to be the Windows 95 of the consumer electronics industry," they chant.

Diba's appliances work with the Internet just like about everything else in the Wired World. They work from the living room through the TV, and in the kitchen through a recipe-holding appli-

---

*Prosumers sitting in front of their Internet TV can buy and sell at electronic bazaars without the benefit of middlemen, returning civilization to a modern form of agrarian tribalism.

†The legend goes like this: After Farzad Dibachi left Oracle, where he was the youngest-ever VP, he bumped into Fred Ebrahim, CEO of Quark Inc., who said, "If you ever do anything on your own, I'll fund you." Farzad and brother Farid took him up on the offer. Larry Ellison of Oracle tells a different story, one that suggests a rip-off of Oracle's NC idea. After all, Farzad was in charge of Oracle's New Media division prior to his departure. Such is life in the fast lane.

ance, and from within intelligent telephones that carry e-mail and do your bidding while your head is disconnected from cyberspace. Diba's approach is to disintegrate the product space, and integrate the market space.

John Busch, vice president of sales, has a vision of computing that differs considerably from that of Microsoft's Bill Gates or Netscape's Jim Clark. While Microsoft and Netscape tear each other apart over scraps of food left on the Fortune 500 table, Busch and company plan to feed the masses. As he sees it, the Next Big Thing is centered squarely on the billion-dollar opportunity called *appliance computers*, like telephones, set-top boxes, personal assistants—even greeting card computers.

Diba's strategy is to make the computer and underlying network as invisible as possible. To John Busch, Windows 95, MacOS, and UNIX are barriers to sales. They are too complex. They are overkill. If computing is to reach the next level, it must disappear, leaving only the human interface. The network appliance is simply an interface to information and services in the Wired World.

Only the interface between human and machine matters. Make the product as small and cheap as possible, and your founder's stock will turn into the gold at the end of the rainbow.

Technology must be less visible. To survive, products must be smaller, cheaper, and easier to use.

CAN'T BUY LOVE

"Consumers don't go shopping for a 24-valve, six-cylinder, 200-horsepower, fuel-injected engine. They shop for a Taurus, Lexus, BMW, Jeep Cherokee, Hummer, whatever," said Eckhard Pfeiffer, CEO of Compaq Computer, the number-one PC vendor in the world. "They shop for well-known, trusted brands. We spend a lot of time, effort and dollars to ensure the Compaq brand stands for quality and useful innovation." Pfeiffer likes to quote Don Quixote: "A good name is better than riches."[10]

Compaq constantly measures changes in perception of their products, according to Pfeiffer's vice president for communications, Jim Garrity. The names given to Compaq's products—Presario and Proliant—are scrubbed down by focus groups, and the company went so far as to challenge Intel in a yearlong tug-of-war over branding. Garrity explains, "Eckhard Pfeiffer views advertising as a long term investment . . . he knows branding is a five-to-eight year proposition."[11]

When Intel unleashed its "Intel Inside" branding campaign, Compaq's Pfeiffer angrily denounced Intel's business practices at a conference and in subsequent printed articles. He feared the "Intel Inside" logo would place Intel's brand name above Compaq's. The feud lasted over a year.[12] Finally the two companies kissed and made up in 1996.

Why has marketing become commoditized? Why is selling a high-tech product like a PC just like selling toothpaste? The answer is simple: Time and attention have become more valuable than money. The consuming public is under too much time pressure to care whether a computer has an Intel or PowerPC processor inside. So instead of making informed decisions, they make comfortable decisions.

Most people who buy complex products don't understand how they work. Nor do they care. How, then, do they make a "good" decision? They rely on a "feel-good vignette." Consumers may not know what Intel is, but they know that a computer with the logo "Intel Inside" pasted on the lid is good.

Time and attention have become a more valuable commodity. Therefore, businesses must increase branding, the formation of tribal communities, and sharply decrease price-learning curves.

ZERO-BILLION-DOLLAR BUSINESSES

Technological change broadens, rather than narrows, consumer choice. Internet TV will not replace ordinary TV any more than the

VCR replaced movie theaters. When a new product, service, or idea hits Main Street, it rarely eliminates older products, services, or ideas. Rather, change adds to the cornucopia of products, services, and ideas. The friction-free economy embraces change by absorption rather than elimination.

Better mousetraps displace older mousetraps, just as faster computers render slower computers obsolete. Obsolescence is not the same as elimination. And renovation can be as profitable as innovation. Every business should consider renovating its products as well as thinking up entirely new ones.

As technology broadens choices, it also introduces opportunities for new products to supplement the old. In a sense, technology is the spawning ground for new businesses—*zero-billion-dollar* businesses. These are the unproven opportunities which drive the ever-expanding friction-free economy. Instead of constantly striving for a revolution, revise existing products to be smaller, cheaper, faster, and more personal. Look for new ways to improve existing products, services, and ideas.

Renovate as well as innovate. Older technologies will often persist—even prosper—despite the arrival of newer rivals.

CHAIN GANGS

Segmentation, declining price-learning curves, and the consequent inverse economics that reduces everything to a commodity, all conspire to make profiteering more and more difficult in the friction-free economy. To make things worse, businesses must invest heavily just to keep up with change.

How does a product get into more markets? Segmentation is one way, but segmentation in the computer industry is difficult because the high-end business has been saturated for nearly the entire life of the industry.

This leaves the low end as a target for expansion. But the low-end market implies a market with very large volumes. A vendor must sell lots of PDAs (Personal Digital Assistants) at $10 profit each to equal one PC at $100 profit. It also implies declining prices, which squeeze out profits as products become commodities. The same $10 PDA profit margin declines as the product is commoditized, which wipes out all profit.

Even so, the low end is where the action ultimately takes a business. Products must be low-priced, specialized, consumer-oriented, designed to consume little power, require little training to use, and implement a compelling value proposition to entice the hordes into buying like crazy. The challenge is to make money from such low-priced products.

As products disintegrate into segments such as video game machines, game cartridges, telecommunications networks, cellular telephone sets, and services, companies enter into joint ventures so that they can live off of the same food chain. Product disintegration makes value chain integration necessary, because the whole is greater than the sum of the parts.

How will businesses survive on thin-margin products? The answer is to tax the food chain—the so-called value chain of the consumer electronics market space. But the go-it-alone approach won't work, so businesses must band together—form value chain gangs, or digital *keiretsu*—in order to survive. Joint venture deals with friends and foes alike supply greater value than vertical integration. In the friction-free economy, value chains are worth more than the sum of their parts:

> *As products disintegrate, their value chains integrate. Form joint partnerships, leverage consortia, and look for ways to siphon profits from entire value chains.*

THE TRANSFORMATION

Only once in a few millennia does one get the opportunity to observe a transformation of society as profound as the industrial revolution or the postmodern paradigm shift. We have been privileged to observe the Next Big Thing in civilization—the transformation of an economy based on things into an economy based on ideas. The friction-free economy is far more abstract than previous economic systems—hence the difficulty in understanding it. Yet, it is clearly under way. It will define the twenty-first century just as the industrial age defined the nineteenth century, and the postindustrial age defined the second half of the twentieth century.

An entire book could be written about the social structures that will crumble in the friction-free economy. The most obvious institutions, law and government, are two of the key structures that will be dramatically altered by the friction-free economy. But it will take some time for these changes to get into high gear. In the meantime, they will act as a hindrance to businesses.

Change will follow close on the heels of changes in the legal system, as traditional institutions like education, government, and centralized organizations begin to transform. Distance learning, wired government services, and just-in-time bureaucracies are on their way and will become opportunities for new businesses as they decentralize to homes.

The friction-free economy clearly means the dawn of a new revolution. In the words of Peter F. Drucker:

Every few hundred years in Western history there occurs a sharp transformation. Within a few short decades, society rearranges itself—its world view; its basic values; its social and political structure; its arts; its key institutions. Fifty years later, there is a new world. And the people born then cannot even imagine the world in which their grandparents lived and into which their own parents were born. We are currently living through just such a transformation.[13]

The postindustrial age is transforming into the friction-free economy. This transformation will take decades, and after fifty years have elapsed there will be a new world. The friction-free economy will undoubtedly rearrange our world views, basic values, social and political structures, and key institutions. It will usher in a brave new era of personalization, mainstreaming, volume economics, calculated obsolescence, value chain integration, and other untold miracles of living in the Wired World.

See you there!

Notes

CHAPTER 1

1. Letter to Editor, "Battleships and Aircraft Carriers," *The Red Herring*, April 1996, p. 16.
2. Management Insights, *Upside*, May 1995.
3. *San Jose Mercury News*, April 26, 1995, p. F1.
4. "No Ordinary Joe," *The PriceCostco Connection*, April 1996, p. 15
5. Sinson Garfinkel, "Address Battles Sometimes Find a Home in Court," *San Jose Mercury News*, June 17, 1996, p. 4E.
6. *Fortune*, August 7, 1995.
7. Reuters, "Internet IPO Innovator Floats New Idea: On-line Stock Exchange," *San Jose Mercury News*, April 3, 1996, p. 4C
8. Michael Santoli, "The Program Trading Kit," *San Jose Mercury News*, April 24, 1996, p. 1C.
9. Ian Brown, "Death and Mourning on the Internet," *Macworld*, June 1996, p. 256.
10. Elizabeth Weise, "A Virtual Community for Real Mothers To Be," *San Jose Mercury News*, May 12, 1996, p. 4B.
11. Lisa Picarille, "Apple Users Hang Tough," *Computerworld*, May 6, 1996, p. 129.
12. Mary Hayes, "Seeding the Future," *Information Week*, May 6, 1996, p. 66.
13. "Apple Shines in Customer Loyalty," *San Jose Mercury News*, June 19, 1996, p. 1C.
14. Sanjay Khanna, "The Spin on Designing a Website," United Airlines' *Hemispheres Magazine*, May 1996, p. 40.
15. James Champy, Robert Buday, Nitin Nohria, "Creating the Electronic Community," *Information Week*, June 10, 1996, p. 64.

CHAPTER 2

1. www.economists.com, "Doomonomics," The Economist, May 1996.
2. James Aley, "The Theory That Made Microsoft," *Fortune*, April 29, 1996, pp. 65–66.
3. Aley, "The Theory That Made Microsoft."
4. www.economists.com, "Doomonomics."
5. J. F. Moore, *The Death of Competition*, HarperBusiness, 1996, pp. 89–91.
6. Moore, *The Death of Competition*, pp.89–91.
7. Ken Schultz, "Satellite Weather Firm Heads for TV," *The Monterey County Herald*, April 29, 1996, pp. 1A, 8A.
8. Schultz, "Satellite Weather Firm Heads for TV."
9. Lisa Dicarlo, "IBM Demos New Mac OS Desktop, Other Advances," *PCWeek*, June 24, 1996, p. 116.
10. M. R. Zimmerman, "Notebook King Toshiba Trying to Rule the New World," *PCWeek*, June 24, 1996, p. 116.

CHAPTER 3

1. Shinichi Yano, *New Lanchester Strategy*, Lanchester Press, 1990, http://www.lanchester.com.
2. John Swenson, "Microsoft Still Going Strong," *Information Week*, April 22, 1996, p. 32; also found at http://techweb.cmp.com/is.
3. Eric Nee, "Jim Clark," *Upside*, Oct. 1995, p. 34.

CHAPTER 4

1. Robert Heilbroner and Lester Thurow, *Economics Explained*, Touchstone, 1982, p. 26.
2. Heilbroner and Thurow, *Economics Explained*, p. 26.
3. Heilbroner and Thurow, *Economics Explained*, p. 26.
4. Moore, *The Death of Competition*, pp. 69–70.
5. Moore, *The Death of Competition*, p. 13.

CHAPTER 5

1. Lea Anne Bansari, "Mode and Club Mode," *Interactivity*, Sept. 1996, p. 57.
2. Ollie Curme, "Web Commerce in Transition," *Information Week*, July 15, 1996, p. 94.
3. Moore, *The Death of Competition*, p. 13.
4. Sherri Eng, "On-line Waiters Find Startup Delivers," *San Jose Mercury News*, July 10, 1996, p. 7G.
5. Edith Weiner and Arnold Brown, "The New Marketplace," *The Futurist*, May/June 1995, pp. 12–16.
6. Nicholas Imparato and Oren Harari, "Squeezing the Middle-man," *The Futurist*, May/June 1995, p. 15.
7. Samuel Bleecker, "The Emerging Meta-Mart," *The Futurist*, May/June 1995, pp. 20–22.
8. Michael Parsons, "Narrowcast News," *InfoWorld*, Sept. 16, 1996, p. 56.
9. Julia King, "Retail Project Cuts Supply Chain Costs," *Computerworld*, Sept. 23, 1996, p. 131.
10. Jeff Ubois, Interview with Dan Lynch, *Internet World*, July 1996, p. 80.
11. Broderick Perkins, "Global Village," *San Jose Mercury News*, Sept. 28, 1996, p. 1F.
12. "Merchants Back Smart Cards," *San Jose Mercury News*, Sept. 17, 1996, p. 9E.
13. Mark Leon, "Getting Carded," *The Red Herring*, Sept. 1996, pp. 30–32.
14. Bill Montague, "Hot Money Shifts World Markets," *USA Today*, May 4, 1995, p. B1.
15. Steve Kaufman, "Small Businesses Play Big Online," *San Jose Mercury News*, March 10, 1997, pp. 1F–4F.
16. Mike Langberg, "VeriFone Unveils Personal ATM," *San Jose Mercury News*, Oct. 1, 1996, p. 2E.
17. Eric Nee, "Larry Ellison," *Upside*, Sept. 1994, p. 22.

CHAPTER 6

1. J. W. Zook, "Computer Programmers Lead Us Down a Dark and Lonely Road," *San Jose Mercury News*, July 31, 1995, p. 3D.

2. Nicholas Negroponte, "Products and Services for Computer Networks," *Scientific American*, Sept. 1991, pp. 102–109.

3. Alex Gove, "Keeping Up with the Joneses," *The Red Herring*, Sept. 1996, p. 24.

4. Janet Rae-Dupree, "Women.com Definitely Not Your Typical Ladies' Mag," *San Jose Mercury News*, Aug. 5, 1996, p. 5F.

5. Alex Hulanicki, "C. V. Men to Market Motorcycles," *The Monterey County Herald*, July 29, 1996, p. 1.

6. Randy Whitestone, "Classifieds Without the Ink Stains," *Inter@ctive Week*, Sept. 30, 1996, p. 75.

7. Virginie Pelletier, "The Well Dips into Custom Conferencing," *Inter@ctive Week*, Sept. 30, 1996, p. 10.

8. Natasha Wanchek, "A Web of .COMmunity," *San Jose Mercury News*, Dec. 8, 1996, p. 1E.

9. Beth Berselli, "One Tough Mother," *The Oregonian*, Sept. 1, 1996, p. L7.

10. Mary Hayes, "Platform Zealots," *Information Week*, Aug. 19, 1996, p. 44.

11. Hayes, "Platform Zealots," p. 48.

12. Hayes, "Platform Zealots," p. 46.

13. Katie Maddox, "Web Business Advances to the Next Stage," *Communications Week*, Sept. 30, 1996, p. 53.

14. Janet Rae-Dupree, "Discount Shopping on the Net," *San Jose Mercury News*, Oct. 14, 1996, p. 5E.

15. Robert Levitan, "iVillage," *Advertising Age*, Sept. 23, 1996, p. 42.

16. Steven Vonder Harr, "Excite Goes on Tour," *Inter@ctive Week*, Oct. 14, 1996, p. 78.

17. Arthur Armstrong and John Hagel III, "The Real Value of On-line Communities," *Harvard Business Review*, May-June 1996, pp. 134–142.

18. Larry Slonaker, "Just Their Type," *San Jose Mercury News*, Aug. 21, 1996, p. 1A.

19. Thomas Farragher, "Electronic Village U.S.A.," *San Jose Mercury News*, May 1, 1995, p. 1A

CHAPTER 7

1. Richard Brandt, "Triumph of Showmanship," *Upside*, Sept. 1996, pp. 74–83.

2. Brandt, "Triumph of Showmanship."

3. "IBM's Priority: Network Computing," *San Jose Mercury News*, Oct. 10, 1996, p. 1C.

4. "IBM's Priority," p. 3C.

5. Clinton Wilder, "Netscape's Next Battleground," *Information Week*, September 30, 1996, p. 20.

6. Don Crabb, "DSP is Apple's Comeback to the Intel MMX Scare," *MacWeek*, Oct. 28, 1996, p. 29.

7. Jeff Ubois, "Java: New Roles, New Content, New Money," *Inter@ctive Week*, Oct. 21, 1996, p. 20.

8. Roger B. McNamee, "Fishing on the Internet Sea," *Upside*, Feb. 1996, pp. 74–84.

9. Elinor Mills, "Microsoft-Netscape Legal Battle Brews," *Info-World*, Aug. 26, 1996, p. 9.

10. Mills, "Microsoft-Netscape Legal Battle Brews," p. 9.

11. Virginie Pelletier, "Netscape: Underdog with 80% Share," *Inter@ctive Week*, Oct. 21, 1996, p. 25.

12. Kathy Rebello, "Inside Microsoft," *Business Week*, July 15, 1996, pp. 56–67.

13. Lisa Picarille, "Suite Success," *Computerworld*, Sept. 9, 1996, p. 28.

14. Jesse Berst, "Corel Slaps Microsoft Upside the Head," *PCWeek*, Sept. 2, 1996, p. 63.

15. Paul Kedrosky, "Corel Bites the Big One," *Upside*, Aug. 1996, pp. 30–40.

16. Kedrosky, "Corel Bites the Big One," p. 36.

17. Farhan Memon, "Java: Perfect Vehicle for Corporate Networks?" *Inter@ctive Week*, Oct. 28, 1996, p. 54.

18. W. D. Riley, "No More Cows," *Datamation*, June 15, 1996, p. 31.
19. Lisa Picarille, "Office 97: 'Fat' Is Where It's At," *Computerworld*, June 26, 1996, p. 6.
20. J. Gerry Purdy, "Could IBM Beat Microsoft?" *Upside*, Jan. 1996, p. 18.

CHAPTER 8

1. "Pepsi's Holiday Cheer: Microsoft Cool," *San Jose Mercury News*, Nov. 27, 1996, pp. 1C–5C.
2. Tia O'Brien, "Ahead of the Future," *West*, March 24, 1996, pp. 10–26.
3. Conversation with Douglas M. Robertson, Motorola Multimedia, at DESKCON II, May 22, 1995.
4. Dave Dooling, "Big, Bold, and Expensive," *IEEE SPECTRUM*, Oct. 1996, p. 19.
5. "Home-shopping Programs put Western Wares in Beijing Homes," *San Jose Mercury News*, Nov. 24, 1996, p. 1E.
6. "Home-shopping Programs put Western Wares in Beijing Homes," p. 5E.
7. Steve Morgenstern, "The Allure of Working at Home," *Parade*, Nov. 24, 1996, p. 16.
8. Janet Rae-Dupree, "Through the Looking Glass," *San Jose Mercury News*, March 25, 1996, p. 1F.
9. "Need a Place on the Net? Call a Broker," *San Jose Mercury News*, Oct. 30, 1996, p. 1C.
10. Editors, "Winning the Computer Advertising Wars," *Upside*, Sept. 1996, pp. 39–50.
11. Editors, "Winning the Computer Advertising Wars," p. 48.
12. Dean Takahashi, "On the Outside, Compaqs Will Wear 'Intel Inside,'" *San Jose Mercury News*, Jan. 19, 1996, p. 1C.
13. Peter F. Drucker, *Post-Capitalist Society*, HarperBusiness, New York, 1993, p. 1.

Index

About the Author

TED G. LEWIS is currently chairman of Computer Science at the Naval Postgraduate School in Monterey, California, and president/owner of Technology Assessment Group (TAG), a private company dedicated to tailored research and analysis of computer systems technology with emphasis on the software industry. Lewis earned his M.S. and Ph.D. degrees in computer science from Washington State University and has a varied background in computer technology, spanning academic, industrial, government, and private organizations. His bimonthly *Computer* magazine column called "The Binary Critic" is widely read by the 100,000 members of the Computer Society. In addition, he is the author of many books spanning twenty years, including, most recently, *Client/Server Yellow Pages, Object-Oriented Application Frameworks,* and *Deploying Distributed Business Software.* He is a highly sought after speaker on the new economy of the Web. Formerly the editor in chief of *IEEE Software* magazine and *Computer* magazine, T. G. Lewis is cofounder, along with Professor Charles Petrie of Stanford University, of a new publication of the IEEE Computer Society called *Internet Computing.* His writings frequently appear on the Internet and can be found at www.friction-free-economy.com.